RÉSUMÉ WRITING

Résumé Writing

A COMPREHENSIVE HOW-TO-DO-IT GUIDE

Burdette E. Bostwick

The B. E. Bostwick Company
Management Consultants

SECOND EDITION

175 YEARS OF PUBLISHING

1807 1982

JOHN WILEY & SONS, New York • Chichester • Brisbane • Toronto • Singapore

This publication is designed to provide accurate and
authoritative information in regard to the subject
matter covered. It is sold with the understanding that
the publisher is not engaged in rendering legal, accounting,
or other professional service. If legal advice or other
expert assistance is required, the services of a competent
professional person should be sought. *From a Declaration
of Principles jointly adopted by a Committee of the
American Bar Association and a Committee of Publishers.*

Library of Congress Cataloging in Publication Data:

Bostwick, Burdette E
  Résumé writing.

  Includes index.
    1. Résumés (Employment)—Handbooks, manuals, etc.
2. Applications for positions—Handbooks, manuals,
etc. I. Title.

HF5383.B57 1980   650.1'4   80-18100
ISBN 0-471-09943-0 (Paper)

Printed in the United States of America

10 9 8 7 6 5 4 3 2 1

To my wife Betty who interviewed me and then hired me as the result of my most successful résumé, sent on speculation, expressing my credentials for, and interest in, a lifetime position

PREFACE

This book is about personal kinds of writing—résumés, job application letters, proposals. Who needs résumés? Almost every job seeker. Nearly 90% of all help wanted *display* advertising and some *classified* advertising demand résumés before interviews are granted. Although the book is intended for all job seekers, résumés for the management level are stressed. The complexity of writing grows with job responsibilities and proceeds from "what can I write about?" to "what should I leave out?"

Eighty percent of the job openings available at any time are *unadvertised*. There are two ways to discover these jobs; know someone who knows about them or find them by writing. If your job search is geographically broad, writing is almost the only way to make the discovery. If you call on an employment agency you will be asked for a résumé. A résumé is part of the hiring program in an executive search procedure. Why is a résumé so important? For many reasons, but three in particular:

1. A résumé is a time-saver for a recruiter. It can be read in a few minutes. An interview may take hours. Any executive in a hiring position who does not screen job candidates by means of résumés for upper level jobs is inefficient.
2. A résumé helps a job candidate understand himself or herself. It forms the basis for a better interview. It shows the reader that the applicant can think clearly and logically.

3. A résumé is the basis for other kinds of writing, also effective or required in the job search.

This second edition has been written to include new and important material; that is, new résumés covering a wider variety of occupations; and an expanded treatment of letters and other job search related writings, such as proposals. Nevertheless the whole structure of the job search program begins with your résumé.

A résumé is intended to open the door for an interview. Occasionally it does more—it can affirmatively affect the hiring decision.

Whether you are unemployed, seek a new career, are restless in present employment, wish to test your marketability, or plan to move to greener pastures your résumé or another form of writing can be your magic carpet. A résumé is the best way and largely the only way to disseminate important information about yourself. It is your personal advertising. Just as a picture is worth a thousand words, so a résumé (a portrait of you in writing) speaks eloquently in your behalf.

Surveys of résumé users show that they are successful people. Surveys of those who hire show that résumés are the preferred basis on which to grant interviews.

Finally, why must you read a book to learn to write a résumé? Because the effectiveness of your writing may be worth hundreds of thousands or millions of dollars to you over the course of your career; and because you want your writing to be superior to that of the general run of job candidates. Writing about yourself is a specialized, concise, formal, and analytical art. People who write about themselves without training can usually be recognized by the inadequacy of their writing. There are prizes for writing a good résumé—higher income, greater achievement, increased happiness. (All the résumés in this book are based on actual résumés described as successful by the people who used them.)

The fact is—you cannot successfully look for a job without a résumé! Even if you use other kinds of writings to gain your objective, the résumé is the source from which they are developed. If this sounds too absolute, perhaps it is only 99% true. Some people are so well known or possess such special relationships that jobs come to them rather than needing to be sought.

This book is a distillation of many years of studying résumés to find the best forms and methods of expression, and of management experience with people and jobs of all kinds.

How do companies sell their products? They advertise. The advertising media are television, radio and print, word of mouth. You are a product, advertising yourself for employment. If you could afford it, and had suitable capabilities, you would use a combination of all the media.

Television, for example, is the medium favored by political candidates. Presidential campaigns spend tens of millions of dollars for television spots. No job seeker in industry can afford this kind of publicity. Your primary advertising is usually your résumé.

Another difference is that you are addressing an elite audience. You can't sell yourself the way companies sell toothpaste, detergents, or paper towels.

This is the reason why your résumé—your whole approach to employment—must be forged into a sophisticated tool, honed to accomplish a specific objective: to present you attractively to your market.

Many of the résumés are textbook examples of the route to success. Actually most of the subjects are highly successful; some are not, but all sound successful as a result of careful selection of their best attributes. The future will decide which of the successful ones will stumble or continue to advance and which of the failures will finally succeed. But the résumé can be a magic carpet to opportunity.

Burdette E. Bostwick

New York, New York
August 1980

CONTENTS

ILLUSTRATIONS

SOURCE OF DATA

The data analyzed and reported in this book are taken from a sampling of 1000 résumés in my own files. They reflect confidential information given to me for résumé preparation by individuals in more than 60 employment classifications. To my knowledge, such data have never before been systematized and analyzed. There may well be a bias toward upper and middle management. Those entering the job market may be underrepresented in the data reported here, since they would be concentrated among the 80% of job seekers who write their own résumés. Nevertheless, the charts disclose significant and interesting facts about the persons who prepare résumés. By scientific polling standards a sample of 1000 is amply sufficient for valid conclusions.

ONE

WHAT IS
A RÉSUMÉ?

A résumé is your personal advertisement. It is the most widely accepted medium of communication between a job seeker and a prospective employer. It differs from an ordinary advertisement in that it is not directed to the general public, but to the employer. An employer may receive hundreds of résumés for a single position. If you wish to be one of the few selected for an interview, you must make your résumé superior to the common run.

Writing a résumé is not an easy task, though it is a very important one in terms of personal reward. The difficulty lies in organization and objectivity. It is not as natural to write about yourself as it is to write about a place, an event, or even another person. There are relatively few great autobiographies! At least 70% of the résumés I have read are deficient in some respect. You can make yours a superior document by studying the method of its preparation.

The résumé, crucial in getting an interview, may enter the final decision to hire. Its role is increasing because of more intense competition for jobs and possibly slower job growth as capital formation is restricted and corporations and institutions learn to live without less productive and less necessary employees.

You can use this book in two ways. Preferably you can learn to write an effective résumé, stamped with your own hallmark. Or, possibly, you can preempt one of the résumé examples as a model for your own résumé, though it might then appear "canned." You need not master all of the résumé styles—they are included to show the options. Pick the one best suited to you.

The words *chronological* and *functional* occur frequently in this book. *Chronological* here refers to the arrangement of data in the order of time of occurrence, but, unlike in a biography or history, the order is reversed. That is, in a résumé the most recent experience is described first and older experiences last. (See the résumé on p. 51.)

Thus the main body of our résumé called *Chronological Résumé with Summary Page* (see Chapter 11, p. 57), starting with the second page, is chronological. The *summary page* is a brief interpretation of the *succeeding* pages. It is written last but placed first in the completed résumé.

The word *functional* refers to a style of résumé that describes activities in each area of experience separately without reference to the companies for which the function was performed or to the time of performance. For example:

EXPERIENCE

GENERAL MANAGER	Held P. & L. responsibility for $10 million division. Reorganized production and cost accounting departments. Reduced costs. Set up new marketing strategies. Increased sales. Also consolidated two manufacturing plants for improved efficiency.
MARKETING MANAGEMENT	Surveyed market for power tools. Established share of market goals for each ter-

ritory; assigned quotas; installed new salesmen's compensation plan. Redirected advertising. Increased sales 36% within 2 years for one company, 23% for another company and 10% for a third.

EMPLOYMENT HISTORY

A.B.C. Company, Chicago, Ill.
D.E.F. Company, Portland, Me.
X.Y.Z. Company, Newark, N.J.

These experiences (described in summary form here) might apply to one, two, or all three of the companies.

Brief descriptions of the various résumé styles, together with our recommendations, are given below. Detailed analyses appear later.

1 **Basic Résumé.** The best form for one entering the job market or having very limited experience. (See p. 43.)
2 **Chronological Résumé.** The second best form (sometimes the best) for a middle or upper management executive, since it permits the sharpest delineation of accomplishments. (See p. 48.)
3 **Chronological Résumé with Summary Page.** The best form for a middle or upper management executive—in addition to permitting a clear listing of accomplishments, it also contains a *Summary Page*. (See p. 55.)
4 **Functional Résumé.** An excellent form, especially for one with experience in several job functions, such as marketing, finance, and general management. A preferred form for educators at the administrative level. Some personnel executives profess a liking for this form. (See p. 71.)

5 **Functional-by-Company (or Institution) Résumé.** Advantageously associates function with the company for which it was performed, but loses the impact of the pure *Functional Résumé.* (See p. 81.)

6 **Harvard Résumé.** Has an excellent appearance, but less effective, from both the job seeker's and the employer's point of view, than the styles discussed so far. (See p. 90.)

7 **Creative Résumé.** For special uses only. Has no definite structure. See p. 96.)

8 **Narrative Résumé.** A specialized form that may serve well in situations deviating from the norm. (See p. 99.)

9 **Professional Résumé.** For lawyers, doctors, teachers, and other professionals whose education and accreditation are of primary importance to the reader. (See p. 104.)

10 **Accomplishment Résumé.** Not generally recommended because its raison d'ètre is to camouflage. (See p. 111.)

These evaluations are based on personal opinions and on experience.

The selection of a résumé form may also change with your career. You might start with the *Basic Résumé,* graduate after a few years to the *Chronological Résumé,* and finally proceed to the *Chronological Résumé with Summary Page* or to the *Functional Résumé.*

A *covering* letter is an essential short introduction to a résumé. Of the samples included in this book there will be one more "right" for you than any of the others, which you can then amend to fit your circumstances. A *broadcast* letter—different from a résumé and a covering letter—is also fully explained.

The word *résumé* (from the Latin resumere, "to take up again," and the French résumer, "to resume, summarize"), pronounced ráy zu may, is defined *by Webster's Third International Dictionary* as "a short account of one's career and qualifications prepared typically by an applicant for a position."

Sometimes the term *curriculum vitae,* pronounced ka rick' you lum vi tee, is used. A résumé can also be defined in a number of other ways:

1 A résumé is an essential part of a job search at the managerial level.
2 A résumé, or the tools that derive from it, is the most effective instrument for finding work or for gaining one's desired vocational situation.
3 A résumé is a door opener to an interview.
4 A résumé is a formal document describing the qualifications of a job seeker.
5 A résumé is a self-appraisal that stresses past and present accomplishments in order to indicate future potential.
6 A résumé is a tool for self-evaluation which, when completed, may suggest new steps toward the attainment of goals.
7 A résumé is a brief business biography or vocational history that emphasizes experience, accomplishment, education, and objectives expressed in favorable terms.

Look upon a résumé as being akin to drawing up a contract, writing a will, solving a complicated tax problem. You have all the elements you need. Analyze each one, express it suitably, and place it in logical juxtaposition to the other elements.

A survey of hundreds of companies conducted by the author, shows these ways to get interviews, as specified by the companies:

1 Knowing someone who will interview you or will arrange an interview for you.
2 Answering help wanted advertisements with a résumé or letter.

3 Sending uninvited résumés or other writing to possible employers.
4 Answering help wanted advertisements with a telephone call, if invited to do so.
5 Making uninvited telephone calls to possible employers.
6 Making cold calls on personnel departments.
7 Attending campus interview sessions.
8 Advertising your availability through ads in the employment columns.
9 Sending your résumé to executive search firms.
10 Visiting employment agencies.
11 Job postings or promotions from within.

Of these methods 44.3% demand résumés and some others involve résumés; 8.2% require writing of some kind (letters, proposals) usually based on a résumé; 20.2% of interviews result from knowing the right person, often requiring a résumé during or after the interview.

Campus interviewing is important for entry level jobs with giant companies. Recruiters usually ask for a résumé.

Thus résumés are vitally important in over 50% of methods used to create interviews. In fact, we think a manager cannot normally complete the interviewed/hired succession without a résumé.

Special note: In an executive search capacity, 95% of the résumés we receive are from men and only 5% from women. A survey of professional résumé writers shows about the same proportion. This may reflect the absence of any large percentage of women in the upper reaches of management or, conversely, it may suggest that if women used résumés in the same way men do there would be more of them in middle and upper management. Perhaps we shall stumble upon some other reasons for this disparity.

HELP WANTED DISPLAY ADVERTISING

A survey of 1000 "help-wanted," "positions available" advertisements in *The New York Times* (Sunday) and *The Wall Street Journal* was conducted over a period of 5 to 6 weeks in February and March of 1975. The results were as follows:

1   Ask for résumé specifically   757
2   Ask for reply with full details (probably requiring résumé)   118
3   Ask for reply only   74
4   Ask for reply by telephone   51

Total   1000

Items 1 and 2 involving résumés, came to 87.5%. Adding item 3, for which a résumé would be the most appropriate reply, we find 94.5% of the advertisements to be résumé related.

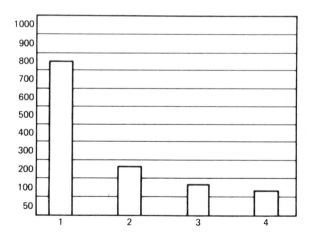

ON THE RISE: Heidrick & Struggles Inc., the Chicago-based consulting firm, found 485 women officers this year in its survey of 1,050 very large concerns. That's up from 416 in 1978 and 325 in 1977. Moreover, 46% are earning over $40,000 a year, up from 33% last year. (*The Wall Street Journal*, December 4, 1979.)

TWO

WHO USES RÉSUMÉS?

Almost every job seeker—whether unemployed or wishing to change positions—needs a résumé. Résumés are prepared by persons at all levels of employment: judges, lawyers, cabinet members, managers, chief executive officers, administrators, bookkeepers, secretaries. In my experience and according to surveys, most résumés are prepared by those looking for management, professional, or performing arts positions. Résumés are not usually required for clerical and skilled labor jobs, though their wider use might possibly expand and upgrade job opportunities in these areas. The only individuals who do not need résumés are those whose outstanding careers make it unnecessary for them to seek jobs—rather, jobs seek them. (See pp. 7, 10, 12, and 18.)

RESUME USERS: BY AGE GROUP

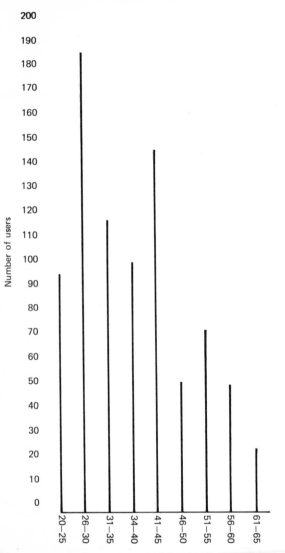

As would be expected, the greatest incidence of résumé use is in the age group from 26 to 45 years (533). The most frequent users are between the ages of 26 and 30; those between 41 and 45 are next. Most of those in the age group 20 to 25 are new to the job market. (From a sample of 1000, of whom 799 gave ages.)

THREE

WHY WRITE A RÉSUMÉ?

A résumé serves to introduce you to the employer and help gain a personal interview. You need a résumé because for most advertised *management* jobs (see p. 4) a résumé is required before an interview will be granted. Employers require résumés because they are executive time-savers. A personal interview takes hours; a résumé can be read in a few minutes.

There are other reasons for writing a résumé:

1 A résumé forms the basis for a mail campaign about yourself, using either the actual résumé or a summary of it in the form of a broadcast letter. The 80% of available jobs that are never advertised must be sought by mail.

2 A résumé can be used to test your marketability while you remain safely employed.

3 A résumé helps you to organize the facts of your past accomplishments, clarifying what you can or wish to do in the future. Many advisors recommend that a résumé be updated every six months or once a year. You thus remain continuously aware of your progress, or lack of it, and of your up-to-the minute responsibilities and achievements. What you did last year may have lost importance by reason of newer accomplishments.

4   A résumé in expanded form may help gain academic cred-
    its for "life work," an important opportunity offered by
    many universities.

5   A résumé may be utilized in buying a business to impart
    information about yourself to the seller.

6   A résumé can serve to solicit business if you are, for exam-
    ple, a consultant, a freelance artist or writer, or a part-time
    worker. A more elaborate brochure explaining your qualifi-
    cations can be based on it.

7   A résumé prepares you for your job interview by forcing
    you to think about and express yourself in an organized
    way. A résumé is your personal guidance manual for speak-
    ing about yourself fluently and unhesitatingly.

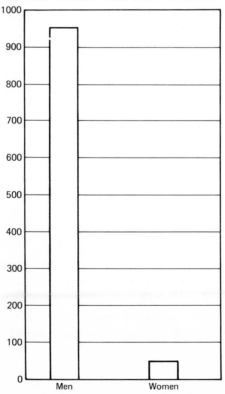

RÉSUMÉ USERS: MEN AND WOMEN

FOUR

THE NATURE
OF THE RÉSUMÉ

A résumé is a sales presentation of yourself. It should not be a mere detailing of past job experiences. It must be alive and interesting and must present your accomplishments to the maximum degree. Make it a portrait in color, rather than a black-and-white photograph. Will it favorably differentiate you from other applicants for the position? The reader of your résumé should be able to infer from your past achievements your expected contributions in a new position. The résumé should be honest—do not inflate your abilities beyond your capacity to produce.

There are many characteristics that make people come alive as individuals—different from the crowd. Accomplishments also can be avocational and interesting to mention. In what ways you are equipping yourself for greater responsibilities in the future is of interest. Your attitudes toward current events might find a brief place in your résumé or covering letter. Political involvement outside your business life can be mentioned if not too controversial. Participation in scouting, your church, your community, your children's school, as an alumnus of your own school or college, successful fund raising, and other activities can be utilized to generate interest if vocational material is inadequate.

FIVE

THE NEED
FOR A
SUPERIOR RÉSUMÉ

To get a job you need not be superior to other applicants; few would have jobs if only ideal applicants were hired! However your résumé should make you appear to be superior. An employer may receive hundreds of résumés for one position. A large corporation may handle 50,000 or more résumés a year. You can improve your chance of being one of the few selected for an interview by studying how to prepare your résumé; a study relatively free of competition and likely to bring great rewards.

In actual fact, you may be superior to other applicants but no one will know it unless you get a chance to explain your qualifications in a personal interview. Words in writing are different from the spoken word. It would be normal for what you say about yourself in writing to seem better to you and to be better, than what you have ever been able to say about yourself orally. This is because in writing about yourself you have had to think more clearly. The chore of writing down, by itself, demands clearer exposition. In a conversation you can repeat yourself or erase previous errors in a succeeding statement. What appears in writing cannot be changed. This also underscores again how important a résumé can be in helping you to express yourself properly during an interview.

The importance of résumés grows daily because of the increased competition for jobs caused by an ever larger population increasingly better educated and better qualified.

What constitutes a good résumé?

A good résumé is one that qualifies the subject for the job sought—as concisely as possible, literately, interestingly and honestly—and causes an interview to occur if a position is available.

To a degree, also, a good or a bad résumé is in the eye of the beholder. Some readers of résumés look for seeming perfection.

For example, the ideal candidate for a high management position from the point of view of some résumé readers would have these qualifications: age 43, a successful career with broad experience, showing continuous rapid progress with two or three multidivisional companies recognized nationally for management excellence. He or she would have graduated with honors from a Midwestern college, majored in economics, shown leadership in extracurricular activities, attended Harvard Graduate School of Business Administration (or Stanford or the University of Chicago), and earned an M.B.A. If a man, he would have an attractive wife and three children. If a woman, she would be single by divorce or separation, attractive, and career oriented (except in government employment).

For a recent graduate, again ideally, mix in a similar educational background, show undergraduate leadership, broad interests, motivation, well delineated career objective, single status.

Fewer than one tenth of 1% of job seekers have such ideal qualifications for any job at any level on the organizational scale.

Practiced résumé readers are noted for the ability quickly to identify the hole in the doughnut; or they read résumés subjectively rather than objectively. In any event, to the extent possible, the résumé writer must include in his document all the material and experience relevant to his or her job area and hope that "holes" will be offset by other qualities.

It is of course possible for a job applicant with poor qualifications to have a good résumé if the element of "honesty" in the definition is omitted; in this event the writing is more in the nature of a novella than a résumé and the overqualifications expressed will be discovered early in employment leading to the job hopping that is another red flag to a résumé reader; or a well phrased honest résumé might gain an interview even if the work background is poor.

You become qualified in your job area if, in employment, you continue the learning process to include all that any reasonable person would expect you to know and, from a résumé focus, present your qualities in appropriate language and form.

SIX

RÉSUMÉ LENGTH

There is no standard résumé length. A résumé should be as long as it needs to be to present important information concisely and interestingly. Successful résumés have been as short as one page and as long as six pages. It is conciseness, relevance, and interest that matter. A six page résumé can be concise; a three page résumé, verbose.

For example, there are many individuals who have extensive achievements over a period of 20 or 25 years or more. Achievements follow patterns. Some résumés could almost be textbooks for others to follow in climbing the ladder to organizational success. Of course they must include a personal method of expression and word usage to avoid textbook dullness. The point is that one can hardly compress a lifetime of achievement into a page of writing. Most employers of upper level managers are interested in what you have done if it has been well done.

Résumés directed toward gaining a specific job may be longer than résumés written for general distribution. One reason is that you will probably know more about a particular job in which you are closely interested and therefore can relate your special qualifications more expansively in terms of what you could or would do.

High level administrative nonprofit positions in a governmental or educational environment may also be more extended. Managers in these areas with the power to appoint tend to want qualifications fully expressed. Where political influence is involved it becomes very important that every ability and experience related to the function is fully delineated so that competitive influences are blunted.

If you are a Henry Ford, a William Simon, a Henry Kissinger you will not need to write much; but if you are not widely known you must explain yourself. There is a happy balance between too much and too little.

The search for a perfect résumé will never end. A perfect résumé is almost impossible, but the following would be:

To Whom it May Concern:
    Available.
        William Shakespeare

RESUME USERS: BY JOB CLASSIFICATION

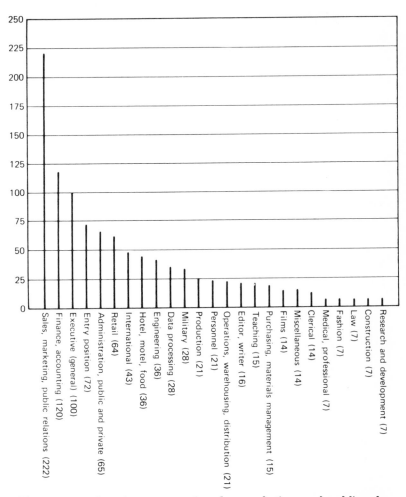

The greatest résumé use occurs in sales, marketing, and public relations. Persons employed in these areas may be more accustomed to writing, more aware of the benefits of advertising, or perhaps merely more restless than are other groups. (From a sample of 1000.)

SEVEN

RÉSUMÉ
LANGUAGE

The language of a résumé must be succinct, crisp, trenchant, expressive, interesting, and personal. Words, phrases, sentences, and paragraphs illustrating this type of writing appear later in this book (Appendix B). Use the specialized vocabulary of your job area. Scientists, data processors, lawyers, financial people, economists, engineers, social workers—each specialization has its own nomenclature. However, a résumé must never be so technical that those outside your discipline fail to understand it. If you have experience in a vocation, your language will naturally reflect it. If you have little or no experience, ignore this aspect.

There are more languages or dialects in English than you might think. To name just a few: academic, conversational, vernacular, bureaucratic, poetic, formal, jargon, argot, Gullah. They arise from education or lack of it, from environmental exposure, from the desire to confuse, from the combined use of two or more other languages to supplement English.

The fact of a résumé language arises out of a need for clear expression in a minimum number of words to create a maximum impact. There is no time for relaxed prose. The average résumé must make its *impression* in 20 to 30 seconds. If the first impression is good the entire résumé will be read. If the first impression is poor, it will be discarded. Average reading time is about four words per second.

There is the hope to lend excitement and create an urgency to make a decision. Most of all, there is the need of discipline to attain your objective which dictates the "language" or mode of expression.

EIGHT

COMMON RÉSUMÉ FAULTS

In my experience, the nine résumé deficiencies listed below are the most common ones and should be guarded against when writing a résumé.

1 A mere listing of the positions you have held, without further explanation.
2 Failure to state your objective early in the résumé.
3 Failure to describe your accomplishments.
4 Stating an objective for which you are unqualified.
5 Omitting a description of your responsibilities in the positions held.
6 Wordiness, incorrect spelling, and bad grammar.
7 Incomplete vocational history.
8 Omission of vital statistics (except for reasons discussed later).
9 Poor physical appearance.

NINE

THE ELEMENTS OF A RÉSUMÉ

WHAT TO OMIT

The following information is usually best omitted from your résumé:

1 Omit date. Your résumé should remain current for an extended period of time. Place the date in your covering letter.

2 Omit race, religion, political affiliation, and the like, unless part of the main thrust of your résumé. Though the law forbids discrimination for such reasons, you should not offer them as a basis for selection, which you do if you include them in the résumé. Disregard this advice if you know your prospective employer to be partial to certain kinds of people. Thus a Catholic parish would not only employ a Catholic priest rather than a Baptist minister, but might also tend to hire Catholic clerical workers—a tendency that holds equally for any religious institution.

3 Omit matters that are negative, detrimental, or awkward to write about.

4   Omit salary requirements.

- A leading reason for seeking new employment is to improve compensation. Avoid being restricted by your past salary level.
- You are entitled to the income level of the position being offered. The company should indicate what it is prepared to pay.
- Salary is negotiable—based on the nature of the position and your expected contribution to it.
- It is unwise to commit yourself to a salary level before the interview; you might underrate your potential.
- In the same way a salary that the employer finds unacceptable from a mere reading of your résumé (causing the résumé to be discarded) might become acceptable after the interview.

Some qualifications are in order, however. If an advertisement asks for salary information, you might supply it. Write it in by hand at the end of the résumé, together with bonuses and fringe benefits, if substantial, or combine all in an inclusive lump sum. I am ambivalent about this. In a very strong résumé salary disclosure can probably be avoided even when specifically requested.

Furthermore, very significant salary growth—from $12,000 to $40,000 within a short time—shows that your employer has recognized your merits in the most important possible way, and this in turn indicates strong functional progress. In such a case, making salary data known, showing your salary growth by percentages or graphically, is another way of buttressing your accomplishments.

Finally, if your earnings are or have been at a certain level that you are confident you can match in your new position, you might safely include your income expectancy in your covering letter.

5 Omit references.

- An employer should have no interest in your references until after he has become interested in you—after the interview.
- A prospective employer might consult the persons given as references before interviewing you. This is undesirable because you wish to be the first one to describe yourself.
- Persons named as references can become irritated by too many calls.
- You will not wish to have your present employer called as a reference before employment interest in you has been indicated.

However, any extraordinary references that you might have can be included. Extraordinary references would include famous people, individuals of stature in your area of competence, important political figures, and the like.

WHAT TO INCLUDE

The elements to be included in résumés are discussed below. The starred items are those essential to any résumé.

*1 **Your personal directory.** Name, address (with zip code), and telephone number (with area code) are obvious essentials that must appear in your résumé. The only exception is the case in which the employer is dealt with by way of an intermediary for reasons of confidentiality. The third party approach is of course less effective than the direct approach and should not be used without good cause. Make sure that the intermediary disclaims any right to compensation for services rendered.

MAGNITUDE OF RÉSUMÉ USE: A SPECULATION

The New York Times and *The Wall Street Journal* carry about 250 display "jobs available" advertisements each week. Assuming that these "bibles" of the job market account for 10% of all management jobs advertised throughout the country, 2500 jobs are listed weekly; 130,000 annually. If advertised jobs reflect only 20% of available positions, there are about 12,500 openings each week or about 650,000 each year. Each of the advertised openings must attract at least 10 résumés, or 1,300,000. Some of these résumés are sent by the same people in answer to several different advertisements; so reduce by half to 650,000. In addition, 200 leading companies receive 25,000 a year (a few as many as 50,000) sent by 125 to 200 writers. Another 2800 companies receive 1000 a year (2,800,000 résumés) sent by 28,000 writers. Dun and Bradstreet list 67,000 additional companies in the million-dollar and middle-market categories which may receive a number of résumés each year; assume two. Add to these the résumés circulated by new graduates just entering the job market to bring the total written each year, to more than 1,000,000 and 100 million mailed out. About 1% may be prepared professionally.

A sampling of about 2000 résumés found 80 to 90% of them to be deficient in one or more respects, doing the subject less than justice.

If you are employed, list your business telephone number, provided that privacy of conversation is possible. Repeated unanswered calls to an applicant's home may negatively affect the prospective employer's interest. Immediate availability can be crucial in the decision to hire.

*2 **Objective.** Your résumé should be geared to your job objective. State the objective clearly at the outset. If you know the experience and qualifications needed for a job, direct your résumé to describing, as specifically as possible, your ability to meet the criteria. Most applicants lack such information, which sometimes can be obtained from friends, acquaintances, bankers, competitors, annual company reports, and similar sources. Usually, however, a résumé is intended to meet the requirements of more than one specific job and must be written more broadly. Among the objectives toward which a résumé can be directed are the following:

- An entry position in marketing, finance, or production.
- A management position in marketing, finance, or production, or in any subdivision of these functions.
- A career change—from a profession to business, from military service to business, and the like.
- An office administrative position.

There are general categories. For your résumé choose as specific a job classification as possible from the thousands of categories in existence. A prospective employer should not have to guess what kind of a job you want.

3 **Qualifications: A brief summary, a paragraph long summary, or an expanded full page summary.** Having stated your job objective, you must present your qualifications for it. Qualifications include courses of study, past work experience, and even character traits that can be supported:

- *Ambition* can be indicated by having worked one's way through college.
- *Motivation* can be manifested by having achieved good grades.
- *Commitment* can be shown by a long term ambition to pursue one's objective and enrollment in training toward that end.
- *Intelligence* might be indicated by a high class standing and receipt of awards.

If you have substantial work experience, a summary page is in order. The method of preparing such a page is explained later.

You can describe your qualifications either objectively or subjectively. Allowing your personality to come through will add warmth to an otherwise sterile document, especially if the résumé is short. Objective evaluations can come from official reports on personnel, such as those used by the armed forces and increasingly by many private companies that review their personnel annually, making the results available to the employee.

RESUME USERS: EMPLOYED AND UNEMPLOYED

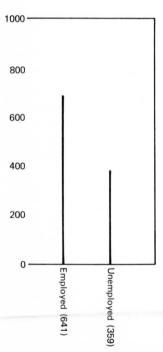

Those who are employed use résumés almost twice as much as do the unemployed. (From a sample of 1000.)

*4 Experience. In describing your experience give the dates on which you began and terminated the job. Use the phrase "to present" to indicate current employment. State the name and location of the company, except when present employment must be kept confidential. "Name of Company on Request" may suffice in such cases. It is not necessary to include a company's street address. Describe briefly what the company makes, sells, or does, how large it is, and how many employees it has.

Then list your responsibilities at the company. Use the company's job description of your position or create your own. A corporate job description can be a formidable and necessarily tedious document. Extract from it the highlights of your responsibilities, using key words and sentences, to avoid burdening your résumé with unneeded, though technically relevant, verbiage.

The description of responsibilities should always be followed by a statement of accomplishments. For example:

> Responsible for planning entry of Company into chain store distribution. Accomplishments: developed program, hired salesmen, implemented program, contributed new volume of $1 million in first year of operation.

> Responsible for transcribing dictation from three advertising agency account executives. Accomplishments: became expert with IBM Executive typewriter; increased typing speed from 50 to 75 words per minute; increased accuracy to 97%.

What you are responsible for doing takes on significance when you describe what you did about it. Ask yourself, "What needed to be done, and what did I do? What happened as a result?"

Follow methodology described for each position you have held in a company and for each company you have worked for. Describe your experience first in chronological sequence; if another style is preferred, rearrange the items later.

*5   Education.   As a rule education appears near the beginning of a résumé if one has no work experience, and after experience when experience begins to outweigh education after a year or so in a job. One exception is the *Professional Résumé* for reasons explained later.

An academic degree or attendance at a college makes any mention of graduation from high school superfluous, though you might wish to list a "name" preparatory school. The high school graduate who did not go to college must mention the fact of graduation. The noncollege graduate should deemphasize education as early as possible in the résumé. Any continuation of education should be noted and described, regardless of the level.

Show your class standing if it is high; otherwise omit it. Mention the honors, awards, and scholarships you have earned.

If your education or individual courses you have attended are particularly relevant to your objective, say so in your résumé (this will be self-evident in the *Professional Résumé*). Advanced degrees should be stated. At this writing a master's degree in business administration (M.B.A.) is the most valuable business degree and commands a compensation advantage of $2000 to $15,000 or more annually. For the nonprofessional a doctoral degree is an advantage if related to the job objective. It is a definite asset for a researcher, teacher, scientist, writer, and public administrator.

6   Extracurricular activities.   Listing extensive extracurricular activities can add flavor to a résumé. Omit them if they are few, however, and after you have gained substantial work experience—their significance tends to erode with time. Do list teaching assistantships, tutoring, waiting on tables, elective student organization offices, sports participation, school newspaper experience, and special distinctions of any kind. They enable the employer to know you better and may strike a responsive chord that might provide an edge in selection for employment.

7 **Summer work while attending school or college.** Employers look with favor on those who have used their school or college holidays for constructive activities. Therefore, summer employment is a worthwhile addition to a résumé, and so is having partially or wholly worked one's way through college. This entry in the résumé is a character building block.

8 **Military service.** Your service in the armed forces, with an honorable discharge, has a place in your résumé. Usually its mention should be brief. Extended description is in order, however, if military service forms a major part of your background—the young man who has been in the armed forces for two to five or more years and has no other employment experience or the career military man who seeks a new career after retirement from the service. Your service record supplies a wealth of information from which interesting, persuasive, and relevant material can be drawn as the basis for a highly effective résumé presentation. Take care to avoid an overlong discussion of your military career, no matter how extensive—stress the factors most relevant to your civilian job objective.

9 **Professional membership.** Membership in professional and trade associations denotes an ongoing interest in expanding one's vocational experience. Some memberships are almost mandatory for certain job classifications. Any industrially, commercially, or professionally recognized membership should be listed in your résumé.

10 **Community activities.** Some companies, highly conscious of their local image, favor employee participation in fund drives, charitable board memberships, and community assistance activities. Participation in community activities may characterize you in the eyes of a potential employer as an individual with broad interests and the potential for greater managerial responsibilities.

11   Accreditation and licenses. Include all accreditations
and licenses related to your vocation in your résumé. Examples are C.P.A., C.L.U., Licensed Engineer, Licensed
Real Estate Broker, and R.N. Honorary degrees should
also be listed.

12   Patents and publications.   Patents, particularly important
to the research scientist, the R.&D. manager or employee, and the engineer, as indicators of original thinking should always be included in a résumé. Publication
carries special weight in teaching, business consulting,
law, and other professions. They serve as tools in evaluating you, and as a basis for a constructive and interesting
interview.

*13   Personal data.   Personal data are date of birth, marital
status, sex (if name is ambiguous), state of health (if excellent), citizenship (if potentially unclear), number of
children, home ownership, willingness to relocate, geographical employment preference (if any), availability for
employment (if not immediate), extensive travel experience, height, and weight.

The laws relating to equal opportunity employment make
it illegal for an employer to discriminate by reasons of
age, color, creed, race, religion, and sex. You must judge
for yourself whether to include all these data in your résumé. Give age if you are young; omit it if you are over
50. On the other hand, if no age is given, the employer
may infer more years than the actual number. Approximate age can be guessed quite accurately from dates of
graduation and from the length of your career. You might
also consider excluding all dates from your résumé. Age
is one of the greatest deterrents to employment for many
reasons, such as pensions and other benefits, which become costly to employers for new employees of advanced age, and the partiality of many large companies
to training their own executives.

Other personal data, we think, need not be excluded from your résumé. The employment opportunities for qualified blacks and other ethnic groups are expanding; an equal opportunity employer may be able to utilize information about your race to your advantage. Employment opportunities for qualified women are growing apace. Your height and weight will be of value only in the entertainment field. We prefer that separation or divorce be stated in a résumé, but this is a matter of personal preference.

14 **Hobbies.** Mention interesting hobbies; omit commonplace ones, except golf and tennis, which accomplish wide rapport. Outstanding excellence in any sport or hobby should be mentioned.

15 **Languages.** A knowledge of languages other than English may be mandatory in an international business and important or helpful in many other activities. Include any language proficiency.

16 **Reason for leaving last job.** Some recruiters consider this information to be an important part of a résumé. We prefer its *omission* because the explanation can be cumbersome and disadvantageous. Furthermore, it can normally have no positive influence on gaining an interview. *The reason for leaving your last job is a matter to be discussed at a personal interview when you can explain it at length.* However, almost everyone has had one disastrous job experience. It may even be an advantage—one story, possibly apocryphal, has it that a large employer receiving hundreds of applications for a position decided to exclude all résumés that did not show one job failure!

There are many reasons for leaving a job either by choice or involuntarily. A frequent reason is personality conflict. Whether your fault or your employer's and colleagues', it is to your disadvantage before the prospective employer has had an opportunity to make a personal assess-

A résumé giving "personality conflict" as the reason for leaving a job may become discarded before a personal interview takes place; it is a reason that can give rise to complicated and unfavorable psychological reactions.

One highly placed manager was dismissed after 20 years because he had accepted a small gift from an appreciative customer four years earlier. In fact, his dismissal was not for this transgression per se. Some of his subordinates had been accepting large bribes from customers, of which he was unaware, but perhaps should not have been. His earlier acceptance of one small gift placed him in an untenable position, which, management felt, could not remain an exception. There was a bit of post-Watergate morality in this corporate action, and near-tragedy for the employee. Many people will find it difficult to understand why a company's chief executive officer is free to spend millions for bribing foreign government employees to get business or hundreds of thousands for illegal campaign contributions while lesser infractions are heavily penalized. It is a subject needing discussion. Certainly most prospective employers would overlook this type of transgression after the applicant's full explanation during an interview—an explanation difficult or impossible to include in a résumé.

The strong trend of merger and acquisition activity has displaced thousands of executives who had thought to be firmly established in their jobs. Being disemployed for such reasons is understandable and without onus. If it is true of you, mention it. It removes a question that is always in an employer's mind.

If an employment agreement was breached, you may say so without going into details.

The sale of a business is usually followed by changes in personnel. Mentioning this in a letter or résumé is more positive than negative.

Divestment of a division, liquidation of a business need but a few words to make clear the reason why you are looking for new employment.

Relocation of a business to a place where you do not want to live is a good reason for you to want to leave a company, but not necessarily from an employer's point of view. The employer may think that this shows employee inflexibility.

Declines in earnings often mean layoffs. If your position was one that did not have an influence on earnings, you may give this reason.

Technological changes or competition can ruin or have an adverse impact on nondiversified companies.

The U.S. garment industry has been adversely affected by competition from the Far East. Hand tailoring has declined with the advent of mass production techniques. If you were in the business of making tailors' shears your livelihood disappeared.

The ball-point pen has superseded the old ink pack pens.

Pocketknives were almost universally carried at one time; now no longer.

Wristwatches supplanted pocket watches.

Cheap electronic manufacturing by the Japanese has replaced U.S. components in television sets and radios.

Overseas auto manufacturers are increasing their share of the market with their compact, high mileage cars.

Such changes have a continuous effect on employment.

Recognition of lack of opportunity in a static business can be used to show high motivation.

Several jobs held in a short period of time need to be explained if the period is important to the chronology of the résumé. The period can be omitted entirely if it occurs early in your career, however.

Employment gaps should be explained or closed as fully as possible. Gaps occurring during a recession will be understood by your prospective employer. For those gaps very difficult to justify you might consult your friends or former employers. Such terms as "consultant" and "freelance worker" are poorly received except in areas where freelancing is common (artists and writers, for example).

17 **Security clearance.**   If your past or present employment is security sensitive, specify the level of your security clearance.

18 **Aptitude and psychological tests.**   Employers tend to think that most tests other than their own have little validity. In fact, such tests frequently are too generalized or diffused to be of significance. Omit test results from your résumé, unless excerpts of singular appropriateness can be used to show qualifications objectively.

19 **Photographs.**   Most of the executives recruiting for business do not consider photographs important. Nevertheless, a résumé impact can be increased by including a small ($2^1/_2$ by $2^1/_2$ inches) clearly defined candid snapshot in color (passport-type photographs are usually of poor quality). Remember that photographs with the subject posed for artistic effect are inappropriate in business résumés. Paste the photograph in the upper left or right hand corner of the first résumé page. Photographs are essential in the résumé of an entertainer or model and should be 8 by 10 inches or larger.

20 **Art decoration.**   Simple decoration can improve a résumé. However, because "one man's meat is another man's poison" use art devices with great care.

21 **Graphs and charts.**   Graphs and charts usually add little to a résumé unless of professional quality. A simple curve showing sales increases is not impressive. On the other hand, a 10 year bar chart of sales and profit increases or a curve of dramatic increases in your income can make valid points.

22 **Testimonials.**   Testimonials can serve effectively as objective evaluations, provided that you can present them without appearing to be boastful. Testimonials can be placed in any appropriate part of your résumé, particularly on a summary page or in a summary paragraph, or when discussing your handling of important responsibilities.

23 **Civil service grades.**   In seeking a job with the government or in indicating the governmental level of your responsibilities to a private employer, mention of the civil service grade is useful.

RÉSUMÉ READERS' CRITICISMS

The criticisms listed below are those most commonly expressed by résumé readers. You will observe that many of them are in exact opposition. There is no way to write a résumé that will appeal to every reader. Fit your résumé to the type of individual whom you expect to be reading it.

1 **Too long.**   The résumé is not concise, interesting, and relevant. A person required to read hundreds or thousands of résumés, however, may find any résumé that exceeds one page to be too long. Keep a résumé short if it is aimed at a lower echelon personnel executive or an employment agency.

2 **Too short.**   The résumé does not give the reader an opportunity to make a proper evaluation.

3 **Too condensed.**   Paragraphs and sentences are too closely written for easy reading. It is preferable to expand spatially sentences, paragraphs, and white space rather than to try to get two pages of easy-to-read writing on one page.

4 **Too wordy.** The description is verbose, with several words used for what could have been expressed in one or two.

5 **Too slick.**   The résumé is so well prepared as to be inappropriate for the individual presenting it and must therefore have been written by someone else. This evaluation leads the reader to suspect that the subject's qualifications are exaggerated.

6 **Too amateurish.**   The applicant cannot express himself, which would be a liability on the job.

7 **Poorly reproduced.**   The résumé is carelessly reproduced, especially when duplicated on poor paper by inferior photocopier.

8 **Misspellings and bad grammar abound.**   Spelling and grammatical errors in a résumé show lack of the primary skills necessary for accomplishment. Poor spellers need not be low achievers, but a poor speller who does not compensate for this deficiency by having another person proofread the résumé shows bad judgment. Bad grammar is inexcusable at the executive and professional levels.

9 **Reason for leaving last job omitted.**   This has been discussed elsewhere in this book.

10 **Date of availability omitted.**   If you apply for a position months ahead of the time when you can start work, include the date of your availability.

11 **Geographical preference omitted.** Any geographical preferences or limitations regarding location of employment should be specified in a résumé.

12 **Objective omitted.**   This has been discussed elsewhere.

13 **Poorly expressed.** If you are unable to prepare your own résumé, have someone else write it for you.

14 **Résumé is boastful.** Boastfulness is an unattractive quality. Be realistic about yourself, but do not bluster, overestimate, or exaggerate.

15 **Résumé is dishonest.** You have claimed to have expertise that you do not possess.

16 **Salary information lacking.** This has been discussed elsewhere.

17 **Résumé is "gimmicky."** It contains words, structure, decoration, or material that departs so much from the norm that it is unacceptable.

18 **Sufficient data lacking.** The material is insufficient for a proper evaluation. You may have tried to condense to one page experience that requires several pages for explanation.

TEN

THE RIGHT RÉSUMÉ— STRONG AND POSITIVE

Most of the individuals whose résumés appear in this book sound like achievers. In fact, some may have had disappointing careers. Others have accomplished something, but not enough, in the companies for which they worked. They might have succeeded in other companies or under other circumstances. The faults measured by the requirements of one position, or by the definition of one management, can be virtues when measured by different criteria.

Your résumé should make you, too, sound like an achiever. Forget your negative aspects and stress your positive attributes. Self-analysis, aided by suggestions in this book, may reveal talents of which you have been unaware. Your chronological job history may disclose accomplishments you have underestimated. When written down, your accomplishments may sound better than you expected. They may be superior when compared to those of others doing similar jobs.

If your career has been less successful than you had hoped, it need not continue to be so. Your résumé is a means of es-

cape from career disappointment or mediocrity to career fulfillment. It is not dishonest to have your résumé accent your
most positive characteristics. No one is perfect. *You* may be
just what some employer is looking for. In another position
your positive attributes may bring you the degree of success
that has eluded you in the past, whatever your present level of
accomplishment.

Your résumé is a way to gain an interview. Make it as strong
as possible to achieve that end. You cannot help yourself or
anyone else with a weak résumé.

A résumé has to be written from the point of view that it is
an evaluation that qualifies you for the job you want.

1 You must show that you meet the requirements of the job.
2 You must analyze your background to find those qualifications.
3 You must express yourself logically, precisely, and with
   individuality.

ANALYSIS OF RÉSUMÉ USERS: ENTRY POSITION

The average age is 24.5.
Females are 20% of sample.

ELEVEN

THE TEN RÉSUMÉ STYLES

There are about 10 recognized résumé styles or forms, with an infinite number of variations and combinations. The examples given in this book should help you in choosing among them. Our recommendations appear on pages 2 to 3. The 10 styles are discussed in detail in the sections that follow.

1 *Basic Résumé.*
2 *Chronological Résumé.*
3 *Chronological Résumé with Summary Page.*
4 *Functional Résumé.*
5 *Harvard Résumé.*
6 *Functional-by-Company (Institution) Résumé. Company* here refers to an incorporated or unincorporated business. *Institution* is an organization with a social, educational, or religious purpose, such as a school, church, hospital, prison, and foundation.
7 *Creative Résumé.*
8 *Narrative Résumé.*
9 *Professional Résumé.*
10 *Accomplishment Résumé.*

The word *form* is used to mean style of résumé. *Format* refers to the physical aspects of a résumé, such as its margins, headlines, underlining, and page size.

Remember that the accomplishments listed in your résumé need not be notable achievements, but achievements within the level of your responsibility only. Whether you are an office boy, a clerk, a supervisor, a manager, or a president, you can have accomplishments that are significant in relation to your job and job objective.

BASIC RÉSUMÉ

The *Basic Résumé,* best suited for those entering the job market, should contain the following items (their order may vary).

1 Name, address with zip code, and telephone number with area code.
2 Personal data (age, marital status, health, willingness to travel or relocate, date of availability).
3 Objectives.
4 Education (honors, awards, high class standing).
5 Extracurricular activities.
6 Languages other than English.
7 Summer jobs.
8 Military service.
9 Hobbies (if interesting).

This is a standard form. We recommend that job qualifications be added, if they can be properly expressed, immediately after objectives. Keep this résumé to one page. Use the *Basic Résumé* whenever work experience is very limited. Any important job experience that does exist should be described before education.

Examples of *Basic Résumé* follow.

INFLUENCE OF COLLEGE EDUCATION
ON LIFETIME EARNINGS

U.S. Department of Labor statistics consistently show that a college education significantly increases lifetime earnings. The 1972 data, for example, indicate the following:

Educational level	Lifetime earnings (ages 25–64)	Increase in lifetime earnings
Four years of college	$668,100	70%
One to three years of college	$461,000	18%
High school	$393,000	

In their recent study, *The Declining Value of College Going,* Freeman and Holloman state that "by all relevant measures the economic status of college graduates is deteriorating, with employment prospects for the young declining exceptionally sharply." This assessment, and its connotation for the future, is not uniformly shared. According to Herbert Bienstock, head of the Bureau of Labor Statistics in New York, long-term government projections show that the demand for college graduates will grow at three times the rate of demand for all workers in the United States labor force. Furthermore, jobless rates in March 1975 were 3% for college graduates and 15% for high school dropouts.

Stephen B. Withey, author of *A Degree and What Else,* writes in a Carnegie Commission on Higher Education report that students going through college increase their interest in esthetic and cultural values and progress on the "social maturity scale" to a much greater extent than do noncollege individuals. They have a greater ability to shape their "material future," greater job security, better career prospect, and greater job satisfaction.

EXAMPLE OF BASIC RÉSUMÉ

21-B Baker Street   (123) 456-/o.-
Fog, CA (zip)

RESUME

of

SHERLOCK WATSON

PERSONAL DATA: Born 3/10/57, single, excellent health.

OBJECTIVE:

Association with a communications or other company in an entry position
with opportunity for general management consistent with ability to
contribute.

QUALIFICATIONS:

Good education, consistently high academic grades, willingness to work
hard to establish capability; concerned with and interested in major U.S.
and world problems; active in causes; experienced in working with general
public during summer jobs and in retail selling since graduating from
college. Volunteer work 1974 to date. Harmonious, articulate, diligent.
Senior year of high school in Thailand. Rudimentary knowledge of French
and German.

EDUCATION:

B.A., Government, University of Pennsylvania, Philadelphia, PA, 1979.
Courses in Government: U.S., South Africa, Latin America, France.
Courses in: Principles of Management, Economics I and II, International
    Business, Business Ethics, Fundamentals of Public Speaking, Oral
    Interpretation.
Dean's list, two years.

EXTRA-CURRICULAR ACTIVITIES:

Football, lacrosse, handball; librarian assistant; mail room messenger;
R.O.T.C.

BUSINESS EXPERIENCE:

Nov. 22-Dec. 24, 1979: THE MAY COMPANY, Long Beach, CA.
TOY SALESMAN for branch of leading department store.

SUMMER JOBS:

1969-1973: DEPT. of PARKS and RECREATION, La Jolla, CA.
June to Nov. 1979, GATE ATTENDANT, beach area; June to Sept. 1978, POOL
GATEMAN; June to Sept. 1977, LOCKER ROOM ATTENDANT; June to Sept. 1976,
LOCKER ROOM ATTENDANT; June to Sept. 1965, PARK ATTENDANT. Collected
revenues, checked residency, painted, cleaned beach.

HOBBIES: Numismatics, philately, chess.

REFERENCES AND FURTHER DATA ON REQUEST

DISCUSSION

Basic Résumé. The Watson résumé arouses interest at once. Here is a young man who knows the general area in which he would like to work and without boastfulness expresses the qualifications he knows he possesses. Probably only a few students could be selected for study in Thailand. He attained academic honors in college. He worked during the summer vacation months. His extracurricular activities were broad. His hobbies are intellectual. His studies were chosen with a business career in mind.

The résumé is patterned for easy readability and logical sequence with education taking precedence over business experience because of its greater importance at this career stage.

If the employment had included important learning experience relevant to job objective it might have preceded education.

MILLARD FILLMORE
1776 Patomac Ave.
New York, NY 11210
(123) 445-6789

RESUME

PERSONAL DATA:

Age 22, single, healthy. Extensively traveled in United States, Europe, British Isles, Canada. Speak and understand some French.

OBJECTIVE:

Position in Financial Department of Corporation, Institution.

EDUCATION:

1978   B.S., Pace University, School of Commerce, New York, NY. Major, Banking and Finance: Corporate Finance, Management, Investment Analysis, Money Markets, Economics, Accounting.

Admitted to Phi Alpha Kappa, Honor Finance Society, for attaining 3.5 index. Cumulative 4 year index: 3.3 of possible 4.0.

Member of Finance Society, Pre-Law Society.

1971-
Present Attending New York Law School (night classes).

EXPERIENCE:

May 1-Dec. 30, 1979 LOST COMPANY, INC.

As ASSISTANT TO THE PRESIDENT, gained practical financial experience in helping to rescue near bankrupt corporation. Involved in decision-making and negotiations.

Met and negotiated with substantial investors from all over the world in connection with Company plans for an underwriting.

Participated in surveys and studies of land development project in Arizona.

Also learned about water desalinization.

Experience in Security Brokerage through part-time work in Uncle's business.

MILITARY SERVICE: 1975 U.S. NAVAL RESERVE, Boatswains Mate 3/C.

REFERENCES AND FURTHER DATA ON REQUEST

DISCUSSION

Basic Résumé. The Fillmore résumé utilizes the same form as the Watson résumé, with different indentation accommodating almost the identical number of words. Again, the form is a matter of choice. The fact that one has traveled extensively is usually well worth including in a résumé because travel is educational and contributes to self-development.

This young man's educational experience was outstanding and easily takes precedence over his business experience even though that was unique and interesting.

Although a legal education is not directly related to finance, it is nevertheless excellent training for any business career and, added to undergraduate studies in finance, will create an individual of substantial educational background that can be later utilized for professional management progress.

This résumé should be well received by executive recruiters.

CHRONOLOGICAL RÉSUMÉ

The *Chronological Résumé* is the one most frequently used by applicants who have job experience. The form offers the writer the best opportunity to "highlight" achievements and the reader the best opportunity to gauge the applicant's qualifications. The work experience is shown in reverse chronological order, the last or present job being given first. The various positions held at one company should also be described in reverse chronological order. This order shows the applicant's growth and development—characteristics of great interest to employers. The elements of the *Chronological Résumé* are as follows:

1 Name, address, and telephone number.
2 Objective.
3 Name of the company of most recent or present employment.

- Brief description of the company.
- Responsibilities.
- Accomplishments (treat each level of assignment as if it were a different employer).

4 Name of the company of next most recent employment.

- Brief description of the company.
- Responsibilities.
- Accomplishments.

Continue as above for each relevant employment, going back to your first job. If earlier employment is unrelated to your present objective, summarize it briefly in a catch-all sentence or paragraph. Omit mention of inappropriate or undignified jobs—jobs that are unrelated to the one being sought, or jobs that poorly reflect your qualities.

5 Military service (delete this heading if inappropriate).
6 Education.
7 Extracurricular activities (including summer jobs).
8 Accreditations (C.P.A., C.L.U., Real Estate Broker, Licensed Engineer, and so forth).
9 Professional memberships.
10 Community activities.
11 Hobbies.
12 Personal data.

The *Chronological Résumé* may be two or more pages in length. Remember the rules: conciseness, relevance, and interest.

Examples of *Chronological Résumé follow:*

JOB COMPETITION

Here is a typical response to an attractive advertisement for a senior marketing executive in a Tuesday edition of *The Wall Street Journal.*

Number of answers	310
In the New York area	186
Outside the New York area	124
Résumés received	294
Letters received	16
Applicants who are employed	257
Applicants who are unemployed	19
Not clear whether employed or unemployed	34
Salary stated	198
Salary not stated	112
Undergraduate degree	180
Master's degree	80
Doctoral degree	7
No degree	43

SMALL AND LARGE COMPANIES AS JOB SOURCES

Fast-growing smaller companies are among the best targets for employment; they have no reservoir of staff and *must* hire at all levels from outside. Many large corporations prefer to promote from within if possible. They are very important employers at entry levels. This does not mean they are not a target of an employment search at any level; it means only that fast-growing companies should be sought out in addition to the very large companies.

1676 Old Saw Street   (123) 456-7890
Boston, MA (zip)

RESUME

of

PATIENCE VIRTUE

Employment Objective in the Following Areas:

INVESTMENT BANKING: Municipal financial consulting; new issues; new
                        business; private placements; financial services;
                        institutional sales; research.

COMMERCIAL BANKING: Urban affairs, money market, municipal lending,
                        financial services.

Education includes:

M.B.A., B.S., superior grades, 3.7 on the 4.0 scale. Finance major.

Personal data:

Age 32, divorced, excellent health; interested in financial analysis,
riding, sports, travel, writing.

Record of Experience:

1972-Present   KUHN MARX & CO., 5 Hancock St., Boston, MA.

ANALYST, Institutional Department for investment banking company and full-
service retail and institutional brokerage. This department over the past
5½ years handled approximately 35 new capital projects per year for municipalities in Connecticut involving general obligation or revenue bonds
of about $200 million.

Responsible for:
- preparation and dissemination of information to facilitate new issue
  financings by serving as intermediary between municipality and investor.
- assistance to debt issuer to obtain best credit rating possible, together with lowest interest cost.
- creating environment to provide maximum marketability of bonds.
- preparation and finalization of all Official Statements including
  organization of all pertinent economic and financial data needed for
  evaluation

51

The above responsibilities entailed:

- participation in all preliminary financial discussions with architects, bond counsels, house counsel, municipalities, solicitors, trustee banks and/or paying agents, syndicate members, issuers, investors and major banks and insurance companies, financial firms and salesmen.

- risk analysis, financing concepts and closing sales. Personally responsible for many salesmen's orders up to $2.6 million.

- examination of feasibility of capital proposals, reviewing feasibility reports prepared by consultants and major accounting firms, suggesting modifications as necessary to assure successful underwriting, inclusion of security provisions, rate covenants, earnings tests, reserve capitalization, analysis of financial statements including balance sheets, breakeven points and rechecking to assure validity of risk/equity relationships.

- contacts with regulatory agencies at State and Federal levels.

The carrying out of these various responsibilities resulted in:

- saving issuers thousands of dollars in basis points by achieving higher ratings from rating services through personal presentations, i.e., upgrading ratings, holding marginal ratings, reversing lower ratings, sometimes getting a higher rating from one service than another and thereby mitigating the lower rating.

- ability to underwrite issues in difficult markets.

- specifically, for example, causing both Moody and Standard & Poor's to upgrade one $15.9 million Refunding School Authority Issue in 1977, which otherwise might have produced an underwriting loss.

- reduction of underwriting and other market risks.

- protection of firm against civil or criminal suits for nondisclosure with concomitant result of full profit.

- repeat business for the firm.

<u>1968-1972</u>   DUN AND STANDARD CORP., 27 Wall Street, New York, NY.

Member of EDITORIAL STAFF, WRITER and ANALYST of and for "Bond Outlook" for publisher of financial data on securities with well-known investment advisory service to clients.

- prepared weekly analysis of new bond issues.

- reviewed and evaluated municipal credit.

- analyzed economic, social, political and geographical data.

- reported on city and state general obligation, revenue and construction bonds.

- studied and evaluated annual municipal financial statements, audits, budgets, capital improvement programs.

- evaluated debt structures, histories and trends.

- reviewed and weighed qualitative factors of administration, organization, structure, efficiency and growth factors.

- utilized all types of financial data, Federal Reserve and Census Bureau publications.

Accustomed to personal interview and liaison activities with municipal officials, business managers, financial advisors and consultants and bank executives. Experience additionally included:
- training analysts.
- analysis of Standard & Poor's ratings on 8,000 issues.
- development of advertising themes.
- providing data and story lines for financial writers.
- diversified special reports, summaries and analysis.

<u>1965-1968</u>   WACHOVIA TRUST CO., New York, NY.

RESEARCH ASSISTANT after starting as Statistical Clerk for one of largest banks in the U.S.
- worked directly with Senior Municipal Analyst and Senior Vice President.
- prepared analytical reports on municipal securities for Officers Investment Committee and Board of Directors.
- provided reports forming a basis for portfolio decisions.
- utilized all sources of financial and economic data as appropriate.
- maintained financial and economic charts.

<u>REFERENCES AND FURTHER DATA ON REQUEST</u>

DISCUSSION

Chronological Résumé. The Virtue résumé is very comprehensive and could have been written in several other forms, such as a *Functional Résumé* or *Chronological with Summary Page Résumé*. The chronological form was chosen because the sequence of experience shows continuous growth.

The summary page was omitted in this instance to keep the résumé short; no summary is really needed to explain the obvious high qualifications of the subject.

The résumé is written in the language of a professional expressing knowledge of her subject with literacy and compactness. Her work is specialized and complicated. Any reader will know at once that here is a highly capable individual. Despite the résumé's comprehensiveness there is still much that remains to be explored in a personal interview.

Age, education, and personal data are clearly and briefly expressed at the outset because most are highly favorable and need no extended comment.

ANALYSIS OF RÉSUMÉ USERS: FINANCE

Chief financial officer, treasurer, controller, accounting, brokerage, financial research, and intermediate positions.

The salary range is $7000 to $80,000.*
The median is $19,000.
In percentages:

45% earn from $18,000 to $26,000.
25% earn from $12,000 to $18,000.
10% earn over $26,000.
20% earn from $7000 to $10,000.

The age range is 24 to 61.
The average age is 38.3.
Some 50% are in their 30s.
Females are 2.5% of the total.

* These figures are based on 1976 salaries.

CHRONOLOGICAL RÉSUMÉ
WITH SUMMARY PAGE

The *Chronological Résumé with Summary Page* is the most effective form of résumé for middle to upper business management as well as in some other vocations. The summary page interprets the résumé and quickly provides the gist of the applicant's case. Remember that the summary page is always the *first* page of the résumé. It is written *last,* however, because it is based on the material appearing in the chronological part of the résumé, which must be written *first.*

A summary page establishes rapport and interest and creates the curiosity to learn more about the applicant's background in the subsequent pages. Psychologically it compliments the reader by recognizing that his or her time is valuable and by providing the opportunity to make a quick appraisal.

The summary page can also be used to "beef up" a basically weak résumé.

The summary page, however, is an extra page. If you are concerned about the length of your résumé, eliminate the summary page or reduce its content to a brief paragraph or two to be placed at the beginning of the résumé. You will find examples of résumés with full summary pages and with reduced summaries.

Because *Chronological Résumé with Summary Page* is difficult to prepare, it is explained in detail in the pages that follow. In our annotated example page 2 appears first because the summary page, page 1, is *written last.*

The summary technique is used by many writers of reports and other long or technical analyses to permit a reader to know the conclusions arrived at before studying the details.

1800 Trafalger Square   (177) 377-4777
Admiral, NC 43215

RESUME

of

WELLINGTON DUKE

Qualified as

SENIOR MANAGEMENT EXECUTIVE

---

* * *   Record of consistent profit contributions amounting to
           millions of dollars in general management, marketing,
           production in the U.S., Canada and internationally;
           accustomed for the last ten years to autonomous multi-
           division P.&L. responsibility and responsible for at
           least eight turnaround situations involving significant
           figures.

* * *   Equipped to use latest management sciences including
           PERT, CPM and other network techniques to accomplish
           Company goals.

* * *   Intimately familiar with the metalworking industry and
           with sophisticated machinery and equipment in a broad
           area of manufacturing.

* * *   Characterized by others as an inspiring leader, incisive
           in identifying problems, imaginative in finding and im-
           plementing solutions, strong in comprehensive, accurate
           planning to improve profitability.

FOR FURTHER DATA PLEASE SEE FOLLOWING PAGES

BUSINESS EXPERIENCE

1975-Present   MIXED COMPANY, INC.
                Winston-Salem, NC

VICE PRESIDENT, GENERAL MANAGER of $45 million tobacco machinery manu-
facturing division of $700 million leisure products conglomerate. Re-
ported to parent corporate Group Vice President. Supervised V.P., R.&D.,
Controller, Director of Marketing, European and South American Directors.

Responsibility:
- P.&L. for U.S. division and plants in France, U.K., Brazil, and
  marketing headquarters in Switzerland.

Achievements:
- U.K. Division lost $250,000 first quarter 1970; by August, Division was
  operating profitably with earnings of $80,000.
- Reduced inflated U.S. payroll by $235,000.
- Successfully introduced three new products of complex technology.
- Increased Division revenue 21% and pretax profits 13%.
- Improved return on assets from 13.8% to 14.6%.
- Prepared, submitted and implemented five-year plan yielding compounded
  annual growth in pretax profits of 13.3%.

These accomplishments were engineered by the use of PERT, Critical Path
Method and other network techniques to improve production, eliminate bottlenecks; by repricing; by implementing plans which had been made but not
acted upon; and by creating a new sales program.

1972-1975 KEEPING COMPANY, INC.
           Springfield, MO

1974-1975 ASSISTANT to the PRESIDENT of $80 million manufacturer of
meters, electric subassemblies, fractional horsepower motors and other
products.

1972-1974 PRESIDENT of autonomous Canadian Division with sales of
$15 million. Responsible for:
- Management of complete staff: finance, sales, manufacturing.
- Divisional profit and loss.
- Assisting the President of parent company.
- Presiding at Directors' and Stockholders' meetings.

Accomplishments:
- in 1972 losses were above $1/2 million annually; by end 1969 losses
  were eliminated and profits stood at all-time high of $1.137 million.
  This was accomplished by consolidating motor operations, reducing
  overhead, eliminating ineffective department in production area,
  realigning production facilities, changing sales plans and reassign-
  ing sales responsibilities.

58

1967-1972 DINNER CO., Harrisburg, PA

This company manufactures castings, wire, rod and strip, electrical wire and cable, fractional horsepower motors and other industrial products. Volume of $300 million.

 1969-1972 VICE PRESIDENT, INTERNATIONAL OPERATIONS. Reported to President. Supervised Director of International Marketing and Managers in Canada, Mexico, Brazil, U.K., Europe, Australia.
 Responsible for:
 - Profit and Loss for 17 international plants, and all exports.

 Accomplishments:
 - Increased pretax profits from $1.07 million to $1.69 million including complete amortization of start-up costs in five new plants.
 - Increased volume of manufactured product from $40 million to $45.5 million.
 - Restored profitability to Canadian plant operating at a loss of $52,000.
 - Achieved turnaround in SARE Division from loss of $350,000 to profit of $120,000; similarly in Netherlands and Brazilian companies.

 1967-1969 VICE PRESIDENT, Dinner Co. of Canada, Toronto, Ontario. Supervised General Sales Manager, Controller and three Plant Managers.
 Responsible for:
 - Profit and Loss for three manufacturing locations and six product lines in $12 million division.

 Achievements included:
 - Improvement in pretax profit from $396,000 to $578,000.
 - Increased revenue from $13.0 million to $15.1 million.
 - Reversed severe loss trend at Canadian wire plant to profit over a period of three years rising from $127,000 to $374,000.
 - Improved operation at Rubberoid Plant from loss of $50,000 to a profit of $400,000.

1958-1967 VANADIUM METAL WIRE WORKS, Alloy Division, E. H. Humbolt & Co., Pittsburgh, PA

GENERAL MANAGER with supporting staff of Assistant Works Manager, Plant Superintendent, Accountant, Metallurgist, Production and Quality Control Managers and Chief Industrial Engineer.
- started as District Sales Manager and progressed successively to Regional Sales Manager, Assistant General Sales Manager, Sales Manager.

Accomplishments:
- in first year of responsibility as General Manager turned loss of $20/30,000 per month to annual profit of $300,000 with subsequent increase to $600,000.

Offered and accepted position with Vanadium (as described).

MILITARY SERVICE:

1946-1945 UNITED STATES AIR FORCE, Captain.

EDUCATION:

B.S., Engineering, 1954, University of Pittsburgh, Pittsburgh, PA.

Graduate work in Business Management at Northwestern and Michigan State.

COMMUNITY ACTIVITIES:

Chairman, Board of Directors, National Hospital, Winston-Salem, NC.

Chairman, Community Chest, Winston-Salem, NC.

Member, National Presidential Committee to Study Government Options.

HONORS:

Winston-Salem Citizen-of-the-Year Award.

HOBBIES:

Tennis, golf, shooting (National 12-Bore Champion).

PERSONAL DATA:

Born 3/31/33, married, two children, excellent health, willing to relocate.

REFERENCES AND FURTHER DATA ON REQUEST

ANALYSIS OF RÉSUMÉ USERS: GENERAL EXECUTIVES

Vice-presidents, general managers, chief executive officers, and individuals who provide no clue to their specialization.

The salary range is $14,500 to $200,000.
The median salary is $33,600.
The age range is 28 to 62.
The average age is 43.3.
There are no females in the sample.
Age in percentages

28% are in their 30s.
33% are in their 40s.
28% are in their 50s.

DISCUSSION

Chronological Résumé with Summary Page. The Duke résumé is a good example of a true executive résumé, as opposed to a run-of-the-mill résumé. It is longer than most because the subject has a long history of accomplishments. The form of résumé was selected because there is nothing to hide in his chronology, with achievements increasing in each successive position. The résumé provides a strong basis for selection for an interview and for an interesting interview discussion. A résumé of this kind could be written only by a man who is supremely confident that there is no area of management in which he does not have experience and knowledge and that he can support all his claims.

This man creates a favorable attitude even before an interview. If his interview techniques and his actual experience as brought out in an interview are as good as his writing, he is assured of employment.

The summary page is used in this instance to express the highlights of his career and offer some material contributing to his total image. It should make the reader want to read the main body of the résumé.

Following the résumé is an explanation of how it was developed.

THE PRECEDING CHRONOLOGICAL RÉSUMÉ WITH SUMMARY PAGE ANNOTATED TO SHOW HOW IT WAS WRITTEN

WELLINGTON DUKE   PAGE 2

Page 1 is written last.

BUSINESS EXPERIENCE

1975-Present MIXED CO., INC.,
              Winston-Salem, NC

Period of employment and name
of company.

VICE PRESIDENT, GENERAL MANAGER of
$45 million tobacco machinery manufac-
turing division of $700 million leisure
products conglomerate. Reported to
parent corporate Group Vice President.
Supervised V.P., R.&D., Controller,
Director of Marketing, European and
South American Directors.

Title.
Description of kind and size of
company; reporting relationship;
supervisory relationships.
Evaluation of a candidate is improved when one knows in what
areas he or she worked.

Responsibility:
- P.&L. responsibility for U.S. division and plants in France, U.K.,
Brazil, and marketing headquarters
in Switzerland.

Nature of responsibilities.

Achievements:
- U.K. Division lost $250,000 first
quarter 1970; by August, Division
was operating profitably with earnings of $80,000, a swing of more
than $½ million.

Turnaround no. 1.

- Reduced inflated U.S. payroll by
$250,000.
- Successfully introduced three new
products of complex technology.
- Increased Division revenue 21% and
pretax profits 13%.
- Improved return on assets from 13.8%
to 14.6%.
- Prepared, submitted and implemented
five-year plan yielding compounded
annual growth in pretax profits of
13.3%.

Got rid of nonproductive employees.
Managed production, marketing,
finance.
Contributed profit increase.

Measured company progress in
terms of financial executive.
Made plans and carried them out.

These accomplishments were engineered
by the use of PERT, Critical Path
Method and other network techniques
to improve production, eliminate
bottlenecks; by repricing; by implementing plans which had been made but
not acted upon; and by creating a new
sales program.

Although this man does not have a
graduate degree, the tools he used
show a continuing study of management techniques. Potential employees can gauge an applicant better
if a brief description of the
methods used to gain the results
described is provided.

63

1972-1975   KEEPING CO., INC.
            Springfield, MO

1974-1975   ASSISTANT to the PRESIDENT of   The same sequence and method
$80 million manufacturer of meters, elec-   are used for each separate em-
tric subassemblies, fractional horsepower   ployment.
motors and other products.

1972-1974, PRESIDENT of autonomous Canad-
ian Division with sales of $15 million.
Responsible for:
- Management of complete staff: finance,   Administered Chief Executive
  sales, manufacturing.   Officer responsibilities.
- Divisional profit and loss.
- Assisting the President of parent com-
  pany.
- Presiding at Director's and Stock-
  holder's meetings.

Accomplishments:
- In 1972 losses were above $½ million   Turnaround no. 2.
  annually; by end 1974 losses were elim-
  inated and profits stood at all-time
  high of $1.137 million.
This was accomplished by consolidating   Methods used in accomplishing.
motor operations, reducing overhead, elim-
inating ineffective department in production area, realigning production facilities, changing sales plans and reassign-
ing sales responsibilities.

1958-1972   DINNER CO.
            Harrisburg, PA

This company manufactures castings, wire,   Description of what Company
rod and strip, electrical wire and cable,   made and its volume.
fractional horsepower motors and other
industrial products. Volume $300 million.

1969-1972, VICE PRESIDENT, INTERNATIONAL
OPERATIONS. Reported to President.
Supervised Director of International
Marketing and Managers in Canada, Mexico,
Brazil, U.K., Europe, Australia. Respon-
sible for:
- Profit and loss responsibility for 17   Multidivision responsibility.
  international plants and all exports.

Accomplishments:

- Increased pretax profits from $1.07   Increased profits.
  million to $1.69 million, including com-
  plete amortization of start-up costs in
  five new plants.
- Increased volume of manufactured product   Improved production.
  from $40 million to $45.5 million.
- Restored profitability to Canadian plant   Turnaround no. 3.
  operating at a loss of $52,000.
- Achieved turnaround in SARE Division   Turnaround no. 4.
  from loss of $350,000 to profit of
  $120,000; similarly for Netherlands and   Turnaround no. 5.
  Brazilian companies.

1967-1969, VICE PRESIDENT, DINNER CO. of
CANADA, Toronto, Ontario. Supervised General Sales Manager, Controller, and three
plant managers. Responsible for:

- Profit and loss for three manufacturing
  locations and six product lines in $12
  million division.

Achievements included:

- Improvement in pretax profit from   Increased profits.
  $396,000 to $578,000.
- Increased revenue from $13.0 million to   Increased sales.
  $15.0 million.
- Reversed severe loss trend at American   Turnaround no. 6.
  wire plant to profit over a period of
  three years rising from $127,000 to
  $374,000.
- Improved operation at Rubberoid Plant   Turnaround no. 7.
  from loss of $50,000 to a profit of
  $400,000.

1958-1967   VANADIUM METAL WIRE WORKS, ALLOY DIVISION,
            E. H. HUMBOLT & CO., Pittsburgh, PA

GENERAL MANAGER with supporting staff of
Assistant Works Manager, Plant Superintendent, Accountant, Metallurgist, Production
and Quality Control Managers and Chief Industrial Engineer.

- Started as District Sales Manager and   Sales experience.
  progressed successively to Regional Sales
  Manager, Assistant General Sales
  Manager, Sales Manager.

Accomplishments:

- in first year of responsibility as Gen-   Turnaround no. 8.
  eral Manager turned loss of $20/30,000
  per month to profit of $300,000 annually
  with subsequent increase to $600,000.

Offered and accepted position with Vanadium
(as described).

MILITARY SERVICE:

1946-1948 UNITED STATES AIR FORCE CAPTAIN

EDUCATION:

B.S., Engineering, 1954, University of Pittsburgh, Pittsburgh, PA.

Graduate work in Business Management at
Northwestern and University of Michigan.

COMMUNITY ACTIVITIES:

Chairman, Board of Directors, National Hos-   Took leading role in commun-
pital, Winston-Salem, NC.   ity activities, adding to
                                                   image of corporation among
Chairman, Community Chest, Winston-Salem,   employees and others.
NC.

Member, National Presidential Committee to
Study Government Options.

HONORS:

Winston-Salem Citizen-of-the-Year Award.   Recognized for community
                                                   activities.

HOBBIES:

Tennis, golf, shooting (National 12-Bore   The hobbies are interesting
Champion).   and well worth including.

PERSONAL DATA:

Born 3/31/33, married, two children, excellent health, willing to relocate.

REFERENCES AND FURTHER DATA ON REQUEST

address   telephone

THIS IS WRITTEN <u>LAST</u> BUT WHEN
COMPLETED BECOMES PAGE ONE OF
THE RESUME.

RESUME

of

WELLINGTON DUKE

qualified as

SENIOR MANAGEMENT EXECUTIVE

===================================

*** Record of consistent profit con-
tributions amounting to millions
of dollars in general management,
marketing, production in the U.S.,
Canada and internationally; accustomed for the last ten years
to autonomous multidivision
P.&L. responsibility and responsible for at least eight
turnaround situations involving
significant figures.

This is a concise statement of
the accomplishments described
in the body of the resume and
of the nature of this man's
responsibilities which were at
the highest level (P.&L.) and
covering the major divisions
of a business: marketing,
production, finance.

*** Equipped to use latest manage-
ment sciences including PERT,
CPM and other network techniques
to accomplish company goals.

This is evidence of professional
management.

*** Intimately familiar with the
metalworking industry and with
sophisticated machinery and
equipment in a broad area of
manufacturing.

This statement identified the
general area in which management
has been exercised.

*** Characterized by others as an
inspiring leader, incisive in
identifying problems, imaginative
in finding and implementing
solutions, strong in comprehensive, accurate planning
leading to improved profitability.

An <u>objective</u> evaluation of the
subject's most important
qualities.

275 John Brown's Crossing   Home (212) 321-7654
New York, NY 10012   Office(212) 456-0987

R E S U M E

of

VINCENT BENET

an experienced

EXECUTIVE SALESMAN

* * *   Approximately 15 years of experience with leading com-
        pany in personal sales, marketing and regional sales
        management.

* * *   Record of success in achieving national recognition for
        type, quality and volume of sales produced; received
        bonuses and awards; more important - produced outstand-
        ing profits!

* * *   Experienced in hiring and training salesmen, developing
        quotas and objectives, formulating and implementing mar-
        keting and sales strategies and techniques.

* * *   A record as hardworking winner with a reputation of be-
        ing the man "least wanted to be in competition with."

* * *   Enjoy excellent contacts among key personnel of major
        companies. Adept at establishing and maintaining pro-
        ductive relationships and experience in customer/public
        relations; an exceptional and exciting platform public
        speaker.

* * *   37 years old. Bachelor of Arts Degree with honors and
        considerable graduate work in Psychology.

* * *   In short, achieved all quotas seven times out of ten
        years; in three of these years, quotas had been raised
        out of all proportion to previous historical sales - in-
        creased sales by 400% - boosted profits.

FOR FURTHER DATA PLEASE SEE FOLLOWING PAGES

* Record of success in achieving a 400% increase in sales as a result of effective sales management:

1972-Present   BRIDGE CO., Freeport, NY

This is a major producer of business machines and data processing equipment.

As SALES MANAGER, Office Products Sales and Data Entry Sales, in the Brooklyn and Queens area, have been responsible for:

- Supervision and training of six salesmen.
- Development of schedules, strategies and techniques to develop leads and increase sales. Brooklyn and Queens are unique in that they have relatively few very large customers. It was, therefore, necessary to tap the potential smaller market. This was done and the region generated 10% of nationwide sales.
- Achieved heavy personal sales and won sales bonuses year after year; became one of the highest producers in the company.
- Participated in the establishment of sales quotas and product mix and developed promotional programs.
- Systematically and effectively converted "low-grade sales" to become high-grade sales involving increased profitabilities.
- Instituted a regional policy to require cash deposits on orders and substantially decreased cancellations. So dramatic were the results that this became standard company policy.
- Maintained a "get tough" collection policy without sacrifice of good will or cordial public relations.

* Other experience in maximizing sales through modern sales management techniques:

1964-1972   BRIDGE CO., Boston, MA

As SALES MANAGER, supervised a group of salesmen and achieved sales quotas seven out of eight years.

- Maintained continuing market surveys to determine customer needs.
- Worked closely with key personnel of customers and potential customers to maintain sales of accessories and supplies, upgrade equipment and provide corporate technical and maintenance services.
- Nearly tripled personal earnings.
- Designed retail accounting equipment that ultimately resulted in multimillion-dollar sales.

* Demonstrated talent for industrial and consumer sales; achieved countrywide leadership:

1962-1964   IBM CORP., New York, NY

As ACCOUNT MANAGER/SALES REPRESENTATIVE achieved sales quota each year and was responsible for:

- Development of an outstanding sales record; substantially contributed to my division's becoming the leader on a countrywide performance record.
- Successfully penetrated accounts such as Railway Express, Texaco, American Can and others.

1959 GROLIERE CORPORATION

Sold encyclopaedias door-to-door throughout New York, New Jersey, Massachusetts, Connecticut, Rhode Island, Vermont, etc. part-time while attending college.

Finished seventh out of 1,000 sales people in a national 20-week contest.

* MILITARY SERVICE

1957-1959 UNITED STATES NAVY

Served as Instructor at the U.S. Naval Academy at Annapolis. Received special commendation for class overall proficiency, then the highest in Academy history.

* EDUCATION

1962 UNIVERSITY OF GEORGIA

Received a Bachelor of Arts degree and attained the Dean's List in the senior year.

1973-1977 NEW SCHOOL FOR SOCIAL RESEARCH

Completed several courses in Psychology which contributed to my understanding of human relations and markedly influenced the success of sales activities.

At college, played varsity football, lacrosse, was Sports Editor, worked summers during college.

* PERSONAL DATA

37 years old, married, one child, excellent health.

REFERENCES AND FURTHER DATA ON REQUEST

DISCUSSION

Chronological Résumé with Summary Page with Variation.
The variations from norm in the Benet résumé are a final
paragraph summarizing his most important assets and
headlines emphasizing the outstanding factor in each
chronologically listed position. Either variation or both
can be used. Headlines can serve to unify the items in a
résumé if they are informative, relevant, and important.

This résumé reflects the personality of the subject in
the use of punctuation, quoted phrases, and relatively informal language imbued with a sense of excitement.

The summary page serves an effective purpose in giving
a special dimension to the subject apart from the material in the résumé.

This is a salesman who sounds like a salesman and would
undoubtedly receive invitations for interviews upon sub-
mitting this résumé.

A summary page can often be used to incorporate material that does not fit gracefully into the body of a résumé.

FUNCTIONAL RÉSUMÉ

The *Functional Résumé* organizes work experience by function, such as general marketing, management, production,
finance, or their subfunctions. Chronology is disregarded. To
facilitate comparison, we have refashioned one of our *Chronological Résumé* examples into functional form.

The *Functional Résumé* stresses the scope of experience,
much as does a summary page. It has the disadvantage of not

relating accomplishments to the pertinent company or companies. Most employers are familiar with other companies, especially in the same industry, and take company affiliations into account when judging accomplishments. The same experience is more impressive if gained at a widely known company than at an unknown company.

The writer of a *Functional Résumé,* not being hampered by chronology, can easily change emphasis or camouflage past experience. This is advantageous in cases in which past job experience is best explained in a personal interview, rather than in writing. We reiterate that the main purpose of a résumé is to gain an interview; it is not a substitute for an interview.

The *Functional Résumé* tends to be shorter than the *Chronological Résumé.* The example that follows has been further shortened to avoid monotonous repetition. Both the *Functional Résumé* and the *Functional-by-Company (Institution) Résumé* are well regarded by institutional recruiters.

CONSTANTINE BISHKO
375 Broadalban Road
Ephrata, PA 12345
(177) 377-4777

SENIOR EXECUTIVE experienced in all areas of General Management

SUMMARY OF QUALIFICATIONS

Record of consistent profit contributions amounting to millions of dollars in general management, marketing and production in the U.S. and internationally; accustomed to autonomous multidivision responsibility. Equipped to use all management techniques to accomplish company objectives.

GENERAL MANAGEMENT	Accomplished seven divisional turnarounds leading these Divisions from high five-figure losses to six-figure profits in periods ranging from three months to two years.
PRODUCTION	Successfully engineered and produced four new products of complex technology supervising Manufacturing Manager, Controller, various engineering disciplines and marketing development.
MARKETING	Conceived and implemented new marketing plan which broadened distribution and increased volume 27%; increased profits 9%.
FINANCE	Instituted new financial controls and procedures; increased cash flow 19%; improved R.O.I. 13%; set objectives and achieved financial ratios which became envy of the industry.
TECHNICAL BACKGROUND	Intimately familiar with the metalworking industry and with sophisticated machinery and equipment in a broad area of manufacturing.

FOR FURTHER DATA PLEASE SEE FOLLOWING PAGE

EMPLOYMENT HISTORY

1975-Present   LEAF MANUFACTURING DIVISION, BRF, INC., Winston-Salem, NC.

1972-1975   THOMAS & SESSIONS, Springfield, MO.

1968-1972   W. H. THOMPSON & CO, Harrisburg, PA.

1958-1967   VANADIUM METAL WIRE WORKS, Pittsburgh, PA.

EDUCATION

B.S., Engineering, University of Pittsburgh, Pittsburgh, PA.

Graduate work in Business Administration and Management at Northwestern and Michigan State Universities.

COMMUNITY ACTIVITIES

Chairman, Board of Directors, National Hospital, Winston-Salem, NC.

Chairman, Community Chest, Winston-Salem, NC.

Member, National Presidential Committee to Study Government Options.

HONORS

Winston-Salem Citizen-of-the-Year Award.

HOBBIES

Tennis, golf, shooting (National 12 Bore Champion)

PERSONAL DATA

Born 3/31/33, married, two children, excellent health. Willing to relocate.

REFERENCES AND FURTHER DATA ON REQUEST

Functional Résumé. Mr. Bishko has experience in all four major facets of management—marketing, finance, production, and general management. The *Functional Résumé* is particularly suitable for expressing such experience. It is also suitable for one who has had the following experience:

IN MARKETING

Territory selling
Regional management
Sales or product management
Sales management

IN FINANCE

Accounting
Controller
Treasurer

IN PRODUCTION

Foreman
Superintendent
Plant manager
Director of R.&D.
General manager

IN EDUCATIONAL ADMINISTRATION

Teaching
Curriculum planning
Administration

The subject areas can be further expanded to include, for example, network techniques in production planning, other important financial ratios, and the most important markets.

11 East 81st Street
New York, NY 10000

Home (212) 000-0000
Office (212) 000-0000
X37

R E S U M E

ELOISE LE BEQUE SANTINI

OFJECTIVE: Editor or Assistant Editor, domestic or international.

EXPERIENCE

EDITOR: 1977-Present McGRAW-HILL CO., New York, NY.
Editor of trade magazine, Main Floor Merchandising, with
A.B.C. verified circulation of 90,000; changed format, improved editorial content, organized and balanced advertising space with resulting increase in advertising revenue
of 23%.

TRANSLATOR & 1974-1977 ARCHITECTURAL DIGEST, Boulder, CO.
EDITOR: Translated French and Italian editorial material into
English, selected photographs, and edited for publication
(New York office).

ASSISTANT 1974-1977 NATIONAL GEOGRAPHIC, Washington, DC.
EDITOR: (concurrently) Full- and part-time editor of new geographical reference book (New York office).

ANNOTATIONS 1976 CONSORTIUM OF UNITED MUSEUMS, New York, NY.
EDITOR: (concurrently) Edited computer-generated data, including
annotations to 30,000 films; for verification of names
and addresses for producer's directory; editing for con-
sistency of information.

TRANSLATOR: 1973-1974 MAINSTREAM PUBLISHING CO., New York, NY.
Translated from English into French for all outgoing material to launch international information service. Translated from Italian into English, Source book on Italian
Renaissance structures with photographs and titles, 12,000
entries; for new book.

EDITORIAL 1972 JOVANOVICH & SPEAR, New York, NY.
CONSULTANT: Consultant in preparation of books on conversational French
and Italian.

PUBLICATIONS: A comparative study of Dante's narrative and dramatic modes.

(continued)

EDUCATION: B.A., Bryn Mawr College, Bryn Mawr, PA, 1971.
               Columbia University, New York, NY, doctoral candidate.
               La Sorbonne, Paris, France, Certificat Superieur de Langue
                 Francaise.

LANGUAGES: Fluent in French, Italian and Spanish.

PERSONAL DATA: Age 29, single, excellent health.

REFERENCES: Available on request.

DISCUSSION

Functional Résumé. The Santini résumé resulted in a position, whereas two previous résumés of a different style had failed. The young woman found the job market difficult because she had spent too much time in academia, had never had a full-time job of any importance, and left the impression of being overintellectualized for the give and take of commercial enterprise. Upon analysis, however, a listing of her activities showed an amazing breadth of experience and willingness to handle detail that would unquestionably have value to a publisher, if her scope could be properly expressed. Lack of consistent work experience was glossed over. Only positive elements were stated. There was once a popular song with a title applicable to résumés: "Accentuate the Positive."

This format is sometimes recommended by public library advisors, among others, but in a different way, for example, using character elements—motivated, leader, multilingual, educated, disciplined, experienced, accomplished, and so on—where Miss Santini headlined her work functions. We think that such an adaptation (character elements) of the *Functional* style would be useless, except possibly for one with no work experience, such as a recent graduate. Should that be your status, try this variation and compare it with a more traditional format. We do not recommend the listing of character attributes in this style because it is or can easily become showy, boastful, self-esteeming, subjective, aggrandizing.

EXAMPLE OF FUNCTIONAL RÉSUMÉ

78 Whitney Road   (789) 123-7654
Gastonia, NC 77777
                              R E S U M E

                                  of

                              JOHN KAY

                          TEXTILE EXECUTIVE

Progressive career in textile industry beginning with textile education
and graduation with honors, continuing with important assignments for
major textile manufacturers, culminating in part ownership of specialty
knitting company growing from inception at zero to $7 million in three
years. Recently sold interest in this profitable enterprise to partners;
now available for employment in the industry as Director of Marketing or
Manufacturing or both.

                              EXPERIENCE

As General Manager: Created company, starting with zero sales, climbing
                        to $7 million in three years, operating profitably.
                        Directed building of dye house. Started new depart-
                        ment for giant textile manufacturer ($800 million
                        plus) aimed at Men's Wear market for single and
                        double knits.

                        Purchased complete equipment needed for new depart-
                        ment (reaching $30 million volume). Established new
                        basis for profitable pricing.

                        Set up R.&D. program to promote growth.

As Director of   Departmentalized each phase of manufacturing assign-
Manufacturing: ing efficiency and capacity ratings; established
                        basis for dependable delivery schedules. Imple-
                        mented new procedures for determining true costs as
                        basis for profitable pricing.

                        Initiated improved quality control. Utilized (DKJ/36
                        and other) double knit pattern lock, nonjacquard and
                        interlock machines, rib transfer machines, single
                        knit equipment 18 to 26 cut, tuck bars, wheels, rale-
                        ways, plain jerseys, finishing, dyeing and bulking
                        equipment; with continuous upgrading.

                                                              over please

As Marketing   Developed seasonal lines by market end-use and fiber
Manager: mix.

                      Developed special programs for key customers, pre-
                      sented new programs and lines.

                      Created new sales programs and new advertising. In-
                      troduced "coordinated look" in Men's Wear, achieved
                      dominant market position for new Division of giant
                      textile producer.

                      Maintained close "intelligence" liaison with sales-
                      men and customers.

                              EMPLOYMENT RECORD

1976-1979   NEW WEAVE COMPANY, New York, NY
                      VICE PRESIDENT AND GENERAL MANAGER

1966-1976   INTERNATIONAL FABRICS, INC., New York, NY
                      GENERAL MANAGER, $60 million Men's Wear Division

1963-1966   TERJAVIAN ET CIE, Brussels, Belgium
                      DIRECTOR OF MANUFACTURING for North Carolina mill of
                      $1 billion international knitter after earlier sub-
                      ordinate experience

MILITARY SERVICE: U.S. NAVY, 1962-1964. Served as Flight Lieutenant
                      aboard Aircraft Carrier in South China Sea.

EDUCATION: B.S., New York Institute of Textile Technology and
                      Merchandising, Hamilton, NY, 1961. Graduated Cum
                      Laude.

                      Graduate work at Bennett University, New York, NY, 1962.
                      Scholarship Award from International Institute of Tex-
                      tile Design.

LANGUAGES: French and Spanish (fluent).

HOBBIES: Platform tennis (ranked in first 10), skeet.

PERSONAL DATA: Age 39, married, three children, excellent health.
                      Willing to relocate.

                 REFERENCES AND FURTHER DATA ON REQUEST

DISCUSSION

Functional Résumé. The Kay résumé utilizes language appropriate to the industry. By naming the types of knitwear and knitting machinery the applicant illustrates his mastery of production techniques as well as an understanding and implementation of objectives. The marketing section shows imagination in theme development to create an important share of market.

As all other résumés in this book, this résumé shows what a successful person has done to improve job performance and how such improvement invariably contributes to the profitability and well-being of a company or institution.

The experiences related in this résumé could have been equally well expressed in other résumé styles. The *Functional* form was selected because of some inconsistencies in the chronology of employment and achievements, which would have been disadvantageously disclosed in the *Chronological* form but could easily be explained during an interview.

FUNCTIONAL-BY-COMPANY
(INSTITUTION) RÉSUMÉ

The *Functional-by-Company (Institution) Résumé* lists functions for each employer. In this respect it is superior to the *Functional Résumé*. However, the listing of functions performed for a company need not be chronological, which, though a bit misleading to the reader, may be of advantage to you. Keep in mind that a résumé is an evaluation of you. In taking "poetic license" with your chronology you may improve your résumé and gain an interview, during which discrepancies can be explained.

Preceding comments aside, the *Functional-by-Company (Institution) Résumé* is well suited for teachers and professors and is well received by academic recruiters. Two examples follow, including one for the educational area.

100 Accomplishment Way   Home (123) 456-7890
Erewhon, MN 12345   Office (098) 765-4321

R E S U M E

HORATIO ALGER

EXECUTIVE

SUMMARY OF QUALIFICATIONS

Experienced in all areas of management: Marketing, Production, Finance
and multidivision operations. Record of consistent profit contributions
in identifying and developing new markets, in creating more effective
advertising themes, in reducing manufacturing costs and lead times, in
reducing inventories, increasing cash flow and doubling price of common
stock in a period of 12 months under adverse market conditions.

EXPERIENCE

1967-Present   GENERAL LEISURE PRODUCTS COMPANY, INC., Winona, MN

                 1974-Present, PRESIDENT and GENERAL MANAGER with P.&L.
responsibility for $100 million leisure products manu-
facturing division of $600 million conglomerate. Report
to parent company President. Supervise Vice Presidents of
Marketing, Manufacturing, Human Resources, Planning,
Finance, and R.&D. Department.

R.&D.   - led Research & Development team in development of new
concept in grass-mowing equipment.

MARKETING   - made innovation in merchandising and advertising home
snow removal machine.
- utilized technology developed in mowing machinery to
manufacture snowmobile; captured first place in Alaska
race test.

MANUFACTURING - selected new wholesale organization to concentrate on
Company (with partial financing by Company).
- increased volume from $60 million to $100 million in four
years.

FINANCE   - increased value of AMEX-listed stock from six to 12-1/2
in 1977, based on earnings multiplication.
- reduced inventory by one-third, leading to increase in
ROI.

over please

1972-1974, VICE PRESIDENT, MANUFACTURING

MANUFACTURING
- consolidated manufacture of motors in one plant here-
  tofore distributed among four plants around the U.S.
- closed least efficient manufacturing plant; utilized
  space for needed new warehouse.
- reorganized flow of production for motors, building own
  specialized automated equipment; reduced lead time from
  six to three months and manufacturing cycle from two
  months to two weeks.
- restyled mowers, snow removers, electric garden tools;
  developed, with R.&D., new concept in electric grass
  shears which became nationwide best sellers and contributed $6 million of profitable new volume.

1970-1972, GENERAL MANAGER, Caracas, Venezuela

MANUFACTURING
- recognized application of new technology to manufacture
  of small horsepower motors; increased plant productivity
  by 30%; technology adopted in three U.S. plants with
  similar results.

GENERAL
MANAGEMENT
- met with government officials to gain "favored manufacturer" status in Venezuela, leading to lower export
  duties.
- expanded distribution to Colombia and Brazil with conse-
  quent doubling of volume.

FINANCE
- reorganized accounting procedures; speeded corporate
  monthly reports by ten days each month, leading to
  quicker identification of problem areas and increase in
  profits from 6% to 15% before taxes.

MARKETING
- conducted market research leading to distribution of
  wider group of U.S. manufactured products in South
  America, with only minor changes in styling.

1967-1970, SALES MANAGER for U.S. and South America

MARKETING
- studied marketing procedures in the U.S. and South
  America.
- studied company potential for new products in areas of
  competence.
- increased U.S. sales 25% through new system of regional
  profit centers and improved training methods.
  regional profit centers and improved training methods.

SALES
- switched main distribution efforts from traditional out-
  lets to newer forms of distribution.
- increased sales in South America by 15% and recommended change in product mix which led to accomplishments previously mentioned.

1958-1964 AVERILL & HARRIMAN COMPANY, INC., Dellmore, IL

VICE PRESIDENT, MANUFACTURING for small ($40 million)
manufacturer of marine motors. Responsible for:
- complete manufacturing operations and R.&D. Department.

Accomplishments:

MANUFACTURING   - set up new production line using new automatic equip-
                   ment.
                 - cleared out accumulated inventory of excessive parts
                   and raw material, improved turnover from three to four
                   times annually.
                 - reorganized engineering department, breaking up
                   authority into Quality Control, Production Control,
                   Production Engineering, Methods Engineering.
                 - conducted cost studies leading to 11% reduction in
                   costs.
                 - conducted value studies; made decision to purchase
                   fasteners and other components at a saving of 16% in
                   raw material costs.
                 - accelerated manufacturing cycle time by 17%, leading
                   to a further cost reduction of 12%.

Invited by executive search firm to consider position with General Leisure Products; accepted.

1958-1961 AUTOMOTIVE PARTS, INC., Jackson, MI

           ASSISTANT PLANT MANAGER (one of seven) for $100 million
           manufacturer of small parts for the BIG-3 auto manu-
           facturers.

           Learned automatic and automated production methods with
           one of most advanced companies in the industry.

MILITARY SERVICE: U.S. ARMY AIR FORCE, 1953-1958. Captain. Served in
                     Korea.

EDUCATION: B.S., Engineering, California Institute of Technol-
                     ogy, Pasadena, CA, 1954. Graduate work in Business
                     Management, 1956 Stanford University, Stanford, CA.

COMMUNITY   Chairman, Board of Directors, National Hospital,
ACTIVITIES: Winona, MN.

                     Chairman, Community Chest, Winona, MN.

HONORS: Winona Citizen-of-the-Year Award

HOBBIES: Tobogganing (National Two-Man Champion), skeet, trap,
                     crosscountry skiing.

PERSONAL DATA: Born 3/31/24, married, three children, excellent
                     health.

REFERENCES AND FURTHER DATA ON REQUEST

DISCUSSION

Functional-by-Company (Institution) Résumé. The Alger résumé illustrates how career progression can be effectively expressed using a combination of the *Functional* and the *Chronological* styles.

This applicant started in production, moved quickly to another company utilizing the production skills learned earlier, and became head of manufacturing for a medium size company. Here he demonstrated good management skills in all areas of production. He moved again to a position involving marketing to round his experience and immediately showed talent in this field, advancing quickly to general management of the company's South American division and two years later to the vice-presidency of the headquarters plant. By this time his ability in each position gave such strong indications of the highest qualities of leadership that he was appointed president of the company with results that made a strongly favorable impact on the company and its stockholders.

This is a capsule illustration not only of excellent management but also of career planning, in which the subject determined to make himself knowledgeable in all areas of management.

One First Avenue   Home (212) 332-4455
Brentwood, NY 54321   Office (212) 432-6688

CURRICULUM VITAE

of

SAMUEL JOHNSON

OBJECTIVE

Administrative Position with a Foundation, Educational or other nonprofit organization.

EDUCATION

M.S., Education, Columbia University, New York, NY, 1959.

B.S., History, University of Pennsylvania, Philadelphia, PA, 1961. Cum
Laude.

Doctoral studies in Philosophy of Education.

SUMMARY OF QUALIFICATIONS

Eleven years of experience in the development of sound educational systems,
administration and teaching.

HONORS

Cited in "The Last 20 Years of Education in the United States," 1st ed.
(1950-1970), Langston and Rhodes, 1971.

Named in Who's Who in Colleges and Universities, 1957, 1958, 1959.

Bronze Star in Vietnam, 1962. Silver Star, Vietnam, 1963. Captain, U.S.
Army.

over please

PUBLICATIONS

The Influence of Experimentation on Basic Learning Skills, Barnes and Dunlop, 1973, 342pp.

Basic Education in a Changing Society, Noble and Morrow, 1972, 307pp.

Paper: A Comparison of Test Scores in Reading and Writing. Columbia University Review, 1969.

ACCREDITATIONS

Boston Board of Education, License No. 123456.

New York State Regents License No. 987654.

ADMINISTRATIVE EXPERIENCE

1970-Present: OLIVER W. HOLMES UNIVERSITY, Brentwood, NY

UNIVERSITY PLANNING OFFICER for University with student body of 2500 projected to rise to 3600 by 1977; faculty of 350 projected to 500 by 1977.

- Established plans for operation of University with student body expansion 1977-1987 including organization, functional responsibilities, philosophy.
- Provided plans for space needs, faculty expansion, additional courses of study, new doctoral programs, budgets, sources of income.
- Recommended enlarged emphasis on teaching skills vs. publication and outside consulting activities.

1968-1970: GOVERNOR WHEELOCK ACADEMY, West Falls, MA

ASSISTANT HEADMASTER for small (400 pupils) preparatory school in rural setting.

- Upgraded teaching staff.
- Supervised construction of new gymnasium.
- Participated in fund raising activities.
- Coached football and lacrosse.
- Worked with Headmaster and Board of Trustees on ten-year plan for Academy.

EDUCATIONAL SYSTEMS EXPERIENCE

1966-1968: NEW YORK STATE REGENTS COMMITTEE ON CURRICULUM REVISION

Invited as one of a committee of seven to study, evaluate and recommend changes in existing methods of teaching at the grade levels 7 to 12.

over please

- Instituted study of comparative reading and writing tests among 400 high
  schools chosen by lot in New York State; evaluated data; recommended
  revision in reading and remedial reading to encompass as appropriate
  individual student teaching, group teaching by skill levels and reem-
  phasis on phonetics for nonhandicapped students.

- Instituted study of methods of teaching mathematics; recommended that
  study of "New Math" be taught in grade 12 instead of grade 9. Recommended additional emphasis on computer mathematics.

- Recommended expanded use of E.D.P. recordkeeping, marking, teacher
  evaluation, Beta system development utilizing minicomputers in specialized areas.

TEACHING EXPERIENCE

<u>1964-1966</u>: BENJAMIN FRANKLIN HIGH SCHOOL, New York, NY

<u>History</u>, <u>History of Western Civilization</u>, <u>History as a Guide to the Fu-
ture</u>. Developed and selected materials that were highly motivating,
varied, skill directed, individualized. Rated in annual Board of Education review, "Thorough knowledge of subject." "Superior in instructional
approach." "Effective in discipline."

Appointed by Principal to Policy Committee which participated in making
decisions related to instruction, administration, overall school evaluations.

Helped write Federal Government proposal for creation of a teacher corps
in New York City in conjunction with school district personnel, university
department heads, principals and teachers.

VITAL STATISTICS

Born 3/31/39, married, three children, excellent health.

REFERENCES AND FURTHER DATA ON REQUEST

DISCUSSION

Functional-by-Company (Institution) Résumé—Nonprofit Objective. In an educational or scientific career the pertinent credentials should be given at the beginning. Though essentially *Functional-by-Company (Institution)*, the Johnson résumé starts with education and lists honors, publications, and accreditations immediately thereafter.

The career begins with teaching, proceeds to curriculum planning and to administration, and culminates in a presently held responsible position at a large university.

The job history is progressive, it has led to the formulation of an educational philosophy, and it embraces the kinds of experience most useful in performing the operating functions within the job objectives named at the outset.

Academic degrees, continuing study, an understanding of the student mind, and reseach in experimental and orthodox teaching methods project an individual who can contribute much to the growth and development of a nonprofit institution, particularly in academe.

HARVARD RÉSUMÉ

The *Harvard Résumé* is widely used because of its appearance and its immediate association by sophisticated readers with the Harvard Graduate School of Business Administration. It has narrow margins and long, rather informal paragraphs. The density of writing often makes it difficult to read.

Accomplishments are less sharply delineated in the *Harvard Résumé* than in other types of résumé. An unusually large amount of personal data might be given. The form usually is *Chronological,* sometimes *Functional-Chronological.*

An example of the *Harvard Résumé* follows.

R E S U M E

Tyne E. Tym
3 Dickens Lane
Grosvenor, MN
(123) 456-7890

OBJECTIVE

A general management or marketing opportunity where broad experience in mechanical products would be valuable. Major emphasis in background includes:

- P.&L. responsibility.

- General Management, sales management and field sales experience.

- Extensive experience with wide range of markets and new product development.

EXPERIENCE

Jan. 1976 to Present LIMITED CO., INC., Harrison, MO
Residential division of Keeping Co., Inc., an independent sheet metal contractor, with annual volume in the range of $12 million, serving residential, commercial and industrial markets.

Vice President

Formed and autonomously manage a new division concentrating on the residential market. Sales were increased by 100% in first two years while getting new division started; earned profit from beginning amounting to 12% before taxes in second year.

Accomplishments include:

- Developing and implementing an overall business plan: market analysis; order forecasting; production plan; manpower needs and recruiting plan; training; P.&L. forecast; facilities and equipment; capital expenditure and operating capital requirements.

- Recruited and trained over 300 people.

- Developing product changes, standardized production and standard costs to achieve 16% reduction in product cost.

- Developing consumer financing plans with St. Louis and Kansas City banks to support expanded sales activities.

- Taking the organization into new product areas to expand markets and eliminate seasonal weaknesses.

1973   COMPANY HALT, INC., Joliet, MO
to
1976   A $5 million manufacturer of mechanical equipment for com-
           mercial and industrial use.

General Sales Manager

Responsible for all sales through 23 independent U.S. dealers and 35 overseas distributors; with a staff of five.

Orders were increased by 20% in weakening markets which had shown a de-
cline.

Earnings were increased through:
- price increases.
- reducing expenses through strict budget applications.
- implementing product cost reduction programs to obtain lower costs in
  a period of rising prices.

Also made changes in representation; set up new dealers; instituted new
training program for all dealers retained; redirected advertising.

1959   UNINVITED COMPANY, INC., Middletown, MO
to
1973   A $100 million manufacturer of plumbing equipment for resi-
           dential, commercial and industrial use.

Manager, Dealer Development, March 1972 to April 1973

Responsible for all Crane dealer activities to sell commercial and residential plumbing supplies. New dealers were established through company
financing and long-range plans for growth. This involved management of
internal staff, regional staff and local offices in recruiting and training qualified personnel to own and operate dealerships. It also involved
development of management skills to support business start-up at a profit.

The organization grew from 30 to 60 dealers and the sale of products from
$40 to $50 million.

Manager, Dealer Distribution, March 1970 to March 1972

Responsible for managing three sales districts in the development of a
dealer organization. This involved market analysis, recruiting and training.

Sales were increased from $2 million to $3 million.

Manager, Market Research, 1967-1970

Headed a marketing group to promote and sell all types of plumbing products in the industrial and wholesaler markets. Supervised marketing departments and research department. New marketing strategies and sales
opportunities were created through new product and system ideas.

Sales Engineer, 1966-1967

Given responsibility to increase market share, profitability and new product development. Developed marketing program, coordinated sales and bidding strategies and trained field sales personnel.

Field Sales Engineer, 1959-1966

Sold all types of plumbing products to apartment owners, architects, contractors, industrials, wholesalers and dealers. Increased sales 230% during this period.

1952
to
1959

U.S. NAVY

Assigned to Destroyer, South China Sea. Lt. Commander

EDUCATION

University of Missouri, Columbia, MO

B.S. degree, Business Management, 1958

PERSONAL

Born October 12, 1936, in the small town of Hackett, Arkansas, where father owned and operated a retail hardware store for more than 40 years. Married childhood sweetheart who attended University of Missouri during two of my undergraduate years. We have five lovely children, including two sets of twins. I am 6'4" in height, weigh 230 lbs. and played varsity football during my last three years at the University. Remain in excellent health.

REFERENCES AND FURTHER DATA ON REQUEST

DISCUSSION

Harvard Résumé The Tym résumé features continuing career development from field sales to general management. You will note that achievement started with increases in territory sales. Management was impressed and gave the subject the opportunity to get similar results in a more responsible position. Success here led to market research management and finally to management of all dealer activities. Opportunities apparently did not come fast enough, and Mr. Tym moved to another company. Soon he changed employment again to obtain general management experience, so that now he is equipped for P. & L. responsibilites in addition to those in marketing. The business biographies of successful people are replete with illustrations of the desire to learn leading to employment changes—sometimes at a temporary financial sacrifice but usually to one's ultimate benefit in terms of greater success.

The *Harvard* form of résumé expresses this career exceptionally well. Note the expanded comments under personal data.

ANALYSIS OF RÉSUMÉ USERS: MARKETING

Sales management, advertising, public relations, product manager, salesman, market research. Titles range from vice-president to salesman.

The salary range (exclusive of profit sharing and fringe benefits) is $10,000 to $50,000.*
The median is $23,500.
In percentage:

> 35% earn from $27,000 to $50,000.
> 31% earn from $12,000 to $18,000.
> 30% earn from $20,000 to $26,000.
> 4% earn $50,000 or more.

The age range is 23 to 56.
The average age is 36.
Some 46% are in their 30s.
Females are 2.6% of the total.

* These figures are based on 1976 levels.

CREATIVE RÉSUMÉ

The *Creative Résumé* lacks a commonly recognized form. Instead, the writer *creates* his own form. *Creative* in this sense does not necessarily mean a better résumé, but one different from the norm. Its quality and effectiveness, as always, will depend on the writer's skill.

The creativity in a *Creative Résumé* may consist in paragraphing, layout, decoration, color, method of folding, or drastically different writing—in rhyme perhaps, or with illuminated capitals, or bearing graphic forms and symbols.

Nor is a *Creative Résumé* necessarily associated with the creative professions. An artist, writer, editor, photographer, stylist, decorator, actor, musician, entertainer, entrepreneur might be drawn toward this style of résumé, but others might use it as well. Actually, too great a departure from the norm turns a résumé into a brochure. The simplified example that follows is creative only in its method of paragraphing and its objective-appraisal type of presentation. To that extent it is different, and effective.

90 Divine Towpath   (000) 456-7890
Stage, CT 12345

RESUME

LILY LANGTRY

MAGAZINE EDITORIAL DIRECTOR - EDITOR

Qualifications:	Twenty-five years of successful experience as Managing Editor with unusually broad responsibilities embracing three successful magazines with a largely female readership; and as Executive Editor, Managing Editor, Features Editor, Assistant Editor in reverse chronology; with three different publishers.

> Publishers Weekly said: "The most knowledgeable woman's editor in the field." (June 1979)
>
> Magazine Writer's Digest said: "Miss Langtry has helped more aspiring writers than anyone I know." (Jan. 1978)
>
> Magazine Guild said: "Miss Langtry has identified her markets and hit them in the bull's-eye; without question one of the most talented editors in her field." (Nov. 1974)

Objective evaluation by Corporate Manpower Development Committee on Executive Evaluation:	COMPETENT in all areas of manuscript selection and purchase, production, control, organization and administration, wide author contacts and excellent reputation for judgment, decisiveness and creativity.

> Possesses in high degree ability to lead, supervise, train and gain loyalty and dedication of staff. Oriented to profitable operations.
>
> SENSITIVE to editorial and reader needs; capable of bringing them together to gain optimum circulation and to make changes quickly as need appears. (Dec. 1970)

Employment history:	1959-1980 - National Publications, New York, NY
	1955-1961 - Hillside Publishing Company, New York, NY
	1954-1955 - Rex Magazine Company, New York, NY
Education:	B.S., Journalism, University of Syracuse, Syracuse, NY, 1963.
Personal data:	Single, excellent health, no dependents, willing to relocate.

REFERENCES AND FURTHER DATA ON REQUEST

DISCUSSION

> **Creative Résumé.** Ms. Langtry's résumé is an excellent example of much relevant and attractive material condensed for presentation on one page. Ms. Langtry, a successful writer, was able to describe 25 years of experience in about 200 words while expressing a competence that might easily have required several pages. She has effectively made use of the words of others, permitting discussions of talents that would be ill-received if expressed subjectively.
>
> The résumé does not follow a formal pattern and is therefore a *Creative Résumé.*
>
> Objective statements can often be obtained from such sources as references, personal evaluations, military evaluations, and press clippings. If well expressed, they can be used as shown in this résumé.

NARRATIVE RÉSUMÉ

The *Narrative Résumé* can be a pleasing variation from formal presentations. You might use this format if you write well, including about the difficult topic of yourself, or if your background is unusual, with perhaps a strong academic foundation. The *Narrative Résumé,* because of its relative rarity, can have extra impact. Remember, however, that it will appeal to some résumé readers only.

Examples of situations in which the *Narrative Résumé* might be effective appear in this book. The form is exceptionally suitable for the *vita brevis* ("short life") type of description of one's lifework. Personal statistics and information about education, military service, hobbies, and the like can be woven into the narrative or given in a separate section.

The disadvantages of the *Narrative* form could be lack of unity, coherence, and compactness. There is also the ever-present difficulty of narrating one's personal and professional life history sufficiently objectively.

EXAMPLE OF NARRATIVE RÉSUMÉ

1 Saladin Way   (890) 123-4567
London, UT 12345
                              RESUME

                         WILLIAM LYON HEART

                  PERSONNEL DIRECTOR/MANPOWER DEVELOPER

Born September 30, 1945, single, excellent health. Residence and travel
in Belgium, France, Tanzania, Kenya, Holland, Germany, Switzerland, Italy,
Tunisia, Morocco, Ivory Coast, Uganda.

Educated as follows:

M. Divinity, M.R.E., 1971. St. Christopher's Seminary, Becton, NY.

B.A., 1966, University of Notre Dame, South Bend, IN.

Post Graduate:

1973, 10 months, Sociology, Louvain University, Belgium.
1972, 12 months, Sociology, Anthropology, Social Research, Princeton Uni-
    versity, Princeton, NJ
1970 (summer), Social Change, Social Psychology, Princeton University.
1969 (summer), Anthropology, Cross Cultural Research, Loyola University,
    Baltimore, MD.

Languages include: French, Spanish, Kisukuma, Kiswahili.

Hobbies include: SCUBA diving, mountain climbing, any racquets game.

Employment experience:

1973-1977: INTERNATIONAL CATHOLIC CHARITIES, New York, NY.

1968-1973: Extracurricular activities while studying included: art ex-
hibits, community relations and marriage counseling, labor negotiation,
consulting, initiation of dramatized TV programs on human relations nationally televised on Channel III, New York City.

I give the preceding statements first because they are the raw data forming the platform for my life to the present and can be tied up in a neat
little package and set aside.

In 1973, acting as a Program Developer, Sociologist and Personnel Director
for the Overseas Division of the International Catholic Charities, I conceived the idea of researching two African church organizations of 7000
members to ascertain the level of their functional efficiency. I was
authorized to carry out such research and as a result suggested a program utilizing sociological techniques to provide job enrichment and
stronger support of the Division by the organizations studied. My report
was read with some skepticism but nevertheless the thesis was finally
accepted and I was appointed to implement the suggestions made.

101

Essentially my suggestions involved a program of personnel reformation and membership education to serve as a model for other branches which would ultimately involve as many as 75 organizations with 60,000 members and 500 supervisory personnel. I spent seven years in Africa on this project in the following activities:

- clarifying the objectives and roles of leaders through reexpression in communications and seminars.
- developing a personnel policy embodying employee relationships.
- conducting role-playing sessions and strategy meetings to help bring solutions to administrative problems and improve interpersonal relationships.
- periodic evaluation of activities to assess their effectiveness.

I published the following articles during this period:

Restructuring Pastoral Programs
Catechetical Program
Youth Study Program
Attitudes in Marriage
Aspects of Communication Between Church and People
Attitudes of Youth Toward Christianity and Marriage
Attitudes of Adults Toward Christianity and Marriage
Training Manual for U.S. and African Organization Personnel

These publications appeared in English and appropriate African languages.

As a result of these and related activities we enjoyed a 50% increase in membership, the program was implemented in 35 additional organizations, relationships between local and overseas personnel were improved, tensions among U.S. workers in Africa were alleviated, medical care was bettered and a library for school children was established.

I am not sure what you may think my education and experience fit me for but I wish to leave Church work to embark upon a career in business.

I think my best contributions would be made in the area of personnel although I would be willing to take any position which would be effective for you while giving me the opportunity to establish a new career.

My qualities include an understanding of and liking for people, some creativity, practical experience in working with people, a good education and an ability to conceive and implement progressive plans.

REFERENCES AND FURTHER DATA ON REQUEST

DISCUSSION

Narrative Résumé. William Lyon Heart spent about 30 years of his life in study and service contributing greatly to the expanded usefulness of his organization. At the end of that period he made a reappraisal and deciding that such service need not be a lifelong commitment, chose to try employment in the private sector. This career change required an evaluation of his past to determine the areas in which he might be most effective. His experience in dealing with people logically suggested the areas of personnel or manpower development.

Being a competent, well educated writer, but lacking business experience, Mr. Heart selected the *Narrative* form, thus notifying the reader that his was an unusual situation calling for a different approach to the job market.

As expected, the subject's obvious interpersonal communications skills, combined with an innovative mind, resulted in a successful résumé that appealed strongly to selected readers. Though without the discipline present in more formal résumés, it has the coherence, unity, logical sequence, and interest needed to make it a compelling document.

ANALYSIS OF RÉSUMÉ USERS: ADMINISTRATION

Supervision, college and school administration, public administration, foundation executives, and hospital executives.

The salary range is $8000 to $34,500.*
Median salary is $14,400.
Age range is 21 to 56.
Average age is 35.
Females are 25% of the total.

* The salary levels are 1976.

PROFESSIONAL RÉSUMÉ

The traditional "learned professions" are law, medicine, and theology. More broadly, a professional is one who has special knowledge enabling him to advise, guide, or instruct others. Teaching is a profession, as is any vocation requiring extensive specialized educational preparation, such as accounting, engineering, or military science.

A *Professional Résumé* therefore places initial emphasis on academic qualifications for the profession. Any other form can serve to present the balance of the information, except the *Narrative*. The most appropriate forms, however, are the *Chronological Résumé with Summary Page* and the *Functional Résumé*.

134 Saturday Post Street   (212) 123-5678
Evening, NY 10017

R E S U M E

of

EPHRAIM TUTT

ATTORNEY

OBJECTIVE: Association with law firm in general corporate and
                  securities areas, including litigation.

SUMMARY OF   Awareness of legal needs of business with ability to
QUALIFICATIONS: provide clear answers and effective remedies for corporate
                  legal problems; including litigation when necessary. Inti-
                  mate knowledge of the Securities Act of 1933 and Exchange
                  Act of 1934; the rules of the major stock exchanges;
                  private placements, lost securities, arbitrations. Fully
                  familiar with tax laws and accounting procedures. Effective
                  in client relationships.

                  Admitted to practice in New York State and New Jersey.

EDUCATION: B.A., Princeton University, Princeton, NJ, 1970.

                  J.D., University of Michigan School of Law, Ann Arbor, MI,
                  1974.

PERSONAL DATA: Age 30, married, two children.

(FOR FURTHER DETAILS, PLEASE SEE FOLLOWING PAGES)

PROFESSIONAL EXPERIENCE

<u>1980-Present</u> WILD, SPENCER AND KING, New York, NY

ASSOCIATE with law firm.

Provide services to clients with wide range of problems but with particular concentration on broker-dealer and specialist problems, controversies involving securities laws, sometimes leading to litigation, registrations of public offerings with S.E.C.

- personally and successfully represented clients before N.Y. Stock Exchange, American Stock Exchange and S.E.C. involving disciplinary matters.
- successfully completed and closed a public offering for a corporation.
- prepared broker-dealer applications for N.Y.S.E. membership.

<u>1976-1980</u> HORNBLOWER, BIDDLE CO., New York, NY

ASSOCIATE HOUSE COUNSEL for major Wall Street investment banking firm.

- won arbitration involving large client of firm.
- approved many Rule 144 sales.
- successfully prosecuted or defended firm position in connection with customer clains.
- aided in drafting a compliance manual for firm; completed compliance inspection of branch offices.

<u>1974-1976</u> MIDWEST STOCK EXCHANGE, Chicago, IL

INVESTIGATIVE ATTORNEY for Midwest Stock Exchange.

- investigated violations by member firms and their personnel of Exchange rules and regulations and of other regulatory agencies.
- prepared charge memoranda for prosecutions which led to disciplinary action by the Exchange.
- reviewed lawsuits and arbitrations to find if any violations existed.

REFERENCES AND FURTHER DATA ON REQUEST

Litigation Lane   (203) 100-1111
Cos Cob, CT 12345

R E S U M E

of

HENRY L. ADAMS

ATTORNEY

OBJECTIVE:

"Of Counsel" relationship and general association taking advantage of
Federal Tax expertise.

SUMMARY OF QUALIFICATIONS:

Awareness of legal needs of business and ability to provide clear answers
and effective remedies for corporate legal problems.

Broad background in acquisitions and joint ventures for major corporations
with record of application of fresh and sophisticated approaches to problems, and successful negotiations.

Extensive experience in general corporate work and general practice;
formerly Special Attorney for I.R.S. Expertise in resolution of complex
tax problems.

VITAL STATISTICS:

Born 2/29/35, married, three children.

EDUCATION:

L.L.M., 1966, Harvard University, Cambridge, MA
J.D., 1959, University of Michigan, Ann Arbor, MI
    Article: "Chancery Practice and Procedure"
    77 New Jersey Law Review 162
B.A., 1957, Brown University, Providence, RI

FOR FURTHER DATA SEE FOLLOWING PAGES

PROFESSIONAL EXPERIENCE:

1966-Present   ALEXANDER, BOTTS & CAREY, New York, NY
                RUSKIN & GREENWOOD, New York, NY

SENIOR ASSOCIATE

Experienced, both as Senior Associate with present firm and as outside
General Counsel to a subsidiary of Loew's Corp., in the successful implementation of acquisition and joint venture projects, requiring legal and
business sophistication, skillful negotiation and careful, often innovative restructuring and drafting. Tax planning and imaginative project
revision have been routine elements of this process. Acquisition work has
included "all cash" deals, stock for stock deals, and stock for assets with
deferred payments.

Sound working relationships were established with senior executives and
counsel for such corporations as Remington-Rand, American Home Products,
Standard and Poor, Gimbel Bros. in implementing joint ventures and acquisitions from letter of intent to final closing.

Experienced in corporate tax problems including accumulated earnings tax,
sales of assets, income and asset problems of REIT's, pension and profit-
sharing plans, deferred compensation contracts, accounting methods, stock
options, liquidations, exempt organizations, net operating loss carry-
overs, reallocation of income, stock valuations, state and local tax
problems.

In these matters, engaged in research, planning and counseling involving
the preparation of legal memoranda, opinion letters, protests and ruling
requests; negotiated with IRS at district, regional and national levels.

Experienced in general corporate work, including planning, negotiating and
drafting for incorporations, stockholders' agreements, buy-sell agreements, employment contracts, liquidations and related minutes and resolutions. Corporate real estate work involved purchases and sales, shopping
center joint ventures, tax shelter partnership deals, options, mortgages,
guarantees, etc.

Experienced in general practice matters including wills, trusts, estate
plans, general contracts, trade name and trademark agreements, franchises
and matrimonial settlements.

1962-1966   INTERNAL REVENUE SERVICE, Washington, DC

SPECIAL ATTORNEY, Office of General Counsel. Primary responsibility involved representing the Government in tax disputes:
- Settlement negotiations with corporate and individual taxpayers and
  determination of whether to settle or litigate.

- Preparation of pleadings, motions, subpoenas, stipulations, briefs
  and other documents for cases pending before Tax Court.

- Conducting trial cases in Tax Court.

COMMENDATIONS:

"The Lawyer's Lawyer gratefully acknowledges the contribution of Henry L. Adams to continuing legal education in the U.S. by reason of his author-ship of the article, 'Syndications: Federal Tax Aspects,' published in The Lawyer's Lawyer, April 1976.

Chief Counsel, U.S. Treasury Department, IRS:
"I would like to take this opportunity to express my appreciation for the splendid work you have performed for this office . . ."

Judge of the Circuit Court of the U.S.:
"I can say without reservation that Mr. Adams has been an effective ad-vocate for the Commissioner in extremely complex cases where the peti-tioners are represented by highly skilled attorneys . . ."

ADDITIONAL PROFESSIONAL ACTIVITIES:

Books:

Federal Tax Manual: three-volume set of tax annotated form books, approx-imately. 3,000 pages.

Successful Underwriting for New Companies, 550 pages.

Connecticut Law Journal: ". . . an excellent working tool for the legal practitioner in acquainting himself with all aspects affecting the public issue and sale of securities of a business enterprise . . ."

New Jersey Law Journal: "This work is recommended particularly for the day-to-day practical workings of the business lawyer who needs a quick, good, reliable reference . . ."

Revision Editor of Moody on Wills.

Articles:
On various corporate tax problems, published in 1961, 1962 and 1967.

MEMBERSHIPS:

American Bar Association
New York Bar Association

REFERENCES AND FURTHER DATA ON REQUEST

DISCUSSION

Professional Résumés. The two preceding résumés give objective first and a summary of qualifications second, with education and personal data following thereafter. In the Tutt résumé experience is more limited than in the Adams résumé, in which more detail was therefore incorporated. Both attorneys illustrate their backgrounds with excellent examples that are, as would be expected, consistent with their objectives. Considerable research was needed to select the most relevant and significant cases from scores or hundreds of them.

Both résumés show individuals of considerable expertise, capable of bringing exceptional abilities to any firm.

Note the inclusion of objective commendations and a listing of publications where applicable.

ANALYSIS OF RÉSUMÉ USERS: PRODUCTION

Plant manager, production manager, inventory control, quality control, and the various engineering disciplines.

The salary range is $10,500 to $28,000.*
The median is $19,500.
The age range is 31 to 58.
The average age is 45.
Age in percentages

    35% are in their 40s.
    37% are in their 50s.
    16% are in their 30s.
There are no females in the survey.

* The salaries quoted are based on 1976 surveys.

ACCOMPLISHMENT RÉSUMÉ

The *Accomplishment Résumé* lists accomplishments without reference to dates and companies and without regard for a chronological order. It is often used by individuals who wish to disguise age, length of experience, employment gaps, lack of progress in recent jobs, job-hopping, and other matters that are easier to explain in person during an interview than in writing. Do not let these reasons dissuade you from using this form if you like it, however. Some nonprofit executive employment services favor this style.

The elements of the *Accomplishment Résumé* are the following:

1   Name, address, and telephone number.
2   Summary of qualifications.
3   List of accomplishments (the most important is given first).
4   List of companies by whom employed (no dates).
5   Military service (no dates).
6   Education (no dates).
7   Hobbies, professional memberships, community activities, and honors (no dates).
8   Personal data (omit age).

An example of the *Accomplishment Résumé* follows.

58 Orchid Avenue
Nemesis, NY 12345

(123) 456-7890

NERO WOLFE

OPERATIONS EXECUTIVE

* * * Experienced manager with proven record of accomplishments in creating profits and often innovative solutions to corporate problems, representing tens of millions of dollars.

* * * Record of progress to increasingly important responsibilities in every employment. Accustomed to working with and leading staffs in improving systems and procedures, in developing harmonious labor relations, in organizing projects for most efficient completion.

* * * Excellent in written and oral communication with wealth of experience in construction, maintenance, site selection, leasing, facilities planning, display, floor layout, contract negotiation, organization of diverse departments involving multi-million-dollar programs.

* * * Experience in the activities enumerated has been worldwide.

FOR FURTHER DATA PLEASE SEE FOLLOWING PAGE

ACHIEVEMENTS:

Cost saving of $1 million in one year using reduced level of personnel and no loss of efficiency.

Completed $50 million construction project in five months with four general contractors saving Company from financial difficulty.

Saved $35,000 annually by devising new method of inventory control.

Set up central purchasing for ten units, saving 13% on annual purchases of $12 million.

Planned, coordinated and supervised a multimillion-dollar construction project with cost saving of $183,000 and bonus to contractor for beating deadline by two weeks.

Planned new housewares department (100,000 sq. ft.) for increased traffic and improved merchandise visibility without loss of business during reconstruction.

Saved 12% in electricity and fuel in group of 37 nationally known department stores, saving more than $3 million in annual costs.

Reduced cost of new two million sq. ft. warehouse 25% by creating flexible storage locations, making changes in rack specifications and other creative planning.

Reduced insurance costs for a three million sq. ft. building by a program of continuous maintenance.

Consolidated insurance on a national basis at a cost saving of $10 million over a period of two years.

Devised new security methods that reduced shoplifting and other causes of loss by 75% with a resultant saving of $13 million. And more.

The preceding accomplishments were achieved for the following companies:
Great Atlantic and Caribbean Coffee Company, Vice President.
The International Insurance Companies, Vice President Operations.
Allied Retailers, Incorporated, Buildings Manager.
Hughes Construction Company, Field Engineer.

EDUCATION: B.S., Rice University, Houston, TX.

PERSONAL DATA: Married, 3 children, excellent health. Willing to relocate.

REFERENCES AND FURTHER DATA ON REQUEST

DISCUSSION

Accomplishment Résumé. The material in the Wolfe résumé was condensed from another résumé of about four pages to two for purposes of illustration. It suffers from a lack of relationship between achievements and employers and lack of explanation of work methods (such as determining the flow of information from the point of sale to the computer, making time studies of jobs, and so forth), which would have added greatly to an understanding of this man's value and the reasons for some of his assignments. Nevertheless, it is effective in presenting a man whose every assignment has been so successful that an employer in need of such skills would be inclined to interview him.

Actually the original résumé, written in *Chronological* form, was very impressive. A broadcast letter summary elicited replies from 70% of the companies approached—an unusually high percentage. Not all replies, largely from the top officers, resulted in interviews, but they provided a base for aggressive follow-ups, leading to personal interviews.

GEORGE BURR
1798 Pennsylvania Ave.
Chicago, IL 00000
Phone (000) 123-4567

OBJECTIVE:

MANAGER OF PROFIT CENTER FOR MAJOR HARD GOODS MANUFACTURER OR CHIEF
OPERATIONS OFFICER FOR NATIONAL INDEPENDENT WHOLESALE DISTRIBUTOR
to utilize strengths in
Financial Planning/Marketing/General Management

EXPERIENCE

<u>1974-Present.</u>   VICE PRESIDENT for Sales & Distribution, Norge Division,
WHITE INDUSTRIES, Chicago, IL

Held sales, distribution, and profit responsibility for all home appliances;
planning responsibility for developing new markets; for this $320 million
division. Controlled $32 million operating budget and supervised 400 sales,
financial and inventory and distribution personnel through eight regional
managers. Planned and directed sales programs for organization with 63
independent wholesale distributors with central buying facilities, and 29
company-owned branches. Created strategies for markets according to varying conditions, to achieve corporate objectives. Planned and implemented
new distribution programs in 27 markets: additional branch operations, additional distributors, and training programs for existing distributors. Opened
distribution with Sears, Ward and Wickes. Reorganization and other planning
resulted in increasing sales 115% with 21% increase in profitability, during
this five-year period, after rejoining company. Other planning: initiated,
devised and operated opening of new mobile home market, resulting in $35
million of additional sales under private label.

<u>1968-1974</u>   VICE PRESIDENT/GENERAL MANAGER, GENERAL ELECTRIC DISTRIBUTORS,
INC., Pittsburgh, PA

Complete P.&L. responsibility for major appliance distributor (inactive
owner), in Pennsylvania, New York State and New Jersey. Introduced marketing to government agencies requiring liaison with manufacturers' R.&D. departments to effect design changes; negotiated G.S.A. specification advantages. Increased sales from $1.5 million, made at a loss, to $3.3 million at a substantial profit and high R.O.I.

<u>1963-1968</u>   REGIONAL MANAGER, Norge Division, WHITE INDUSTRIES, Chicago, IL

Managed marketing activities in Middle Atlantic states plus Virginia, Maryland, Delaware and District of Columbia. Supervised five district managers
with sales group of 20. Conducted advertising, training, personnel selection, planning. Expanded wholesale distribution and more than tripled
sales during five-year tenure. Promoted to this position in 1965 from
District Manager.

<u>1957-1963</u>   SALES MANAGEMENT positions with Whirlpool, and with Casey
Jones, HVAC distributor in Iowa. In latter position, increased market penetration to achieve dominant market share for company.

EDUCATION

M.B.A., University of Chicago, 1956
B.A., Hudson University, Lakeville, OH, 1953

DISCUSSION

Chronological Résumé—Condensed. The Burr résumé is in a condensed chronological style favored by a well-known career consultant company that offers job finding services at $3000 to $5000 or more. Its résumés never exceed one page, even if crowding results. This résumé would ordinarily require two pages. You may make your own comparison and choose among the various sample résumés. We consider it to be dry, and more difficult to read than other formats. We have seen other résumés of this type that are even more crowded in page/word density.

If the subject's career were of a lower order of achievement, reading it could become a chore, leading to discard. The author personally tested the reading time needed for this and a comparable résumé (*Chronological with Summary Page*). The reading time of this résumé is 3 minutes and 20 seconds, with lower comprehension. The reading time of a comparable résumé of 2½ pages: 2 minutes and 3 seconds, with immediate comprehension of candidate's qualities through the device of the initial summary paragraphs. Age, as well as any personality indicators, is omitted. The names of the companies and all other identifying data are fictitious.

Note that, as with any résumé, analysis of one's work background and its proper expression is always of chief importance, regardless of physical format. But physical appearance, as with people, can help.

TWELVE

GETTING READY
TO WRITE
YOUR RÉSUMÉ

All the preceding sections in this book have been preparing you for writing your résumé. The key to this task is the analysis and orderly listing of your job responsibilities and achievements. You must know yourself: what you were or are expected to do, what you actually did or are doing, and how your action affected your job, your section, your department, your division, or your company or organization.

To help you organize these facts, we have prepared an analytical questionnaire. We suggest that you use it. It has been carefully set up so as to make you think about yourself, recall forgotten activities, and focus on actions instrumental in your vocational life. You must first recall events, and then describe your recollections. The second task is eased if done after you have performed the first. Jot down the things that you have accomplished in the form of informal notes, using single words, phrases, and sentence fragments. These notes will serve as the basis for the actual résumé.

SIX BASIC STEPS

Follow these six basic steps in writing your résumé:

1 Assemble the raw data (from your answers to our analytical questionnaire).
2 Refine the data (initial draft).
3 Select the most relevant data.
4 Translate the data into suitable language. Your sentences and paragraphs are the building blocks that you can move around to fit your chosen résumé form.
5 Select your résumé format.
6 Write your résumé.

YOUR ANALYTICAL QUESTIONNAIRE

Before starting on your résumé, gather the data for it by answering the analytical questionnaire below. Your answers will serve to give your résumé focus, direction, and the proper "slant." If you have difficulty in answering a question, skip it for now and return to it later. Take plenty of time to think about yourself and to make a thoughtful self-analysis. Depending on your background, completing the questionnaire will require a half hour to several hours.

1 Your name, address, and home office telephone numbers.
2 Titles of jobs desired, if possible. If you cannot supply them at this time, briefly *describe* the job you want. Identify several jobs by assigning to them the letters A, B, C, and so on, using the same code in Question 3 below.

Turn to Question 11 and answer it before answering the questions that follow.

3 Qualifications that you believe you should have for the jobs A, B, C, and so on, listed in Question 2. (Most data should be in answer to Question 11.) *For example,* your answer to Question 2 is "sales manager," you might answer question as follows:

a Appraise pricing and distribution policies.
b Recruit and train sales staff.
c Maintain distributor liaison.
d And so on.

Now *underline* the qualifications you have *and* list any other qualifications you feel you should have for the jobs you desire.
4 Your age, marital status, number of children, home ownership, car ownership, and so on.
5 Military service

a Dates, branch of service, rank.
b Special training, courses, responsibilities.

6 Education—dates, schools, academic degrees, and proficiency in languages.
7 Major and minor courses. List courses relevant to the jobs desired. State your class standing if possible. Describe scholarships, awards, and honors.
8 Extra-curricular activities at school (sports, jobs, social activities, etc.).

9 Hobbies and your degree of proficiency in them, travel (if extensive), memberships in societies and community activities.

10 A summary of your employment history. *Work backwards,* giving the last job first. Use three columns to assemble the following information:

Dates of beginning job and leaving job (years only) titles	Company and address	Job

11 For each job listed above, starting with the *last* job, give the following data. Treat each position or important assignment with the same company, or with important clients of your employer, as though it were a separate and distinct job. Answer *each* question carefully.

  a Job title.

  b Dates of beginning and leaving job (by transfer to another company or by promotion or change within a company).

  c Beginning and ending salaries or earnings.

  d Name of company and division or department within company.

  e Description of what the company makes, sells, or does.

  f An indication of size of company—by sales volume, number of employees, number of plants, and number of branches or stores, for example.

  g The title of the person for whom you worked (president, foreman, sales manager, etc.).

  h The number of persons you supervised (if any).

  i The kinds of employees you supervised (engineers, clerks, etc.).

  j The types of equipment you used (or that was used under your supervision) and for what purpose. This will be relevant for such jobs as production manager and computer executive, but irrelevant for others.

k Your responsibilities. Describe them briefly but fully; give facts, rather than abstract generalities. Consult page 29, Chapter 9 under "Experience" before answering this question.

l Your accomplishments. Describe them briefly but specifically.

- The problems you were faced with.
- What you did about them.
- What you achieved and how.

That is, what did you see that needed to be done, what did you do about it, and what happened as a result? Do not list mere claims, such as "I increased sales." Give facts: "I found that sales were only $150,000. I made a market survey and determined that the market needed a 'widget.' I introduced a new line of widgets. I trained salesmen by doing X Y Z. Sales increased in six months by $50,000." Such an analysis is important. You need it in your résumé if you are to stand out from other job applicants. It will also reassure you that you are qualified for the job you want, in addition to refreshing your memory and providing valuable *rehearsal and training* for your job interviews.

12 References: name, title, company, address, and telephone number (and extension). Do not include references in your résumé; assemble them for use at interviews.

GUIDANCE IN ANSWERING THE QUESTIONNAIRE

The two sample answers to this questionnaire appearing below illustrate what you should *not* do. Here is how one man answered Question 11:

> 1972-present (name of company). AREA SUPERVISOR. Began February 1972 as restaurant manager in failing unit. The unit started to show profit after four weeks. I was promoted to supervisor of two units after three months. In the following months I was given the entire Maryland area to supervise (five units). A new type of concept was developed, and I was picked to bring it into a profitable operation. At that point the larger volume (Philadelphia) units were given to me to supervise. At my request, I was moved to the New York area as supervisor in July 1973. Since that time I have opened three large volume units for the chain, both in New York and in Pennsylvania. All of the six units now under my supervision gross $1 to $1.5 million per year.

This very successful man needed much prodding before supplying additional information vital to his case. In the final résumé below the portions with data initially not disclosed are underlined.

> 1976–present (name of company)
>
> AREA SUPERVISOR for a rapidly growing, limited menu, full service, $30 million <u>AMEX-listed restaurant chain with 30 loca</u>tions; earlier single unit manager. Responsible for New York and Pennsylvania area supervising six $1 to $1½ million units each with a staff of 60 to 90 people.
>
> — Indoctrinated company with new cost concepts which have contributed significantly to <u>rapid growth from nine units in 1971 to 30 units currently.</u>

— Reduced food cost from 40% to 35%.
— Opened three large volume units: hired, trained complete staffs, installed systems.
— Accustomed to exercising controls through analysis of computer printouts daily on food, liquor, payroll. Trained managers in use of cost analyses.

Earlier managed failing unit; turned it from loss to profit in four weeks by exercise of proper controls, by establishing incentive system, and by gaining cooperation of employees. Personally contributed to success of 15 of existing 30 units and set standards for entire operation.

Prod yourself for the type of detail that, as just demonstrated, can turn a poor résumé into an effective one. What did you see that needed to be done? In this case the corporation was in need of profitability. What did you do about it? In this case the man created better cost concepts. What happened as a result? In this case the units became profitable.

In our second example of how *not* to answer the analytical questionnaire the subject took a shortcut. The result again was the omission of vital information.

1. Simon Le Pie, 5 Mother Goose Path, Childhood, N.Y. Home (123) 456-7890. Office (321) 654-0987.
2. Sales manager.
3. a. Styling of line.
   b. In charge of all shipping.
   c. Distribution of goods to the factory—what goes into work at the machines.
   d. Production.
4. 36—married—3 children—own home and car.
5. U.S. Naval Reserve 1960–1968—2 years active—6 years reserve.
6. High school graduate—4 years—with some college.
7. Academic.
8. Worked in specialty shop—worked in bowling alley. Sports—bowling, football, baseball, horseback riding.
9. Horseback riding, photography.
10. Seventeen years in the employ of Toni Co., 1962–1979.

11. a. Sales manager.
    b. 1962–1979.
    c. $45 week to $560 week.
    d. Sales department.
    e. Ladies' ready-to-wear.
    f. 35 employees—$4,500,000.00.
    g. President.
    h. Supervised up to 10 employees.
    i. Salesmen, shipping clerks, production workers.
    j. Sewing machines, cutting machines, taping machines.
    k. Making sure all machines were running in proper order. Responsible for putting them in proper order if not working. Selling, getting orders by phone out of town. Getting merchandise from the factory in time to ship goods. Getting piece goods in on time as per delivery order. Consistently, I had to be after these people to get the goods I needed to run the business in a proper manner.
    l. In the 17 years I was with the company, I worked up from delivery boy to sales manager. The achievement of being able to book $1.0 to $1.21 million a year.

The man omitted the following important information:

1 Business increased from $2 million to $3.5 million during his tenure.
2 The business was discontinued because of the owners' retirement.
3 The company had a sales showroom in conjunction with the factory, where he accomplished a lot of selling to out-of-town buyers.
4 He was in charge of purchasing, inventory control, and sales forecasting and was production manager in addition to being sales manager.
5 He supervised seven salesmen operating nationally and reported to the president.
6 His association with buyers was such that he could book large orders by telephone.

7   He was an excellent salesman himself, in addition to successfully managing a sales organization.

8   He personally sold to most of the major Los Angeles and other West Coast department stores and was responsible for getting business from such national accounts as Sears, Ward, and Penney.

The final résumé, with all information included, follows.

367 Couture Avenue
Pasadena, CA 12345

Home (123) 456-7890
Office (432) 654-0987

R E S U M E

of

JOHN ABRAMS

SALES MANAGER - APPAREL

*** Seventeen years of experience in apparel field with one company, for last ten years as Sales Manager, responsible for increasing multimillion dollar business by 75%. Owners retired and business was terminated.

*** Close associations with leading buyers of women's dresses and pants suits all over the United States, experienced in selling to department and specialty stores, chains, giant national retailers and in maintaining productive contacts with major buying offices.

*** Effective trainer and leader accustomed to managing national sales organization. Management versatility led to expanded responsibilities including production, purchasing, shipping and assistance in styling and pricing in addition to marketing.

*** Excellent personal salesman with ability to get and retain customer loyalty and write business either by personal calls or by telephone, with hundreds of leading buyers across the country.

*** Capable of bringing additional volume and profit to any women's wear manufacturer.

FOR FURTHER DATA PLEASE SEE FOLLOWING PAGE

BUSINESS EXPERIENCE:

1962-1979   TOO MUCH CO., INC., Los Angeles, CA

SALES MANAGER for $4.5 million manufacturer of Women's Apparel with showroom and factory in California; sold nationally to department and specialty stores, chains and such giant retailers as Sears, Ward and Penney. Supervised staff of seven salesmen and Production Manager. Reported to President. Owners decided to retire and business was terminated. Responsible for:

- developing increased sales through leadership and training of seven salesmen, and personal selling.
- sales forecasting, inventory control, purchase of piece goods and trimmings.
- aiding in pricing and styling.
- expediting production as necessary to achieve prompt shipments.

Accomplishments:
- rose from delivery boy to Sales Manager with earnings increases to 12 times starting salary.
- increased volume 87%; opened scores of new customers; developed existing customers.
- personally accounted for sales of $1.0 million to $1.25 million annually to leading accounts around the country.
- improved turnover by rigid inventory controls.
- curtailed price increases by creative piece goods purchasing.

MILITARY SERVICE:

1960-1968   U.S. NAVAL RESERVE. Two years active duty; Airman 3rd Class.

EDUCATION:

Three years at University of California in Los Angeles.

EXTRACURRICULAR ACTIVITIES:

Worked while attending high school and college; **participated in football, lacrosse, bowling, riding.**

HOBBIES:

Riding, photography.

PERSONAL DATA:

Age 36, divorced, two children.

REFERENCES AND FURTHER DATA ON REQUEST

ANALYSIS OF RÉSUMÉ USERS: RETAIL

Assistant buyers, buyers, merchandise managers, store owners, retail advertising, display executives, and store managers.

The salary range is $10,000 to $52,000.*
Median salary is $23,500.
Average age is 40.5.
Females are 11% of the total.

* Compensation as of 1976.

THIRTEEN

WRITING YOUR RÉSUMÉ

To begin with, turn to *your* answers to Question 11 in the analytical questionnaire. Write your résumé first in the *Chronological* form. Write dates of employment (beginning and ending) for the most recent position. Write name of company for which you work (or worked).

Write your title and describe briefly what the company does. Write in the first person, but avoid the use of "I." Describe each responsibility concisely, in a brief, almost terse, sentence or phrase. Omit responsibilities that are unimportant or negative with respect to your objective. For example, if clerical chores are part of your job as an office manager, make no mention of them if your job objective is "office manager." Now briefly and clearly write your achievements. Emphasize contributions to profit, cost savings, new techniques or methods you introduced, mechanical or product improvements, training programs, departmental reorganizations, accuracy, and anything else about you that is positive.

What did you do and what happened as a result? To answer these questions, use the words that are best understood in your field, but avoid overly technical language (study the résumé examples included in this book, as well as the vocabulary section) in Appendix B. Use simple words wherever possible if they say exactly what you mean. For example, the employment of a computer programmer, recommended by the department head, may require the approval of a higher level executive. The chances are that the executive is unfamiliar with computer jargon, but he *will* wish to know whether you can communicate your special expertise to nonspecialists. Such terms as FORTRAN, COBOL, and second, third, and fourth generation identification numbers are all fine, but use them sparingly, except in answering advertisements that are themselves highly technical.

Follow this procedure for each position that you have held. The most recent jobs are usually the most important ones. "Most recent" may mean the past year for a young person or the preceding 10 to 15 years for an older person. Give most space to the areas of your greatest accomplishments. Account for time back to your earliest jobs, unless they are completely irrelevant. For example, if you have been a city administrator for several years, it is unimportant that you were a waiter or a porter at some previous time. Several years can be bunched together as "1954–1959, various unrelated positions as bookkeeper, cost analyst, station agent, prizefighter."

After your business, professional, or other vocational experience list military service. An outstanding military career would require a detailed description; dates, service arm, and rank will suffice for an average one.

Education, extracurricular activities, community activities, awards, personal data, and others follow, as discussed elsewhere and as exemplified in the many résumé samples in this book.

As a final sentence add "References and further data on request."

If you wish to add a summary paragraph or page describing your accomplishments in functional terms first review the accomplishments sections of your résumé and your answers to

Question 3 in the analytical questionnaire. Suppose that you have described your accomplishments as follows:

a. Promoted to manage larger office which was operating at a loss.
b. Increased sales from $5.0 million to $7.8 million.
c. Reduced staff of sales managers from 8 to 2.
d. Brought operation from loss to profit.
e. Assigned to another losing office to attempt similar recovery.

Your front page summary might then read like this:

Assigned successively to branches operating at a loss. Consistently successful in creating profitability in every position, increasing sales and revenues variously from 60% to more than 100%, and reducing costs by streamlining management.

Or you might have made the following listing of accomplishments.

a. Assigned to manage new venture; set up new corporation.
b. Went from groundbreaking to startup in five months, one month ahead of schedule.
c. Worked within forecasted capital and expense budgets.
d. Wrote off all startup expenses and put company in a profit position within five months of startup and three months ahead of schedule.
e. Increased profit from 35% to 40%.
f. Developed cost reducing shift schedules, fringe benefit packages; improved productivity.
g. Program influenced the establishment of a second profitable subsidiary.

This front page summary might then be in order:

Experience as general manager includes all areas of responsibility from original incorporation, site selection, building design and construction, and hiring and training to startup and operation; all work consistently ahead of schedules.

Record of profitability improvement from increased revenues. Cost savings by innovative planning in connection with work scheduling and worker incentive packages. Set viable precedent for further profitable corporate expansion.

Review the *Chronological Résumé with Summary Page* annotated for additional explanation of résumé layout and the preparation of a summary page or paragraph. Under this setup you are essentially turning specific accomplishments into a more generalized description of what you did. That is, you are using specific accomplishments as the basis for an expressive summary—if you increased profits from 35% to 40% (specific) you are a manager who can add profitability to a corporate activity (functional).

A correctly written résumé should flow, one action or achievement leading to the next. You had certain responsibilities. As a result you took certain actions. The actions were of such and such a nature. They culminated in the results described. The results saved time and money. Additional profits were created, morale was improved. Each assignment for a company or a succession of companies brought increased responsibilities. Results were progressive or forward moving.

This evolutionary development of a career is best shown in the *Chronological Résumé* or the *Chronological Résumé with Summary Page.*

FOURTEEN

TYPING
YOUR RÉSUMÉ

Type your résumé on good quality (16 to 24 pound weight) 25% rag paper 8½ by 11 inches in size. The IBM Executive Selectric and many newer typewriters have attractive, readable typefaces. Reproduce your résumé by offset printing to retain its good appearance. The sheet can be folded in various ways to obtain a "different look." We prefer standard size and format, using *content* and *language* to create an exceptional résumé.

White, unembellished paper is best, though a blue legal backing or simple colored borders can be attractive. Whether you are an artist, writer, graphics specialist, or government administrator, the person reading your résumé most wants to know what you can contribute to the company or organization in profit, leadership, initiative, reliability, and the like. As an artist or designer you might best expend your effort in preparing a superior work portfolio rather than in embellishing your résumé. Do not use conformed right-hand margins. Keep the résumé neat, but informal in a nonprofessional format.

Use short sentences. Observe grammatical rules and conventions. Punctuate for readability rather than by strict rules. Use underlining and uppercase letters for emphasis.

Keep paragraphs short. Double or triple space between paragraphs. It is easier to read a properly spaced résumé of three or four pages than one page of closely written, overcrowded copy.

The physical appearance (format) of your résumé matters very much. Typing, layout, margins, headlines, centering, paragraphing, spacing, spelling, punctuation—all have bearing on the effectiveness of your résumé. Poorly done, they wreck a good résumé. Well done, they enhance a poor one.

Choose the format that you consider to be the most appealing from the many résumé examples in this book. Some specific guidelines for typing your résumé and your summary page are given below.

RÉSUMÉ

Allowing 1 inch from the top of the page, type your name in uppercase letters at the left margin. The page number, indicated by an uppercase PAGE and an arabic numeral, is placed on the same line at the right margin.

Triple space before the first category, "EXPERIENCE." Each category is typed in uppercase letters.

Double space and type date of employment of last job at left margin. Company name and address are typed in uppercase letters on the same line at approximately the center of the page.

Double space and start the job description, with the job titles in uppercase letters. The body is single spaced with double spacing between paragraphs and categories.

After the last category and description, triple space and center the phrase, "REFERENCES AND FURTHER DATA ON REQUEST," in uppercase letters.

Choice of margins, positioning of headlines, paragraphing, use of dashes and asterisks, and spacing are largely aesthetic matters.

SUMMARY PAGE

Starting approximately 1 inch from the top of the page at the left margin, type your home address. Your home (and business) telephone number is typed on the same line at the right margin. Margins should be at least $1/2$ inch wide.

The word "RESUME" typed in uppercase letters is centered 5 or 6 lines below the last line of the address. Double space and write the word "of" in lowercase letters (centered). Double space and center the name in uppercase letters. Double space again and center in uppercase letters the position title or objective.

Triple space and type a dividing double line to separate the heading from the body of the summary page.

Triple space and indent each paragraph, setting it off with triple asterisks.

Center paragraphs on the page, with triple spacing separating single spaced paragraphs.

Leave three or more spaces (depending on the position on the page of the last paragraph) before centering the phrase (in uppercase letters) "FOR FURTHER DATA, PLEASE SEE FOLLOWING PAGES."

COMPARISON OF PICA AND ELITE TYPES

The pica type appearing on the Executive typewriter requires about 18% more space, double spaced, than does the elite type. A typewritten page with 1 inch margins at top and bottom would show a difference of 2 inches between the two type sizes. Three inches take in about eight lines of Executive type and nine lines of eite type in double spaced copy. Three more lines of elite type than of pica type would fit into a 9 inch space. Single spacing doubles the number of lines. The size of paragraph indentations will affect these estimates.

Almost all successful corporations use advertising as one of their basic techniques for building business and improving profitability. A resume is an individual's method of advertising him or herself; perhaps the only method of advertising for the great majority. Some people hire public relations firms to gain an image; some have important or newsworthy accomplishments that place their names in the news media. Most must rely on a resume to circulate information about their talents or expertise.

In writing about oneself it is best to be dignified and professional. The modern resume has evolved as a rather formal document. At its best it is concise, informative and literate. Unlike a novel it cannot use the devices of plot, humor, imagination and length to create and resolve situations. It is real and subject to the

Example of pica type. (The IBM Executive Typewriter)

Almost all successful corporations use advertising as one of their basic techniques for building business and improving profitability. A resume is an individual's method of advertising him or herself; perhaps the only method of advertising for the great majority. Some people hire public relations firms to gain an image; some have important or newsworthy accomplishments that place their names in the news media.

In writing about oneself it is best to be dignified and professional. The modern resume has evolved as a rather formal document. At its best it is concise, informative and literate. Unlike a novel it cannot use the devices of plot, humor, imagination and length to create and resolve situations. It is real and subject to the infirmities that each of us has and to the limitations of time, space and honesty. These limitations require the discipline of formality. Add to this the difficulty of self expression and you find another reason to have and follow rules of procedure. That is what this book is all about.

Example of elite type

FIFTEEN

THE COVERING LETTER

Your résumé, when mailed, should be accompanied by a covering letter. It should be dated. The covering letter is a way of introducing yourself, saying what you want, and asking for an answer. Keep it brief, quickly leading to that all important document—your résumé.

It is appropriate to write a special covering letter for any résumé being sent to someone you know or with respect to a job about which you have some knowledge. You can adjust a covering letter to fit a particular person or job while a résumé cannot be that frequently revised. Address the letter to a specific person, with the proper title, address, and salutation.

For a general mailing a general letter is suitable. Though it is always better to address a letter to a specific person, the salutations "Dear Sir" or "Gentlemen" are acceptable in a general letter. Filling in a name might be impossible in a printed letter because of the difficulty of matching typefaces.

Your covering letter identifies you:

> After 14 years as sales manager of a major company in the lighting industry during which time I was instrumental in increasing sales 27%, I am now qualified for full marketing responsibilities in or outside this industry. My résumé discloses the nature and depth of my experience.

It asks for an interview:

> I would like to discuss with you how I can be productive for your company while at the same time creating a satisfactory career for myself.

It requests an answer:

> I look forward to your reply.
>
> > Sincerely,
> >
> > John Smith

A covering letter may also serve as a summary of qualifications if they do not appear in the résumé. We suggest, however, that the covering letter be kept informal and brief, letting the résumé convey your message.

Type the covering letter on a sheet of 8½ by 11 inches, or 7 by 10 inches if the letter is short. Name and address, appearing at the top, can be engraved, in raised letters, printed, or typed. Engraved or printed stationery is preferred, but not essential if you are short on money or time (getting stationery printed can take several weeks).

A résumé that is weak because one's accomplishments cannot be suitably expressed, can be strengthened by a covering letter describing latent abilities, aspirations, and personal qualities that have no place in the résumé itself but might help to obtain an interview.

A disability—one eye, a limp, an arthritic hand, a speech defect, eye sensitivity to bright lights, or anything else that might be noted by an interviewer—should be mentioned in the covering letter so that both you and the interviewer are prepared in advance. Your disabilities are not necessarily a disadvantage, and may sometimes be described in a manner that creates added interest.

Unsolicited letters should be addressed to the most appropriate individual within a company:

1   In a small company it is usually the president or owner who makes or approves all employment decisions.

2   In a larger company send middle management inquiries to the executive in charge of your departmental area (sales, finance, production) or to the personnel director.

3   For a position at the entry level in a medium size or large company address your letter to the personnel director.

4   If you know someone in the company you are approaching, send your letter to that person.

5   If you are an upper level executive with unusual qualifications use a broadcast letter instead of a résumé with covering letter and address it to the top executive or one of the top executives by name.

6   At the clerical level send your letter to the attention of the personnel department.

7   If your case is unusual (you are changing careers, for example) or if you have special credentials (education, background, military career) that you think would be of interest to a top executive, send the covering letter and résumé to him or her. Your letter will be routed to the proper department head.

8   If you are interested in working in a particular department, send your covering letter and résumé to the head of that department, rather than to someone in the personnel department.

When addressing a corporation, use the salutations "Dear Sir" or "Gentlemen." When addressing an individual, use his or her name and title, as shown below. Information about unusual forms of address can be found in most dictionaries.

Mr. John Smith, President
Roland Smith Co., Inc.
1 Bridge Street
Cohama, Nevada

Dear Mr. Smith: [or]   Dear Sir:

Roland Smith Co., Inc.
1 Bridge Street
Cohama, Nevada

Gentlemen: [or]   Attn: Mr. John Smith

Mrs. John Smith, President
Roland Smith Co., Inc.
1 Bridge Street
Cohama, Nevada

Dear Mrs. Smith: [or]   Dear Madam:

Ms. Eleanor Smith, President
Roland Smith Co., Inc.
1 Bridge Street
Cohama, Nevada

Dear Ms. Smith:

In typing your covering letter, place the date three lines below the last line of the letterhead (the heading containing your name and address), slightly to the right of page center.

Start the address four or five lines (or more if the letter is short) below the date, at the extreme left margin.

Salutation starts on the third line after the address.

Double space before typing the body of the letter. The letter text is single spaced, with double spacing between paragraphs. When completed, the body of the letter should be centered on the page, with all margins being equal.

Double space between the body of the letter and the complimentary close. The complimentary close should be aligned with the date.

The name (aligned with the complimentary close) is typed five spaces below, allowing sufficient room for the signature.

Reference initials of the writer are indicated on the same line as the typed signature at the extreme left margin, typed in uppercase letters.

Examples and a layout of a covering letter appear below. A *block margin* is without indentations. *Indented* margin means that the first line of each paragraph is indented.

EXAMPLES OF COVERING LETTERS

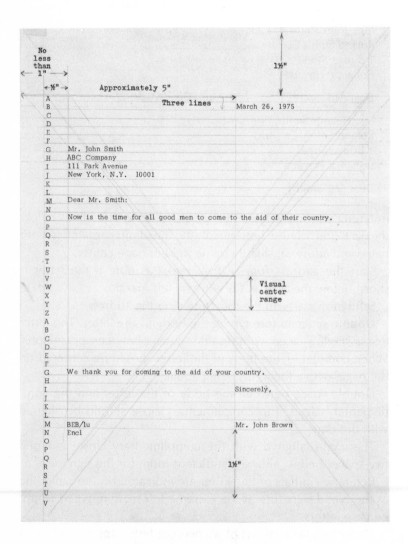

Layout of Covering Letter

WILLIAM WASHINGTON
300 Rue de la Paix
Paris, France 12AR

Dear Mr. Clark:

I am sending you my resume on the possibility that you may have an assignment to find an individual with my qualifications.

I am now headquartered in Paris with European sales responsibilities, working for an American company. Previously, I had extensive sales experience in the U.S.

My record of contributions to increased sales through improved strategies, my ability to use training skills to improve management at all marketing levels, and my encouragement of people development have been consistent in my background.

My compensation requirement is in the high thirties. I return to the U.S. about every two months and can arrange to meet personally with you when necessary.

If you have anything of interest I shall be most happy to hear from you.

Sincerely,

William Washington

WILLIAM ADAMS
37 Main Street
Braintree, MA 00000

Gentlemen:

For the last five years I have been actively engaged in
mergers and acquisitions/corporate development in the U.S.
currently, earlier in Brussels, Belgium. I have identified,
negotiated and concluded six multimillion-dollar acquisitions:
European acquisition of American companies and U.S. acquisition
of European companies; I am competent in this work on an international scale.

My present company is suspending its international acquisition
activities, and I am now seeking a position where such corporate
development remains an important part of management planning.

My resume is enclosed.

If my qualifications are of interest to you, I would welcome
your reply, and an opportunity to meet.

Very truly yours,

William Adams

(000) 913-8765 Home
(000) 926-1234 Office

WILLIAM JEFFERSON
1743 Monticello Avenue
Shadwell, VA 00000

Dear Sir:

After 16 years in public service, I am interested in making a career change to the private sector or to a foundation in a people-related area such as Personnel, Recruitment, College Administration, Manpower and Program Development, General Administration.

My work in Africa for the past five years and prior to that has involved personnel and general management in addition to pastoral duties and has provided a broad social relations understanding reinforced by education.

For example:

- I am experienced in the establishment and implementation of programs for training, education, health, medical and guidance services for more than 100 overseas U.S. personnel and 10,000 Central African mission members; in organizational development, advising, compensation, providing leadership and motivation.

- I conceived and instituted a new system of team ministry to overcome frustration and low morale among U.S. expatriates.

- I trained local members to become self-sufficient in and to understand committee work, decision-making, budgeting, banking functions, the drawing of contracts, self-education.

- I personally conducted a fund-raising drive and raised nearly $1/2 million for the Society.

- I coordinated medical services for 30,000 population.

As a result of these experiences, I am sure that I can be effective in private enterprise. My resume is enclosed.

Age 44, single, excellent health; B.A., M.Div., Ph.D., one year of Business Administration.

May I discuss the opportunity to be contributory to your organization while creating a new career for myself? I look forward to your reply.

Sincerely,

William Jefferson

WILLIAM MADISON
1780 Port Conway Road
King George, VA 00000

Gentlemen:

I am seeking a position in research and analysis of statistical and quantitative data and have been pursuing my education in this field, as an Economics major, since 1972. I expect to earn my Master's Degree in June 1979 from New York University, where I am an evening student.

In order to get started in my chosen career, I am willing to accept any position where I can demonstrate my competence and move upward according to my abilities.

My studies have suggested to me that the creative analysis of data can provide an important key to better management planning. I think I can be useful in this area.

My resume is enclosed.

If there is an appropriate opening in your company, I would enjoy a personal meeting to further express my qualifications.

Your reply will be appreciated.

Sincerely,

William Madison

ELIZABETH MONROE
1786 Westmoreland Road
Charlottesville, VA 00000

Dear Sir:

It is necessary for me to create a full-time career. I have
tried to assemble my experience and abilities in the enclosed
resume.

It would be easy to remain in the travel business, for which I
am well qualified, but I am seeking a more challenging opportunity.

I prefer a position where I can utilize skills in researching
projects and writing about them (such as new and interesting
lifestyles, food and travel) for a magazine, public relations
firm, or airline; or acting as an administrative assistant to
a busy executive.

My experience covers a wide range of activities in all of which
I have been successful, though lacking, due to home commitments,
the dedication to a career that I am now able to provide. (My
son is about to enter college.)

I am highly creative and I believe that I could be an asset to
any company in the areas in which I am interested and efficient.

If you have an opening for an individual of my background, I
can promise a high level of efficiency, enthusiasm and vigor
applied to any assignments given.

An opportunity to meet with you personally would be a privilege
and a pleasure.

I look forward to your reply.

Sincerely,

Elizabeth Monroe

A COVERING LETTER IN ANSWER TO A DISPLAY ADVERTISEMENT

ABIGAIL ADAMS
1767 Braintree Street
Oklahoma City, OK 12345
(123) 456-7890

Mr. Giles Blass, President
Automatic Equipment Company
Industrial Park
Dallas, TX 34567

Dear Sir:

In re: your advertisement the <u>Wall Street Journal</u>,
3/30/78:

I am a personnel executive with eight years of
achievement and increasing responsibilities.

I am expert in personnel administration, training,
labor relations and executive recruiting.

My resume is enclosed.

May I discuss with you how I might be contributory
to your Company? I look forward to your reply.

Sincerely,

Abigail Adams

AA

The XYZ Corporation
666 Springfield Avenue
Westfield, NJ 07901

Mr. John Q. Adams
Vice President, Marketing
Executive Vitamin Co., Inc.
300 Pennsylvania Avenue
Durham, NC 12345

Dear Mr. Adams:

You can employ this man whose career highlights are described on the attached page for effective contributory work in sales management in the fields of pharmaceuticals, proprietary drugs, cosmetics, appliances, accessories.

We have researched his references and they are, without exception, excellent.

There is no obligation to this Company in connection with his employment by you.

If you are seeking an M.B.A. with related business experience you can save search, advertising or other fees by interviewing this man who is available for immediate employment. He is willing to relocate for a good opportunity.

You may phone him direct at (123) 567-0987 to set up an interview, or you may write to him at the above address.

Sincerely,

Andrew Jackson

JM/ds

WILLIAM JACKSON
1767 Hermosa Street
Hermosa Beach, CA 10000
(321) 098-7654

Dear Sir:

I have been attending Cal-Tech since 1977, evenings, and most recently full time, to gain a B.E. degree in Chemical Engineering which I have just been awarded.

Engineering has been my vocational objective for many years, particularly Process Design and Development, chemically related, or Chemical Engineering. I believe I am now qualified to make positive contributions in these areas for any corporation, particularly since I have had previous administrative experience and a career in the U.S. Army which will enable me to adapt easily to responsible assignments.

The training in Engineering has been both rigorous and enjoyable and I look forward to utilizing the knowledge I have acquired in a productive way.

My resume is enclosed. May I have an interview to establish my credentials?

I look forward to your reply.

Sincerely,

William Jackson

WJ

A COVERING LETTER FOR MAILING RÉSUMÉS TO EXECUTIVE SEARCH FIRMS

WILLIAM H. HARRISON
100 Whig Road
Boston, MA 02108
(617) 789-0987

Gentlemen:

I am currently employed and have enjoyed a career of substantial success as a Sales Manager for a $20 million division of a large corporation.

My situation has been somewhat unique in that I have had almost autonomous responsibility in operations.

My income is in the middle $30s with comprehensive fringe benefits. I am willing to relocate for any good opportunity.

My resume is enclosed.

If you have a search in progress for someone of my qualifications, I would like to explore mutual interests with you at a personal meeting.

Sincerely,

William H. Harrison

WHH

Note that the covering letter mentions the salary desired. Executive search firms must know a job applicant's compensation suitability for their clients.

                    William Tilden
                       Lob Lane
                  Oldwick, NJ 07000

Dear Sir:

I have a 15 year record of success in leading the R&D
Department (as Corporate Vice President) of a major
consumer products company which leans heavily on expertise
in electronics and mechanical engineering.

I have made many contributions to new art (for which I am
co-patentor) and have developed products which are the
leading products in my industry as you will see from my
resume, enclosed.

I am looking for broader horizons and it is possible that
my abilities would be of interest to your Company. May we
discuss it?

When I visit you, you will observe that I walk slowly due
to a broken hip which has not set properly, sustained in
a tennis accident. This has no effect on my productivity.

Your reply setting up a date for a personal meeting will
be appreciated.

                              Sincerely,

WT   William Tilden
                              (201) 123-5678

100 Petticoat Lane
Far Hills, NJ 07100

Mr. Hamilton Beach, Chairman
Bankers Holding Company
100 Wall Street
New York, NY 10001

Dear Sir:

From time to time some of your larger customers, clients
or friends may ask you if you know of an available,
competent executive to guide a corporation effectively.

On the possibility that you have or may have such a request,
I am enclosing my resume which describes a successful,
contributory career.

I shall appreciate your referring to me any opportunities
which may come to your notice; or passing this along to
someone else who might have interest.

Sincerely,

WT   William Tyler
Encl.   (201) 321-7654

Lewis Carroll
57 Mirror Road
Denver, CO (zip)
(123) 456-7890

Mr. Henry Gladstone, Pres.
Senator Playing Card Co.
30 Mosswood Avenue
New Orleans, LA

Dear Sir:

I have a consistent record of profit contributions arising from competence in general management, marketing and production for major companies in the U.S., and overseas; accustomed to P. & L. responsibility.

I am widely experienced in power tools and sophisticated machinery. My resume is enclosed.

May I discuss mutual opportunities in your company with you?

Your reply will be appreciated.

Sincerely yours,

Lewis Carroll

LC

SIXTEEN

USING
YOUR RÉSUMÉ

You can make use of your résumé in a number of ways:

1 Use your résumé to answer suitable advertisements in newspapers, trade magazines, and wherever else help wanted advertisements appear.

2 Distribute the résumé among friends and acquaintances.

3 Send your résumé to members of boards of directors of local businesses.

4 Send your résumé to the companies for which you think you would like to work. Distribute as many as you can afford (at least 100) in this manner. Address the résumé to the personnel manager—either by name or by title.

5 Send your résumé to executive recruiters if you are seeking a middle or upper management position.

6 Have the résumé on hand when visiting employment agencies; they may want several copies.

7 Take the résumé to your banker, your insurance agent, your lawyer, your accountant, your broker.

8 Send your résumé to directors of trade associations related to your experience.

9 Supply a résumé to everyone who you think might be influential in getting you a job or, if you are employed, the job you would like to have.

10   Use the résumé as the basis for your presentation at an
     interview.

As a rule your résumé will be handled with confidentiality. Exceptions do occur, however. Thus in answering a blind advertisement you may unknowingly send a résumé to your own
employer. The possibility of a breach of confidence must be
considered when soliciting a position from a company other
than your current employer. Weigh the potential dangers
against the benefits. Though a breach of confidentiality can
have disastrous results, it has on occasion served to make a
company aware of a valuable employee's restlessness, leading
to increased rewards for the employee. Labeling the résumé
"Confidential" will not assure its confidentiality. A breach of
confidentiality is usually beyond your control.

ANSWERING ADVERTISEMENTS

The leading newspapers are primary sources of job availabilities—classified advertising for lower level jobs and display advertising for executive levels. *The Wall Street Journal* and *The
New York Times* have national distribution and carry ads in
their various sections from all over the country. These newspapers are the bibles of the job market. Many people are un-
happy with the responses, or lack of responses, from their answers to ads. It is true that frequently ads do not properly
describe the job openings, that people use ads for other reasons than to find employees, and that for some openings so
many résumés are received that it is impractical to respond to
more than a few. Again, you cannot afford *not* to answer appropriate advertisements, however, because one of them might
provide just the future you are looking for. Don't overlook
your industry trade magazines.

Some of the effective ways to answer ads are discussed below.

If you are employed and your job search is confidential, you must be careful about answering "blind" ads (no company name given). The ad may have been placed by your own company. You may be able to discover the identity of a "blind" advertiser by calling the newspaper carrying the ad. You can also answer with a statement of your qualifications and an explanation of the confidentiality necessary and in turn provide a box number for the answer.

Always, if you can find out exactly what the advertiser is looking for, you can write a better letter in answer to an ad. Most job seekers do not bother to call the advertiser (if the name is disclosed), though often a telephone call to the person named or to the personnel manager will elicit valuable information. If you do make the call, be sure that you have your own story letter-perfect in generalities; avoid specifics until you have found out as much as possible about the job requirements.

The general rule in answering ads is that the more specific you can be with respect to your qualifications for the exact job involved the better will be your chance of success.

Frequently the ad itself discloses information from careful analysis that is not apparent from a first reading.

HOW TO READ AND ANSWER
NEWSPAPER ADVERTISEMENTS

Advertisement for senior systems programmer:

Major job functions will require you to support communications software in a TCS/VS/CICS environment, and analyze and resolve technical problems. Your background should exhibit a detailed and complete comprehension of VS operating systems,

TCAM knowledge, 3–5 years systems programming experience in an OS/VS shop, specific knowledge of CICS internals and SMP, good verbal skills, and a willingness to perform goal maintenance skills.

Forward your résumé and salary history in confidence to [name of company and individual follow—a brokerage company].

This ad means:

1 You must have substantial experience in programming and systems packages.
2 Your experience should have been with IBM software.
3 The symbols are all within the communications area, not in applications programming.
4 The advertiser is a brokerage company.
5 You must be able to express yourself with respect to EDP in nontechnical language for the understanding of general executives, and be able to write and speak clearly in providing instruction manuals and training sessions.
6 You must be continuously aware of the rapid changes in computer technology, hardware, and software and show evidence of your continuing education.
7 The age range sought is 30–35.
8 Previous experience in brokerage accounting systems will be a plus.

When answering any ad it is worthwhile to list the elements appearing in the ad, to clarify, if possible, anything that you are unsure of, and to incorporate in your answer everything that is relevant. To answer this particular advertisement you may in your covering letter use technical language to express your qualifications. You will stress your exposure to IBM equipment. You will tell about brokerage-related experience. You will refer to your verbal and writing skills and give examples of the communications efforts in which you have been involved. If your age is favorable, make a point of it—if not, don't mention it. Indicate your continuing studies.

This advertisement is best answered with a résumé that permits a fuller expression of technical qualifications than a letter.

43 Ocean Gap   (123) 456-7890
Hermosa Beach, CA 98765

R E S U M E

WILLIAM FRANKLIN

EDP SYSTEMS DESIGNER
and ANALYST

SUMMARY

* * *   Qualified to design on-line systems, implement and
          operate at optimum capacity. Record of providing
          cost savings in time, manpower and equipment and
          utilizing advanced technology to accomplish objec-
          tives within expedited time frames.

EXPERIENCE

<u>1975-Present</u> PACIFIC CONTINENTAL TELEPHONE CO., Los Angeles, CA

ONLINE SYSTEMS DESIGN and PERFORMANCE ANALYST for one of nation's largest
computer installations.

Responsible for:
A. justifying and devising plan for the following:
   1. conversion of Disbursement Accounting Department's TCAM (Telecom-
      munication Access Method) data collection system to CICS (Customer
      Information Control System) and centralization of on-line program-
      ming
   2. CICS on-line inquiring to IMS data bases via DL/I interface
   3. eventual migration to mixed CICS-IMS/DC-VTAM environment and
   4. selection of an on-line text editor to replace TSO for source pro-
      gram development and maintenance by application programmers

B. (earlier) headed task force of three analysts to improve Disbursement
   Accounting on-line CICS Data Entry System.
   1. converted from CICS Release 1.2 to Release 1.3 and fine-tuned CICS
   2. redesigned and reprogrammed the major Data Entry Application
      Module
   3. established Data Entry Problem Determination procedure
   4. fine-tuned CICS system to a half-second response time and cut CICS
      CPU resource requirements by 50%
   5. installed PAII for workload and performance tracking and capacity
      planning
   6. converted CICS 2260 terminal support to 3270 Native-Mode support

   Accomplished B. above in 6 weeks vs. estimated time frame (by IBM) of
   16 weeks.

C. initial assignment to:
   1. redesign department's Mechanized Work reporting TCAM Data Collec-
      tion System
   2. act as team leader of four Assembly language and COBOL programmers
      during design and implementation of system

Accomplishments overall:
- initiated formation of committee to determine requirements of Disbursement Accounting Department for next five years
- designed data collecting system that facilitated maintenance and provided additional flexibility
- expanded capacity of system; increased productivity by 100%, eliminating
  the need for additional hardware

1972-1975   GREAT WESTERN INSURANCE CO., Los Angeles, CA

SENIOR PROGRAMMER for major insurance company.

Responsible for:
- creating a workload Statistics Report program for the Online Data Entry
  System
- batch program to convert data entry records to card image record for batch
  processing
- INTERCOMM systems programming
- conversion of Data Entry Application Modules from 2260 to 3270 native-
  mode
- a table-driven, basic editor for online application

1970-1972   EQUIMETRO LIFE INSURANCE CO., Los Angeles, CA

PROGRAMMER assigned to COBOL and BAL program maintenance group after employment as trainee.

EDUCATION and PROFESSIONAL TRAINING:

B.S., Mathematics, California Western University, San Diego, CA, 1970

Stanford University graduate training: 30 hours of Computer Applications
Information Systems (Computer Management).

IBM training includes: Performance Evaluation and Capacity Planning; all
   CICS courses; all IMS/DC courses; TCAM application and systems courses;
   TSO training; BAL and COBOL programs; 3600 Finance System training,
   INTERCOM (TP Monitor) training; over a period of eight years.

Worked at various jobs throughout college years.

HOBBIES: Basketball, track, football, chess, skiing

PERSONAL DATA: Age 30, separated, excellent health

                 REFERENCES AND FURTHER DATA ON REQUEST

Advertisement for specialty apparel buyer:

M. M. Deen, nationally known retail and catalog merchandiser, is expanding its buying group. Live and work in a small town near the Maine coast, mountains, and forests. Experience with traditional specialty outdoor apparel for men and women to include textiles in general, casual sportswear, and active outdoor apparel and accessories.

An exciting position you can only find in a small and professional organization. Responsibility for product development (test products on trips and expeditions), vendor selection, merchandising, buying, and staff development. Position requires strong analytical skills; minimum of 3–5 years experience with major retail/catalog merchant; knowledge of fabric construction.

Attractive salary and benefits.

Write to [name of company and recruiter]

This advertisement discloses the following information:

1   Name of company, and name of person to whom to write.
2   Position: apparel buyer—men and women.
3   Outdoor sporting specialties—apparel.
4   Knowledge of textiles required.
5   It is a small but national organization.
6   Product testing ability is needed.
7   Personal outdoor interests important.
8   3–5 years buying experience = 25–30 years of age (possibly to 40).
9   Retail/catalog experience (major company).
10 Basic textile buying experience desirable.
11 Degree probably expected.
12 Must be happy to live in small town.
13 Analytical skills required.

From other sources you can discover that the company has a sales volume of about $30 million, is located in a town of 1822 population about 15 miles north of Portland on Route #1, has 380 employees and three officers, and in addition to buying also manufactures footwear and sporting and athletic goods. Sales per employee are $79,000, a high ratio, suggesting that the executives probably apply themselves to a variety of responsibilities.

It deserves an answer something like the following:

REASON FOR LETTER	This is in response to your advertisement in The Wall Street Journal (date).
EXPRESSION OF ANALYTICAL SKILLS	In a ten year career with Abercrombie, Sears, Penney & Co., famous national retail and catalog merchandiser, where I am presently employed, I tripled women's sportswear sales over a period of seven years, increased markup 11% and gross margin 7.5% on a total departmental volume of $75 million. During this period, we have achieved a national reputation for sports and casual wear.
DESCRIBES EXPOSURE TO OUTDOOR SPECIALTY ATTIRE	I have done extensive research on sports apparel, fabrics, linings, weight, closures, durability, warmth, and other aspects of correct clothing for scores of activities ranging from casual use to use under the most rigorous conditions of climbing, hunting, fishing, exploring, and the like. I have also been involved in outfitting complete expeditions to the North Pole, Africa, the Himalyas, and other exotic areas.

DESCRIBES TECHNICAL FABRIC KNOWLEDGE	I have taken intensive courses at the New York School of Textile Design and am thoroughly knowledgeable about fabric wear, count, texture, sources, and the methods of achieving desired qualities according to end use.
TELLS OF APPAREL TESTING EXPERIENCE AND OUTDOOR LIFESTYLE	In connection with my work and for pleasure I have traveled extensively in wilderness and white water areas and overseas to Kashmir, the lower reaches of Mt. Everest, and in Kilimanjaro.
EMPHASIZES BROAD RETAIL AD-MINISTRATIVE EXPERIENCE	My background includes buying for both stores and catalog, merchandise presentation, distribution, automatic shipping systems, profit projections, budget administration, promotion planning, and market testing.
GIVES REASON FOR INTEREST	I am interested in moving from a giant corporation to a less structured atmosphere where opportunities for greater career and personal development are present.
	My résumé is enclosed.
ASKS FOR INTERVIEW	If there is a meeting of my qualifications and your need I would welcome a chance to explore it personally with you.
ASKS FOR REPLY	I look forward to your reply.
	Sincerely

SEVENTEEN

SALES AND BROADCAST LETTERS

Sales and broadcast letters are the equal partners of the résumé. They are easier to write after the résumé has been prepared because they epitomize the résumé. They have a special place in the job campaign. The word "broadcast" is widely used to describe one way in which a sales letter can be used. Your sales letter is a "broadcast" letter generalized for mailing to many companies; it is a "sales" letter when you tailor it for sending to a specific company as a solicitation for a position or in answer to an advertisement.

The broadcast letter is a special type of employment application that is widely circulated to top company executives, rather than the personnel department. Its role derives from the fact that 50% to 75% of available jobs are never advertised and must be tracked down by mail.

When using the broadcast technique, whether for résumés or for letters, you judge the effectiveness of your mailing by the percentage of response, as would be the case with any mail order product. A response (inviting you to an interview) of 2% is fair; 15% is excellent.

Broadcasting is one of the quickest and most effective ways of finding a position. Send out at least 100 and preferably as many as 500 broadcast letters. The broadcast letter is used in such cases as the following:

1 Your career level makes it appropriate to bypass the personnel department.
2 Your talents and experience may have special appeal to a company executive.
3 Your special abilities may cause an executive to employ you now for a position that will actually become available only later.
4 Your qualifications might exactly meet the requirements for a position that the company has been unsuccessfully trying to fill for some time.
5 Your unusual qualifications may be particularly appreciated by a particular executive.
6 You might be well and favorably known at the top executive level of many companies.
7 Your qualifications might lead to an executive reorganization, making a place for you that did not exist until your letter acted as the catalyst to initiate such action.
8 Many top executives, including chief executive officers, like to be made aware of the availability of certain kinds of people.
9 Recruiting an executive by way of a broadcast letter can save a company thousands of dollars in search fees.

The use of a résumé in these conditions would nullify your objective—résumés are almost automatically routed to personnel departments. Your broadcast letter might lead to requests for your résumé, which, sent at this point, serves the positive function of satisfying the company's affirmative interest in you.

By using the broadcast letter approach you are not depreciating the personnel department. Many personnel departments do not handle the employment of personnel at higher levels where the subtleties of character and required expertise are difficult to gauge. Employment ideas, amorphous at first, often may be formed only after an interview. Many corporations do not even list employment directors by name in the standard directories.

The rules for writing a good sales or broadcast letter are these:

1 Start either with (a) a point that you think will be interesting to the addressee or (b) with your reason for writing. If you use the first alternative follow with the second; if you begin with the second alternative follow with the first.
2 Give examples of other qualifications that show how specially qualified you are to provide superior services in your area of expertise. Give four or five carefully chosen examples. Highlight them in short sentences and paragraphs. Leave white space between each point.
3 Follow with a general statement that sums up your qualifications.
4 Provide personal data if favorable—age, marital status, number of children, education.
5 Ask for a personal meeting.
6 Ask for a reply.

You will write a better letter if you have already completed a résumé. Select the material for your letter from your résumé. Your sales letter is a summary of your résumé.

Start the letter by identifying yourself and your field of specialization:

> I have 15 years of successful, progressive experience in marketing management in the pharmaceutical and health care fields with an $100 million company.

State your objective:

I want to become associated with a medium size company or a division of a large company in the Southwest or Midwest where I will have complete marketing responsibility and opportunity for growth.

List some of your accomplishments:

In six years I increased regional sales of pharmaceutical and health care products from $9 million to more than $30 million while maintaining or improving profitability.

Recruited, trained, and led a sales force of 60 salesmen, 3 field assistants and 7 district managers.

Three of the 7 district managers under my leadership were awarded "Manager of the Year" recognition.

Indicate special qualities:

I have been a successful salesman. I have trained scores of salesmen and managers to sell and manage effectively. I am innovative, motivated, and dedicated and possess the quality of leadership to a degree that has made my region first among all company regoins in four of the last seven years. I am experienced in budgeting, forecasting, advertising, promotion, and compensation administration.

Give favorable statistics:

M.B.A.; B.A. in marketing; age 35; married.

Ask for an answer:

I would like a personal interview to discuss my potential for contributing to your company and opportunities for me to grow within your company. I look forward to your reply.

Broadcast letters may take up too much of the page to leave room for a full heading (name and address). To personalize them, use the salutation only, such as "Dear Mr. Jones."

Preferably use one or two pages of Monarch-size stationery ($7^1/_2$ x 10 inches).

Examples of broadcast/sales letters follow. One broadcast letter similar to those shown produced an unprecedented response of 75%, a significant number of which suggested interviews or left the way open for later follow-up.

WILLIAM J. K. POLK
1795 Mecklenburg Avenue
Maury, TN 00039

1. For most of my career (10 years) I was associated with one company, the last two years as president and general manager and before that as senior vice president.

2. I left that company to enter another as executive vice president, on the assurance that I could acquire it within three years. I reorganized the production and marketing, reducing costs over 20% and expanding sales by more than 100%, within a year and a half, resulting in unprecedented profits. The owner has declined to sell at any reasonable price, and I am now seeking another position with a small- to medium-size company offering growth and compensation consistent with my abilities.

3. Here are some examples of my record:

4. - as president of $50 million company developed a new division from zero to more than $10 million, over a period of four years, with a pretax profit of 20.3%

5. - doubled the sales of a second division $10 million (now grown to $20 million) by stimulating technical progress and introducing new products

6. - reorganized marketing strategies of a third division, introduced installment sales, increased volume 63%, reduced overhead 15%, expanded computer facility, and designed a plan to reduce the impact of fluctuating currency exchange

7. - adapted a product, developed for internal use, to meet market needs and added a fourth division to the company which, within two years produced $3 million of sales at pretax profit of 35%

8. These and other achievements may suggest that I am an innovative manager who could be useful to a company seeking management and growth.

9. I am married, have three children, attended Cornell University (B.S. Administrative Engineering), received my M.B.A. from Columbia. Honors include Phi Beta Kappa and Tau Delta Pi.

10. If there is interest on your part, I would enjoy a personal meeting. I look forward to the pleasure of hearing from you.

Very truly yours,

12. William J. K. Polk
Home (201) 000-0000
Office (201) 111-2222

DISCUSSION

1 Mr. Polk starts with his occupational level to help the reader understand immediately who he is. The length of his career suggests his age.

2 He relates an interesting set of circumstances that differentiates him from the usual and at the same time indicates his executive ability; announces his objective; and recommends a compensation level that is readily understood.

3 Leads into examples of his effectiveness.

4, 5, 6, 7 Examples.

8 Makes general statement.

9 Provides personal data.

10 Asks for personal meeting.

11 Asks for reply.

12 Gives telephone numbers.

This writer will gain executive attention. His level of responsibility establishes a rapport with the reader. After a successful career with one company he did what most people would secretly like to do—made plans to have his own business; but it didn't work out. Rider explains concisely what else he has done. He suggests how one with his background could be useful to the reader. He can afford to understate, rather than belabor, his excellent educational background.

What does this letter convey?

- General management ability of a high order.
- Experience in all facets of general management, and contributions to each.
- Innovativeness.
- A strong sense of profit motivation.

- A record that suggests value to any company in need of management strength.
- Abilities that showed themselves as early as the under-graduate period. ⌐
- An age between 36 and 38 inasmuch as "most" of his career is 10 years: graduation with master's degree at 23; 2 or 3 years in employment not disclosed; 10 years in one company; 1½ to 2 years in present company.
- He chose to write this letter to the C.E.O.s of selected companies (see salutation).

This is an actual letter. It resulted in satisfactory employment.

WILLIAM Z. TAYLOR
1784 Rough & Ready Way
Orange, NJ 12468

1. Currently, I am Director of Marketing and board member for a small ($20 million) chemical company.

2-3. I am looking to upgrade my career in a new position offering broader opportunity either in marketing or general management. Based on my record of effectiveness I can bring dynamic marketing performance and decisive management skills to any company with a need in these areas.

   To illustrate:

4. - for present company, in a period of less than four years, increased volume 150% and provided the earnings base for further expansion and plant modernization; I now participate in all corporate financial, production and marketing planning.

5. - the growth was achieved by means of market analysis, planning, raising plant productivity, setting objectives and creating new strategies; and getting out into the field with customers and salesmen to explain the new programs, resulting in individual orders of as much as $2 million.

6. - in earlier employment with giant international chemical company, progressed from salesman to senior management; tripled regional sales in five years to more than $40 million; achieved rank as No. 1 region in sales and profitability in three successive years.

7. - trained and recommended 15 individuals for promotion to enlarged responsibilities, some of whom are now at top management levels in the company.

8. These are but a few highlights. I have made significant contributions in all marketing areas: advertising, sales, promotion, administration; in financial areas; investment and acquisitions; and in production with cost-cutting innovations, for two employers during my career.

9. I am 41 years of age, married, have three children, earned an M.B.A. at the Wharton School, University of Pennsylvania, and continue my education in new techniques and technologies, regularly.

10. If my qualifications meet a need in your company, I'd enjoy a personal meeting.

11. I look forward to your reply.

   Very truly yours,

   William Z. Taylor
12. (234) 000-0000 Home
   (234) 000-1111 Office

DISCUSSION

1   Mr. Taylor says who he is to set the tone of his letter.
2   Explains what kind of a job he is looking for, to let the addressee know at once the reason for the letter.
3   Makes a general statement about his accomplishments, which are then supported with examples.
4   Example of a very major contribution resulting in the assignment of broader responsibilities.
5   Describes methods used to achieve the results mentioned, which give credence to his marketing abilities and suggest general management caliber.
6   Example of experience in much larger company to give added breadth to his background.
7   Example of his leadership ability by his salutary influence on those who worked for him.
8   Lists the specific areas in which he has had important experience, showing in more detail his areas of particular competence.
9   Provides essential personal data.
10 Asks for a personal interview.
11 Asks for a reply.
12 Provides both home and office telephone numbers for the convenience of his addressee.

These are the elements of a good letter. Such a letter will gain favorable responses from companies that have an opening. The preparation of this letter required several hours of close analysis of this executive's background. The true nature of what he had done for his employers did not immediately surface. When the data supporting point 4 finally emerged, they changed the whole concept of this executive's approach to a new career.

There are many forms. Here are others: Start your letter with a strong statement about an accomplishment or a capability as shown below:

> I made contributions to sales, production and financial management leading to expansion, lower costs, and better profitability while the chief operating officer of a $50 million corporation.
>
> If you are in need of a senior executive who is accustomed to achieving outstanding results you may be interested in the specifics of the above and additional highlights in my background.

or

> With an earlier background as a statistician/data analyst (B.A. and M.B.A. degrees) I have used this ability, now as a manager, to reduce costs $2 million and add sales of $12 million within a period of two years, for a 200 million division of a giant company.
>
> If you are in need of a creative marketer who can use data as tools for developing strong forward progress you may be interested in some of my other accomplishments.

or

> I am experienced in securing a 2000 mile smuggler-infested coastline along a foreign shore; and in maintaining security for 27 manned outposts in the same area.
>
> If you have need of a security officer I have had training with one of the best educators (U.S.M.C.) and experience under the most rigorous conditions (wartime).

This form is more in the nature of a product sales letter; it is also ideal for a consultant seeking assignments. For letters addressed to top corporate officials I consider it a little abrupt.

Examples of additional sales/broadcast letters follow.

BROADCAST LETTER: CAREER CHANGE

Dear Mr. Snow:

I have spent my entire career since graduating from college in 1971 in the U.S. Army. I am now ready to reenter civilian life hoping for a career that will permit me to utilize skills in analysis, management and languages in a domestic or international setting.

As a Major I have been assigned to duties with the Office of Special Investigations (OSI) as Agent in Charge since 1973, acting in connection with frauds, criminal activities, smuggling, homicides and related matters in the U.S.A., Sicily and Korea.

Out of my experience I have formed the ability to see what needs to be done in any particular assignment and how it can be done better. I have been cited for numerous contributions to more efficient operations, cost savings, the curtailment of frauds and criminal activities, and dedication to duty.

A few examples:

- adapted PERT and CPM techniques to train Special Agents to bridge the gaps between the business world and the military environment

- arranged for extensive training of Italian National Police to help contain drug traffic utilizing remote areas of the Adriatic coastline for smuggling

- set up territories for Special Agents in Texas by counties, to reduce unnecessary repeated trips to the same places

- reorganized method of credit and security checks with substantial savings in time and money

I possess B.S. and M.S. degrees in Management Science in addition to much other special training. I am multilingual in Korean, Italian and French (the last needing brush-up).

Of a personal nature, I am 34 years of age, married, with two children, in excellent health; have resided in Korea and Italy and have traveled extensively in Hong Kong, Thailand, Cambodia, Vietnam and Europe.

If this suggests that I might have some qualifications of interest to your company I would enjoy a personal meeting with an appropriate executive.

Your reply will be appreciated.

Very truly yours,

Samuel L. Clarkson
(000) 333-0000

Dear Mr. Roosevelt,

I was called upon to work with a reasonably successful pocket-knife manufacturer, as a consultant. A study of the business showed a number of things to be wrong:

- sales confined to a geographical section
- outmoded displays and packaging
- a sales force that was nonproductive 40% of the year
- lack of accurate cost data
- no budget for sales, advertising or administration
- a line of great breadth of which sales of many items were only a few hundred a year
- product emphasis on numbers which had ceased to be popular 50 years ago
- a completely frustrated sales department
- many employees just hanging on until retirement

In two years' time, devoting one day a week to these and other problems, I was able to achieve:

- national distribution
- a reduction in number of items manufactured of 33%
- a sales increase of 50% with a 25% increase in profit
- a new and popular line of knives
- a new concept of a pocketknife (with patent) of which over 100,000 were sold on the first calls of the salesman on their customers with the new product
- the automation of certain production activities
- budgets for sales, manufacturing and administration

Not many companies are in such bad shape. But these achievements illustrate the breadth of my skills.

If your company could use a "total approach" to your problems with the promise of innovative suggestions to produce higher sales and profits perhaps I could be useful.

A personal exploratory meeting without obligation would be very welcome.

Your reply is keenly anticipated.

Very truly yours,

This kind of letter could be made to apply to many products, many circumstances.

BROADCAST LETTER FROM A GENERAL EXECUTIVE

Dear Sir:

Your investment in the creative mind of an experienced executive can produce greater returns in the next 15 years than almost any other you can make.

I am such an executive. You may be interested in a man competent in Corporate Planning and Economic Development. Here are some of my accomplishments:

- As a negotiator represented an aircraft company for contracts involving over $50,000,000 in sales. I am skilled in management and government agency interface, verbally and in writing.

- As an aerospace engineer I was among the first to introduce and implement Systems Engineering Management procedures. I am familiar with the important methods of profitability management; management by objective, management by exception, PERT and other

- As C.E.O. of a company, I developed programs to assist economic development in the Caribbean through use of Systems Management in accomplishing industrial breakthroughs.

I have a record of adding $100 million in extra profits to three companies by whom I have been employed.

Age 50, married, three children, excellent health, B.A., Economics.

Can you use an Executive with these qualifications in your business? If you can, let's discuss it. I'd like to work for you.

Your reply will be appreciated.

Sincerely,

Dear Sir:

I have 15 years of successful experience in financial areas: six years as bond analyst for a leading underwriter; six years as editor, writer and analyst for a large investment advisory service; three years as a research analyst for a major Boston bank.

My competence includes the ability to make effective underwriting presentations to achieve better bond ratings through restructured analyses, understanding of legal requirements in connection with, and effectiveness in, accomplishing sales closings.

I am accustomed to the orderly presentation of complex financial and economic data, the preparation and finalization of all official statements and have a complete understanding of money and capital markets and exchanges. I am also familiar with and experienced in regional specialization, and have an excellent knowledge of marketing techniques.

I would like a personal interview to discuss the possibility of joining your company.

My educational background includes M.B.A. and B.S. degrees in finance. Personal data: age 36, married, excellent health, prefer Boston location.

Your response will be appreciated.

Sincerely,

WILLIAM FILLMORE
1800 Cayuga Road
Buffalo, NY 123456

I am a broadly knowledgeable general counsel and administration executive seeking association with a corporation that can use strong management and skillful and innovative leadership in these areas.

My current position is Vice President and General Counsel of a major $500 million textile company. Because of a pending merger with a larger company, I wish to make a change in employment. Somewhat ironically, during my tenure I have had major involvement in acquisitions and divestitures amounting to more than $80 million.

I would like to highlight some of the kinds of activities in which I have participated effectively:

- managed domestic and international litigation of diverse matters exceeding $200 million in claims; all cases won or favorably settled.

- saved company $12 million in plant expenditures by seeking and obtaining revised environmental permits.

- held legal responsibility for more than $100 million of real estate transactions.

- operated the international division of West Point Cannon, turning a losing operation into profitability within two years.

- personally negotiated profitable agreements in 16 countries around the world; identified and worked with top legal specialists in 28 countries altogether.

Some other categories in which I have competence are these: corporate strategies, budgeting, antitrust, contracts; secured selling arrangements and security agreements under the U.C.C.; environmental compliance; EEOC and OSHA problems; joint ventures: licensing, profit-making, and avoiding excessive legal spending by doing work in-house. My references are of the highest order.

If this background suggests a personal meeting with you or your designate I would look forward to it.

With kindest regards,

William Fillmore

Gentlemen:

With 15 years of successful experience in marketing management for major companies largely involving power tools and a record of consistent progress from salesman to manager of a $30 million region, I am a qualified marketing executive.

Among my accomplishments:

- over a period of six years increased regional sales from $9 million to nearly $30 million while staying well within profitability guidelines.
- recruited, trained and led a sales force of 60 salesmen with two field assistants and seven district managers.
- of seven district managers under my leadership, two ranked first and second nationally with the first awarded recognition as Manager of the Year.
- planned effective promotions and advertising on the way to achieving sales increases described.
- successfully promoted 25 of my salesmen into corporate positions in various areas: Product Planning, Marketing, Regional and District Management.
- upon assignment to important Atlanta District brought it from fifth to first place in sales and earnings and won Manager of the Year Award.
- earlier developed District which ranked last in sales to fourth position nationally.
- as salesman was routinely among top salesmen in the U.S., winning sales contests and earning numerous awards.

I am an effective innovator, sales leader and trainer, with a solid background in modern management techniques and concepts, banking and finance. B.S., Business Administration, age 40, married, two children, own home, excellent health.

I seek a position as Director of Marketing or General Sales Manager for a medium-size corporation in the tool industry.

If my qualifications are of interest to you, I would like an opportunity for a personal meeting.

Sincerely,

Dear Sir:

I am 35 years old, well educated, motivated, with successful experience in sales, office management, PR/client relations and advertising. I am currently employed with a national temporary employment organization in a management capacity.

I seek a position that provides opportunity for growth to management, preferably in a people-oriented environment where I can utilize abilities in persuasion, communications and leadership such as sales promotion, PR, communications, advertising, film production; willing to travel.

Some of my achievements:

- increased business $100% for present employer by selling services to new accounts.

- worked with PR firm in organizing and producing successful fashion shows, obtaining talent, choosing garments, accessorizing, photography and writing, including press releases.

- supplied effective help in copywriting production of sales films, scripts, story boards; and market research for major consumer goods client of well known advertising agency.

I have extensive training and experience in the performing art under nationally known teachers; was a National Honor Student; have won State awards in writing and mathematics.

I look forward to hearing from you.

Sincerely,

Dear Sir:

I am seeking to associate with a medium-size company or a division of a large company in the Southwest where I will have complete marketing autonomy with senior general management opportunity.

I am accustomed to multimillion dollar marketing responsibilities for corporations in the office equipment industry.

My current responsibility is Marketing Development for Smith & Company, Inc., known worldwide for management excellence.

The following indicate my capabilities:

- increased Company's revenues in the Eastern Region by 53% in three years by identification of new markets and new applications for existing products.

- headed marketing team in the analysis of a new market and its requirements leading to the development of a new multimillion dollar market.

- created complete marketing plan for these new products.

- learned basic selling in door-to-door canvassing on a commission basis for leading manufacturer of photocopiers after earning M.B.A.

I am thoroughly indoctrinated with advanced marketing and management techniques; have received company awards for outstanding contributions; believe that I bring significant profitability and management advantages to a company in the consumer products area.

Age 35, married, excellent health. Undergraduate degree in Economics; Dean's List; Honor Roll; graduated in top 10% of class.

If my qualifications are of interest, I would like to have a personal interview.

I look forward with great interest to hearing from you.

Sincerely,

Dear Sir:

My background is 10 years of intensive training and successful administration in marketing a wide range of consumer products, including major appliances, in South America with profit-center responsibility for $22 to $36 million operations for a billion-dollar international corporation.

- In 1979 I made a profit study which led to the discontinuance of unprofitable operations and a saving of $1 million annually in G.&A. expenses.
- In 1978 I established a new dealer structure and introduced 6 new products recommended by me which added over a million dollars to annual volume.
- From 1976 to 1978 I increased sales with another group of new products from $50,000 to $1 million.
- In 1974-1975 as a retail store manager, I increased sales from $400,000 to $600,000.

I have successfully trained hundreds of sales managers and salesmen. I am experienced in budgeting, sales forecasting, market research, advertising, product analysis. I have a strong profit motivation and have demonstrated high leadership qualities.

Age 33, married, excellent health, B.S. Accounting, fluent in Portuguese, Spanish and French.

May I have an interview to discuss my potential contributions to your Company?

I look forward to your reply.

Sincerely,

WILLIAM PIERCE
1804 Congress Street
Hillsboro, NH 10543

Dear Mr. Jones:

I have been employed by two multibillion dollar companies in progressively more important duties over the past 11 years, involving marketing and economics research encompassing the creative interpretation and extrapolation of data resulting in new marketing strategies, sales increases and cost savings amounting to millions of dollars.

My experience includes projections, financial analysis, cost studies, territory analysis, product and line studies, advertising effectiveness, analysis, feasibility studies, computer utilization and systems and long-term (25-year) economic planning.

Because my work has been effective for major companies I would like now to have expanded responsibilities and new challenges in a multinational company - my reason for writing to you.

Here are some specific examples:

- after conducting a marketing analysis, I recommended a new sales approach to drugstores, which has resulted in a 20% increase in retailer inventory turns and a $15 million increase in volume.

- developed a marketing strategy for selected items based on extrapolations of model territories resulting in raising share of market by 10%.

- studied trade promotions, couponing, and test market results and made other evaluations leading to a rescheduling of promotional activities and an annual increase in one line of products of $13 million a year over the past three years.

- recommended a capital improvement program (accepted) improving return on investment by 7%.

- restructured forecasting technique to accomplish an $18 million reduction in inventory with improved product availabilities.

I have been extensively commended for these achievements, but the present organization does not provide room for the expansion of my responsibilities in the near future.

I am 34 years of age, married, with two children, possess an M.B.A. from the Tuck School at Dartmouth and am multilingual in German, French, Spanish, Romanian and Hungarian.

If my qualifications suggest that I might have interest to you, I would enjoy a personal meeting.

Your reply will be appreciated.

Sincerely,

Mr. James Eastland, V.P. Finance,
Equitable Prudential Co.
1000 Third Avenue
Chicago, IL 10020

Dear Mr. Eastland:

One of the greatest opportunities existing today for the enhancement of
return on investment (and capital gains) lies in real estate.

I have been in this business for seven years as instructor, salesman,
appraiser, analyst - most recently Associate with a prestigious real
estate consulting firm working with "Fortune 1000" clients.

In my present position I have become expert in restructuring all the
components of a real estate income statement to estimate the market
value of income producing properties for the purposes of investment,
divestment, or use.

I have been able to identify opportunities which have been put to use,
with considerable success, by such companies and institutions as General Motors, A.T.&T., I.T.&T., Koger Properties, Prudential Insurance
Co., Yale University, Texaco, 245 Park Avenue, Loew's, and many
others.

My methods include the following studies:
- physical description, underlying fees, air and subsurface rights
- lease analyses (terms, tax and escalation liabilities; caps)
- debt structure, costs, discounted cash flow analyses (I do my
  own computer programming for this purpose), yields
- demographics, trends, projections, comparisons

In addition to the careful and precise exposure of value for all kinds
of real estate I have had special experience in the analysis of regional
shopping centers.

My value would relate to companies with large pension or other funds to
invest for whom I could provide reliable analysis and creativity in the
identification of real estate investment opportunities to produce optimum yields.

I have both J.D. and B.A. degrees. Age 34, married.

If this background is of interest to your company, I would enjoy a
personal meeting.

Sincerely,

Dear Sir:

For fifteen years I have been successful and innovative for a multi-million-dollar company as Manager of Research and Development in the consumer products field.

My general assignment is to provide my Company with a continuing and timely supply of new designs and competitively superior products relating to all aspects of development of mechanical and electrical consumer products.

I have advanced consistently through the organization to increasing responsibilities starting as Project Engineer and successively as Chief Development Engineer, Development Manager, Project Manager to present position as Assistant Manager, Research and Development.

My accomplishments include:

- Design and development leadership in creating famous product now marketed internationally.

- Cost reduction projects that saved Company millions of dollars and resulted in the revitalized marketing of established products with a substantial contribution to corporate volume.

- Patents involving new art.

- A new approach to research and development evaluation procedures providing full performance functioning not before available and contributing both to better product and to improved customer relations.

- Consistent operation within budget and for 1978 a budget saving of $765,000, while maintaining full and effective services.

My experience includes management and leadership of large technical groups, technical writing, product evaluation procedures, project programming, budget administration, computerization of data and primarily the exercise of pragmatic creativity in the appraoch to successful product development.

Hold B.S. and M.S. degrees in Engineering. Age 48, married, three children, own home, excellent health.

Sincerely,

RESULTS OF A TYPICAL JOB CAMPAIGN UTILIZING A BROADCAST LETTER

CANDIDATE PROFILE

Functional area: Marketing
Age   50
Geographical employment limitation: Eastern half of U.S.
Employment History:
  Early career: 18 years very successful
  Recent career   12 years, 4-5 job changes; effective
                                          executive, but work not attended by
                                          recent success

NATURE OF CAMPAIGN

Number of letters sent: 191
Selection of addresses: Careful selection of companies suit-
                             able to subject's background, rang-
                             ing in size from $40 million annual
                             sales to large conglomerates over
                             $1 billion

[Note: for smaller companies, subject wrote to President or Chairman. For larger companies, he wrote to Vice President, Marketing. For giant companies, he wrote to Vice President of Marketing or Vice President of Personnel. All letters were addressed to selected individuals by name.]

TECHNICAL DETAILS

Stationery used: 24 lb bond, Monarch size
Color of stationery: White
Method of reproduction: Offset
Heading on letter: Letterhead typed
Method of addressee fill-in: Same typeface as body of letter
Length of letter: 1-1/2 pages
Signature: Personally signed
Replies: Sent to third party to avoid residence
                             disclosure

RESPONSES

Number of replies: 101, with 43 different titles grouped
                             as follows:
                                15 Chairmen and Presidents
                                18 Vice Presidents
                                25 Directors of Personnel variously
                                   titled
                                14 Managers of professional staffing
                                 (and various titles)
                                29 Miscellaneous

<u>RESPONSES</u> (continued)

Number of interviews: 6*
Number of job offers: 3

<u>RESULT</u>:

Accepted job offer as head of marketing for division of multibillion-dollar company.

---

*The number of invitations to interview was reduced by the extreme caution of this candidate in protecting his identity; nevertheless, his campaign worked.

The author's personal experience shows that mail campaigns are successful in eliciting job offers at least 75% of the time.

Dear Mr. Billingsley:

A few years ago I made a study of our sales (consumer products) by individual product. We manufactured 250 numbers with sales ranging from a few thousand to several hundred thousand of each. I found that our sales fell into patterns according to end use. These end uses were distinctive, although our sales strategy, our tradition, as well as our salesmen and their customers tended to blur these distinctions.

I created a personality for each of seven numbers and developed a comprehensive presentation and a national advertising program. The result was orders for these seven numbers in a period of six months, equal to more than our entire year's sales of 250 numbers and many times the annual sales of the seven numbers.

This is but one of the many ideas I provided for my company to give it the position of owning a 75% share of market nationally.

There is a good chance that I could help your company similarly.

It interested, let's talk about it.

Very truly yours,

SALES OR BROADCAST LETTER TO MANUFACTURER

Dear Mr. Bush:

Hedge, grass, pruning and lopping shears (hand operated) make up a line of cutting tools recognized as a product group. Their sale was highly seasonal, concentrated in the spring months. I studied this line and discovered geographical preferences. I found that consumers were influenced by what professionals used. I discovered that we, as manufacturers, were hidebound in our designs as well as our price structure. By a study of horticulture I learned that pruning in much of the United States should be done in the fall and not the spring. I recognized that our marketing department had become overawed by the advent of power tools.

Without burdening you with details, when these facts and others were properly assimilated, it changed the whole concept of our marketing strategy, leading to our ultimate complete dominance of the market and not less than a 15% increase in unit sales each year.

This is the kind of leadership and analysis that I can bring to any line of products.

If such achievements would be of interest to your company I'd welcome a personal meeting.

I look forward to your reply.

Sincerely,

*Other products can be substituted according to one's experience.

191

Dear Mr. Corning,

If you make a list of department stores according to annual sales and relate your company sales to store size you will probably discover a tremendous variation in sales. To give an example, store A in Morristown, NJ, did $10,000 per year of our product, while a much larger store in Des Moines, IA, purchased only $5000 per year. We analyzed the reasons, restructured our sales strategy and smoothed out these variations to become the dominant force for our product throughout the nation, over a period of 3-4 years.

This is but one example of creative marketing which I provided for my company. I could name twoscore more of equally effective projects which I have accomplished. I could do the same quality of work for you.

If you would like to grow faster, increase your profits and possibly become the major factor in your industry, it is highly probable that I can help you toward these objectives.

If this is the kind of thinking you are interested in, let's meet for an exploratory discussion.

Sincerely,

Other products can be substituted according to one's experience.

Mr. J. Russell Stout, Vice President
Colgate Cyanamid Co., Inc.
Colgate Park
Bright Bond, NY 08967

Dear Mr. Stout:

I retired last year as Vice President of the Empire Bank, but
continue my association as a consultant to the bank and as
a member of the Board of Directors. One of my assignments
has been upgrading our manpower development department. In
this capacity I have had an opportunity to meet a large
number of promising executives both in and out of this
company.

I have also become aware of your own change in marketing
strategy from product to market departmentalization with
which, incidentally, I agree.

The purpose of this letter is to tell you about a young man
who has had substantial success in his own company but now
faces an uncertain future because of his company's acquisition
by a much larger one.

He has had a ten-year career since gaining his M.B.A. degree
at Stanford and is widely recognized in his industry (chemicals). In the last couple of years he has been credited
with increasing share of market for his company's major line
of proprietaries by more than 50%, and at an increased R.O.I.
He also introduced the same marketing moves in which you are
currently involved.

It occurred to me that such a man might be of interest to you.
If so, call me or drop me a line and I'll set up a meeting.
Needless to say, I have no personal or financial involvement
in this other than an interest in seeing a highly talented
individual find the right spot for his career development.

Kindest regards,

William Van Buren

PROPOSAL LETTER

Here is an example of a letter that might have been written following a meeting initiated as an informal discussion of mutual interests, rather than as a job interview.

Dear Mr. Buchanon,

Thank you for the opportunity to sit down with you two weeks ago and explore interesting aspects of the hand tools business. I have been interested in this area for many years, for special reasons, although my experience has been in consumer soft goods. It was good of you to give me your sales figures broken down by territory and states.

Just as an exercise for my own edification, I have used Department of Commerce figures on sales in the hand tools classification, expressed in percentages by states. Using your figures for New Jersey, your best state, as 100%, I have extrapolated what each state would do in sales if it were as well handled as New Jersey. Calculating your potential sales in this way and allowing for certain distributional aberrations of which I am aware, I find that *you have a potential national market 327% greater than your present sales.* I know you sense this, but these figures prove it.

Furthermore, using Florida as an example, where your sales of circular saws are greater than all the rest of the United States together because of special circumstances (a retiree with an encyclopedic knowledge of saws, selling direct to retailers), an opportunity of huge dimensions is uncovered.

You might be interested in studying these figures. I have also noted some of the steps that would need to be taken to move toward such objectives. My experience in marketing tells me they would not be easy of accomplishment, but very possible in, for example, a dedicated five-year program.

I have had personal experience in implementing programs of this kind, and know that their achievement is possible.

I will 'phone you in a few days. I will be glad to find the time for an in-depth discussion of these findings if you are interested.

Again thank you for the opportunity to learn more about your business. My hobby is business analysis.

Kindest personal regards,

Note: There are many small businesses, such as this one (sales about $1.8 million) that reward their owners and a few others with substantial incomes. I know of one company president, operating a business of only $750,000 annual sales, who paid himself $125,000 a year 15 years ago. The comforts of operating in a small niche often settle into inertia and becloud substantial opportunities well within reach. These smaller company executives are often easier to meet than those in the upper echelons of giant companies.

This letter resulted in a job offer.

EIGHTEEN

USING LISTS

To conduct a job search campaign by mail you will need to refer to directories and lists of various kinds to develop your personal mailing list. Your list should be tailored as closely as possible to the kinds of companies, geographical areas, and other characteristics that reflect your personal needs or preferences.

The names and addresses of corporations and organizations and the names of their personnel can be obtained from the following sources found in most libraries:

1 Dun and Bradstreet *Reference Book of Corporate Management.*
2 *Telephone directory Yellow Pages* (company and organization names and addresses only).
3 Standard and Poor's *Register of Corporations, Directors, and Executives.*
4 State industrial directories.
5 Industry association (almost all major industry classifications have one).
6 Thomas' *Register of American Manufacturers.*
7 *Martindale-Hubbell Law Directory.*
8 *Moody's Handbook of Common Stocks.*
9 *The Value Line Investment Survey* (published by Arnold Bernhard & Co., Inc.).

10 *Rand McNally Bankers International Directory.*
11 *Fortune's* annual supplement listing the 1000 largest corporations (no individual executive names) and other listings.
12 Forbes annual list of 2500 corporations (no individual executive names).
13 *Hardware Age Directory* (published by Chilton Co., Radnor, Pa.).
14 *Pharmaceutical Handbook.*
15 *The Standard Advertising Register.*
16 American Management Association publications (such as Executive Search Firms).
17 *The Literary Marketplace.*
18 *MacRae's Blue Book.*
19 *Standard Rate and Data Service.*
20 *United States Government Organizational Manual.*
21 Trade magazines.
22 *Directory of Foundations in Massachusetts.*
23 *College Placement Annuals.*
24 Association of Consulting Management Engineers (New York City).
25 *The Wall Street Journal* daily list of corporate operating reports.

Standard and Poor's Register of Corporations, Directors, and Executives contains an alphabetical listing of the names of about 35,000 corporations, 300,000 officers, directors, and principals, and 70,000 officers, directors, trustees, and partners. *Fortune* magazine annually lists the 1000 largest industrial corporations as well as the largest financial institutions and the largest overseas corporations. *Stores,* a National Retail Merchants Association publication, annually lists, by volume, the leading department stores. *Forbes Magazine* has an annual listing of 2500 major companies.

If you prepare your own list of companies to write to, make use of the S.I.C. (Standard Industrial Classification) numbers to identify a company's business. Many companies have multiple S.I.C. numbers. The first two digits of the four-digit S.I.C. number show the major industrial group to which a company belongs:

01 to 09 Agriculture, forestry, fishing
10 to 14 Mining
15 to 17 Construction
20 to 39 Manufacturing
40 to 49 Transportation, communications, utilities
50 to 59 Wholesale and retail
60 to 68 Finance, insurance, real estate

The last two digits classify each company more closely; for example, 3172 and 3199 refer to leather goods and 2844 to cosmetics. A cross-reference to the main body of the register (Standard and Poor's for example) will then give you the address and size of the company and names of executives. Many fine companies are unexpectedly missing, as are some divisions resulting from mergers. Most lists, as distinguished from directories, do not include location, area code, names of executives, and products. Creating your own list is an arduous and time-consuming task, but the result is invaluable. You may also purchase lists containing the information you need from specialist list companies and other sources such as some of the better résumé writing/career guidance companies.

The executives of the 500 or 1000 largest companies are bombarded with résumés. You might find it worthwhile to address your mailings to smaller, equally fine and growing companies.

The *Yellow Pages* is another good source of local company names, but does not provide names of executives and area codes.

In using lists and "broadcasting" your availability you take the best, quickest, and surest route to employment, other than knowing someone who can place you or having some other "inside track" to a position. Note the following in mailing your material:

- Address your letter or résumé to a specific individual by including the name on the envelope.
- If possible, include the individual's name on the letter as well, though this is not mandatory.
- If you are an upper middle or top level executive or administrator, send a sales or broadcast letter to one of the top executives or to the chief executive officer (by name).
- If you are a lower middle executive earning, say, $18,000 or less a year, send a covering letter and your résumé to the personnel director (by name if possible).
- Make your initial mailing to 200 or 300 companies, or more if possible, in order to obtain a satisfactory number of useful responses.
- Select as special targets for individualized letters companies in which you are particularly interested.

In choosing companies to which to apply for employment, you must consider for which type of company you prefer to work and are best qualified to work.

One factor is company size, which can range from small $1 million to $2 million to very large multibillion dollar concerns. Some large companies are conglomerates, containing many surprisingly small units. Some small businesses are highly profitable, and many are the giants of tomorrow, taking advantage of the continuously emerging new areas of technology.

Large single product companies are apt to be highly structured, with formal channeling (job descriptions) for all functions (some small companies seek to copy the structure). The units of large multidivision companies that allow operational autonomy within their divisions, however, can run the full gamut of management philosophies.

Small companies generally tend to be less rigidly structured, allowing greater participation in more areas. Smaller companies are also more subject to the vicissitudes of the marketplace. Single product companies can be eliminated almost overnight by technological changes. Companies in trouble need better management. You might be able to supply it.

APPENDIX A

SUPPLEMENTARY RÉSUMÉ EXAMPLES

In this appendix we reproduce 31 résumés, in addition to the 20 résumés scattered throughout the book. To find the résumé you want, consult the Index of résumés at the end of the book.

300 East Avenue
New Orleans, LA 00000

Home (000) 000-0000
Office (000) 000-0000

R E S U M E

of

ANWAR S. BLOUNT, C.P.A.

OBJECTIVE

Position as Financial Vice President, Controller,
Treasurer at corporate level

SUMMARY AND QUALIFICATIONS

***   Ten years experience as Manager, Supervisor and Accountant for major and "Big 8," public accounting firms.

***   Provide consulting services for client management in corporate financing, ERISA and pension plan practices, investments, information systems (computerized and manual).

***   Fully familiar with FASB-APB, SAS, taxation, S.E.C. requirements (10K, 10Q, 8K, etc.) and other regulatory agency requirements.

***   Competent in the preparation and analysis of financial statements, corporate tax returns (federal, state and local), financial and operational audits, budgeting, and in tax planning.

***   Experience with wide variety of industries and commercial enterprises ranging up to $100 million in size.

***   Capable recruiter, trainer and motivator.

(FOR FURTHER DETAILS SEE FOLLOWING PAGE)

EXPERIENCE

<u>1968-Present</u>   "Big 8" firm since 1977, and international C.P.A. firm since
              1968. Names on request.

SUPERVISOR, MANAGER; report to partner; earlier Accountant.

Responsible for:
- various clients $20-150 million in size in publishing, real estate, whole-
  sale, distribution, manufacturing and commercial banking
- audits, taxes, financial statements and management services
- training accountants
- supervision of accountants

Accomplishments:
- provided advice with respect to prospective acquisitions and audits upon
  completion of acquisitions
- acted in advisory capacity on compensation for clients
- advised clients with respect to debt vs. equity financing
- advised and aided clients in setting up management information systems
- reduced client tax liabilities in such areas as subscription expense
  method; completed contract vs. percentage of completion method; installment sales tax program; inventory systems
- gained reputation as an authority in areas of deferred income taxes,
  leases, publishing and real estate
- early proponent and user of sophisticated EDP auditing techniques
- sought by clients for management advisory services

<u>EDUCATION</u>:

<u>B.S.</u>, Accounting, New York University, New York, NY, 1968

<u>ACCREDITATIONS</u>:

Certified Public Accountant, 1970

<u>MEMBERSHIPS</u>:

American Institute of Certified Public Accountants
Louisiana Certified Public Accountants

<u>HOBBIES</u>:

Skiing, history of Louisiana

<u>PERSONAL DATA</u>: Age 33, married, excellent health

<u>REFERENCES AND FURTHER DATA ON REQUEST</u>

27 86th Street   (212) 777-7777
Staten Island, NY 10000

R E S U M E

of

JOHN GRANT HEFNER, C.P.A.

OBJECTIVE

Tax Manager, Supervisor or Director for financial,
service or industrial corporation.

SUMMARY

***   Extensive successful experience as Tax Manager and
        Supervisor for "Big 8" certified public accounting
        firm for 13 years; credited with significant con-
        tributions to tax law interpretations in aid of
        clients, including large and small corporations,
        and individuals.

***   Earlier, for five years, agent with the Internal
        Revenue Service responsible for initiating and
        winning a precedent-setting action in a famous
        case.

***   Although a tax specialist, possess credentials and
        competence in all areas of accounting services.

(FOR FURTHER DETAILS SEE FOLLOWING PAGES)

EXPERIENCE

TAX MANAGER   <u>1965-Present</u>:   CROON, BABSON & CO., New York, NY
                              Certified Public Accountants with 60
               partners, staff of 375 and diversified corporate clients
               from large to small in a great variety of industries.

               Responsibilities:
               - as manager, below partner level, supervise entire staff
                 on tax matters

               Contributions to firm:
               - added about $3 million in new clients to firm's volume
               - conducted seminars on regular schedule for entire staff
                 on tax matters; prepared advisories used by entire firm
                 on tax procedures
               - acted as personal tax consultant to high elected political
                 figures, senior partners of international law firms, fa-
                 mous designers, realtors, stock brokers, television per-
                 sonalities, and sports figures in addition to corporate
                 work
               - provided solutions for complex tax issues
               - was recognized authority in certain tax areas
               - expedited intraoffice paperwork; improved quality of
                 correspondence

               Areas of activity include tax shelters (oil and gas, com-
               modities, real estate, equipment, cattle), joint committee,
               farm losses, accumulated earnings tax, travel and enter-
               tainment, officers' salaries and loans, leasebacks, bad
               debts, etc.

               Contributions to clients (examples):
               - increased pension benefits by restructuring a corpora-
                 tion into six corporations
               - saved $½ million in connection with a proposed dividend
               - saved $20,000 in the use of a yacht for business enter-
                 tainment
               - liquidated a real estate corporation that did not have
                 an attorney
               - saved $1 million for famous designer with a plan in-
                 volving a personal holding company
               - arranged substantial tax and personal benefits to two
                 feuding family officers; represent both of the two
                 surviving corporations
               - and much more

I.R.S. AGENT   <u>1960-1965</u>   U.S. INTERNAL REVENUE SERVICE,
                              Office of International Operations,
               Washington, DC, and at Camden and Trenton, NJ

               - examined returns of U.S. citizens residing abroad, non-
                 resident aliens, and foreign corporations

I.R.S. AGENT (continued)

                  – as agent in New Jersey, audited returns of corporations, partnerships, and individuals

                  – assigned also to tax problems involving celebrities such as John Wayne, Clark Gable, Clara Bow, Mark Twain, Norman Rockwell and others

                  – initiated a precedent-setting case involving income exclusion for a U.S. citizen residing abroad; position was sustained

EDUCATION: <u>B.S.</u>, Drew University, Madison, NJ. Elected to Honor Elected to Honor Society

                  Graduate work in Accounting at University of Pennsylvania

                  Continuing education with NY State Certified Public Accountant Society

ACCREDITATION: Certified Public Accountant

PROFESSIONAL   American Institute of Certified Public Accountants, Board
AFFILIATIONS: of Examiners

                  New York State Certified Public Accounting Society, Committee on Federal Taxation

                  Columbia University Tax Study Group

PERSONAL DATA: Age 42, married, excellent health

REFERENCES: On request

DISCUSSION

Accounting Résumé. The résumés of public accountants (if they are not partners) are often difficult to write using the formula of "what were your responsibilities?" and "what did you accomplish in the exercise of those responsibilities?" In practice, accountants do segments of a client's work—payroll, audits, reconciliations, taxes, investments, consolidations—and are unaware of the total influence of the package on the client's affairs.

The two preceding accounting résumés have interest because the subjects analyzed their involvements carefully. Blount listed experience in a wide range of activities.

Hefner, in his tax work, had many interesting experiences, including his tenure as an IRS agent, and named some of the people (fictional here) whose returns he had worked on. He also became such an expert in the tax area that he was called upon to give seminars for the entire staff of his large firm.

In accounting résumés, experience in a variety of industries or institutions lends breadth, advisory work with clients provides authority, and work on tax shelters, EDP techniques, estate advisories, corporate reorganizations, and reversing IRS decisions shows a sophisticated competence.

EXECUTIVE SECRETARY

510 Governor Clinton Apartments   (212) 867-3410
New York, NY 10009

R E S U M E

of

TUESDAY WELT

OBJECTIVE: Position in private industry as EXECUTIVE SECRETARY to busy manager.

QUALIFICATIONS: Skills include ability to plan and organize work for expeditious completion; to work under pressure; to accept responsibility; to supervise effectively and coordinate the work of others. Harmonious with people at all employment levels. Possess typing speed with accuracy of 75-80 wpm; shorthand speed of 100-120 wpm. Experience in research. Able to handle correspondence with minimum supervision when desirable. Accustomed to summarizing important happenings during absence of executives; to setting up agendas, acting as liaison among executives, making itineraries, scheduling travel. Administratively competent in record-keeping, forecasting work loads, arranging and reporting meetings. Multilingual. Have highest nonprofessional Civil Service rating.

EXPERIENCE: *1952-Present* Rockefeller Foundation, New York, NY
EXECUTIVE SECRETARY, Office of the Chairman, Council on National Alternatives (1974-present). Responsible for preparing summaries of committee meetings; coordinating work of secretarial staff; often under pressure, sometimes throughout the night to draft reports, resolutions and amendments for distribution prior to next day's meeting; for organizing and processing document publication. Responsible for attending conferences in Mexico City, Rio de Janiero, Buenos Aires; monitoring results.

PERSONAL ASSISTANT to Executive Director of Grants (former U.S. Ambassador to Albania) (1971-1974), requiring attendance each year at Economic and Social Council meetings in Berne, handled protocol at official dinners.

PERSONAL ASSISTANT, formerly Secretary, to Director of South American Trade and Development (1967-1971). Responsible for coordinating and supervising work of secretaries. Aided in setting up conference committees. Attended conferences in New Delhi and Geneva.

208

EXPERIENCE: SECRETARY to Director of Public Information Division
(continued)   (1952-1967). Responsible for keeping Director briefed
                     during extended absences; for supervising office staff.
                     Attended meetings in Paris and Mexico City.

LANGUAGES: Fluent French and Spanish.

EDUCATION: King's University, London, England, 1947-1948.
                     Pace Institute, New York, NY, 1948-1949.
                     Hold certificate in report and letter writing.

PERSONAL DATA: Divorced, age 40, excellent health. Want to relocate.

REFERENCES AND FURTHER DATA ON REQUEST

27 Alexander Hamilton Hill   (201) 618-7423
Hoboken, NJ 07000

CURRICULUM VITAE

CAROLYN COMFORT

OBJECTIVE: Administrative or Consulting position in health care in-
                  stitution (recruiting, management, research) or admin-
                  istrative or teaching position in university (Associate
                  Dean, Assistant Professor, Department of Nursing).

QUALIFICA-   Doctoral, Master's and Bachelor's degrees; nursing ex-
TIONS: perience in medical departments of large medical centers,
                  intensive care burn unit, chronic rehabilitation hos-
                  pital, public and private psychiatric hospitals; ex-
                  perience in supervising nonprofessional hospital staffs
                  and professional nursing students in the environments
                  mentioned above. Experience in teaching and curriculum
                  development. Competent in research and statistical
                  analysis.

PERSONAL DATA: Born 2/24/46, single, excellent health.

EDUCATION: PhD., Psychology, Teachers College, Cornell University,
                  New York, NY, 1979.

                  M.S., Nursing, University of Chicago, Chicago, IL, 1970.

                  B.S.N., Saint Aloysius College, Cincinnati, 1967.
                  Graduated Cum Laude.

HONORS,   Rhodes multidisciplinary scholarship, Psychology, 1972-
AWARDS &   1977. Rhodes graduate traineeship, Nursing, University of
SCHOLARSHIPS: Michigan, 1968-1970. Elected to Kappa Gamma Phi for
                  achievement in academic work at the college level. Thesis
                  selected for presentation at Eighth Annual Nursing Con-
                  ference (1970), Albuquerque, NM.

PROFESSIONAL   1976-1979   See EDUCATION
EXPERIENCE:
                1979-1975   COLUMBIA UNIVERSITY - PRESBYTERIAN HOSPITAL
                             Medical Center School of Nursing

                1974 ASSISTANT PROFESSOR, part-time, teaching Life-Span
                Psychology, Adolescence through Senescence; 110 students

                1973-1975 RESEARCH ASSISTANT and INSTRUCTOR
                - jointly with Dean, and in collaboration with faculty,
                  established new curriculum for Department of Nursing
                  focusing on the range of physiological and behavioral
                  states in consideration of preventive care, chronic care,
                  and acute care
                - and development of course in life-span psychology

210

<u>1970-1972</u>   INSTRUCTOR. Supervised nursing students in spectrum of hospital settings (rehabilitation, public and private psychiatric, medical department)
- taught chronic neurological and psychiatric conditions of patients
- established group dynamics sessions to promote professional peer evaluation of nursing care
- alleviated chronic friction between nonprofessional nursing employees and professional nursing students

<u>1969</u> (summer) UNIVERSITY HOSPITAL, Kansas City, MO
STAFF NURSE, Burn Intensive Care Unit
- part of interdisciplinary team implementing range of life-sustaining care for severely burned patients

<u>1968</u> PRESBYTERIAN MEDICAL CENTER, Denver, CO
STAFF NURSE, medical. Team leader for nonprofessional personnel. Provided nursing care for acutely ill patients

<u>1967</u> UNIVERSITY HOSPITAL, Kansas City, MO
STAFF NURSE, medical. Team leader and nurse, as above

MEMBERSHIPS: Federal Association for the Advancement of Science
American Association of University Professors
New York Nurses Association
American Psychological Association
Society for the Research in Premature Births

HOBBIES: Tennis, gourmet cooking, skiing

44 Tracay Avenue   Home (321) 098-7654
Kansas City, MO 12345   Office (123) 456-8765

R E S U M E

of

ROBERT SOLON

PUBLIC ADMINISTRATOR/FOUNDATION EXECUTIVE

Skilled in creating programs, setting and accomplishing goals for the
alleviation or elimination of minority group grievances by persuasion,
conciliation, arbitration dealing with administrators at the highest
levels of City, State and Federal Government and with minority groups;
with effective results in averting crises, resolving disputes, developing
mutual respect in confrontive situations.

As Regional Director U.S. Department of Justice	Over a period of four years hired, trained and led a professional, racially mixed staff of 30 and 12 clerical employees in the handling of conflicts, disputes, demonstrations in the North Central United States.
	Motivated staff to encourage and accomplish problem solutions by the citizens themselves in a matter of their own best self-interest.
	Established Agency liaison with Governors of various States and their staffs to use Agency programs to handle potential crises.
	Accomplished liaisons with major businesses, major Federal funding agencies and with Departments of Labor and Transportation to ensure that solutions were fully understood at all levels.
	Averted riot in Detroit, Michigan, by use of Department "Task Force" approach.
	Resolved school conflict in Cleveland, Ohio, by coordinating administrators, teachers, community groups and students under a program that identified areas of mutual interest before attacking areas of disagreement.
As Community Relations Specialist, U.S. Dept. of Justice	Aided in averting violent confrontations in Watts area, Los Angeles, California.

Settled conflict regarding Indian hunting and fishing rights in New Mexico. Chaired group to set up critical analysis of methods of solving urban problems in Newark, Paterson and Plainfield, NJ; developed modus operandi; established training seminars for administrative officials under Federal auspices; techniques now being extensively utilized by local and state governments.

As Trial Attorney U.S. Dept. of Justice

Prepared, filed and conducted civil rights cases, involving police restrictions of freedom in connection with demonstrations by large groups.

Analyzed litigation procedures and developed new procedures for expediting litigation. Worked with U.S. Supreme Court Administrative Assistant to create plans for a sublevel of jurisdiction to eliminate case overloads. Plan is under consideration.

Chronology of Employment

1972-Present: U.S. Department of Justice, Community Relations Service

1969-1972: U.S. Department of Justice, Inter-Government Liaison Service.

1968-1969: U.S. Department of Justice, Civil Rights Division.

1962-1968: U.S. Department of Justice, Administrative Division.

Military Service

U.S. Army, 1954-1964, Aide-de-Camp to General Symington, Tenth Combat Division, Vietnam.

Education

L.L.B., Harvard University School of Law, Cambridge, MA.

B.A., Political Science, University of Denver, Denver, CO.

Accreditations

Member of the Bar, District of Columbia, Maryland and Virginia.

Personal Data

Age 39, married, three children, excellent health.

REFERENCES AND FURTHER DATA ON REQUEST

Olympic Tower
391 Fifth Avenue
New York, NY 00000

Home (000) 000-0000
Office (000) 000-0000

R E S U M E

of

RALPH W. EMERSON

ADVERTISING EXECUTIVE

OBJECTIVE   Percentage ownership and profit sharing in large, suc-
               cessful advertising agency.

EXPERIENCE

CREATIVE   1974-Present   RUBICAM, THOMPSON, AYER, WELLS & DOYLE,
DIRECTOR   New York, NY

               Credits:
               - created Alka-Seltzer compaign
               - developed Miller Light campaign
               - received Anny award for Coca Cola campaign
               - established Joe DiMaggio and other celebrities in bank,
                 coffee, Fortunoff and other campaigns
               - continued A.T.&T. account direction
               - conceived Marlboro campaign
               - 27 awards in five years for copy, art, concepts,
                 leadership, best advertising campaigns, and best indi-
                 vidual advertisements

COPY   1970-1974   RUMRILL, FOOTE, McCANN, D'ARCY ADVERTISING,
CHIEF   New York, NY
               - copy and lyrics, Chrysler Corp.
               - copy for Rolls Royce and Volkswagen
               - copy for XEROX Corp.
               - campaign for British Airways
               - developed theme for A.T.&T., still used
               - received 18 awards for excellence.

ACCOUNT   1966-1970   OGILVY, MARSTELLER, GUENTHER INTERNATIONAL,
EXECUTIVE   New York, NY

               Responsible for the following accounts:
                 Chemical Bank, XEROX Office Systems, United Technol-
                 ogies, TV Guide

214

ACCOUNT   <u>1960-1966</u>   HICKS & DeGARMO, New York, NY
SUPERVISOR
Aided in market analysis campaign development and new
business presentations. Assisted in handling such
accounts as Welch Grape Juice, J. Wiss & Sons Co., Time
Magazine and State of West Virginia. Wrote copy, recommended media, participated in concept planning, met
with clients.

PUBLICATIONS: The Thorn Birds (national best seller)
The Advertising Murders (selected by The Crime Club
Advertising Made Easy (Macmillan Book Club)
Sex and People (co-author with Chapman and Jong)
Back Packing Around the World (selected by the Wilderness
  Club)
Official handbook, U.S. Department of the Interior and
  the U.S. Army)
Extensive published writing for trade publications

EDUCATION: <u>M.B.A.</u>, Harvard Graduate School of Business Administration, Cambridge, MA
<u>B.A.</u>, English, Bucknell University, Lewisburg, PA, Phi
Beta Kappa, Summa Cum Laude

HOBBIES: Platform tennis (runner-up, national championship, men's
doubles); tennis, court tennis, squash (A player)

PERSONAL DATA: Age 37, married, three children, excellent health

REFERENCES: Anyone in the advertising business

12 Duse Street   (516) 000-0000
Liberty Square, NY 11000

R E S U M E

of

WILLIAM R. STOCKHOLM

BANK OFFICER

* * *   Entire career in banking as Assistant Vice President and
        Branch Manager (earlier Teller and Chief Clerk), with
        responsibility for new business and operations. Record
        of developing significant volume of new business in
        every branch assignment and of effective management and
        good judgment.

* * *   Experience and competence also include accounting
        financial analysis, branch location planning, commercial
        and consumer lending, foreign transactions, money market
        operations, mortgage loans, personnel administration,
        municipal finance.

* * *   Qualities include leadership, innovativeness, selling
        skills, ability to train and motivate, analytical ability,
        broad financial acumen, comprehensive branch bank opera-
        tions management knowledge.

(FOR FURTHER DETAILS, SEE FOLLOWING PAGE)

EXPERIENCE

__1955-Present__   BENJAMIN FRANKLIN TRUST COMPANY,
New York, NY, with 2,000 employees.

__1977-Present__   ASSISTANT VICE PRESIDENT, MANAGER of Radio City Branch,
Superville, NY. Supervised assistant and ten clerical employees. Reported
to Senior Vice President.

Responsible for:
- profitability, policies and procedures, carrying out the precepts established by general management to recapture losses resulting from the
problems of an acquired bank

Accomplishments:
- with aid of staff recovered more than 40% of the lost deposits

__1955-1977__   ASSISTANT V.P. and MANAGER, successively appointed to larger
branches rising from start as Teller, Chief Clerk, Manager, Assistant V.P.

Responsible for:
- new business, operations, profitability, policies and procedures

Accomplishments:
- directed three branch openings; managed branches and brought them to
profitable operating levels
- developed new business programs; met potential customers; multiplied
membership in local organizations to widen business potentials
- opened Selden office (1959); started at zero, built deposits to $6 mil-
lion by 1964, increasing to $15 million by 1969
- opened Lefrak City branch October 1970; from zero gained deposits of
$2.5 million in five months

__1951-1955__   BANK OF SMITHTOWN, Smithtown, NY. TELLER.

MILITARY SERVICE:

U.S. ARMY, 1943-1948. Graduated from O.C.S. as 2nd Lt. Graduated from
Pilot School. Assigned to European theatre; promoted to Captain division
artillery, Air Section; supervised 30 officers, 50 enlisted men. Awards:
Air Medal with four Clusters.

EDUCATION:

Rutgers University, New Brunswick, NJ, two years
Major: Accounting, Business Management
Graduate: American Institute of Banking

LANGUAGES:

Fair Spanish

HOBBIES:

Local community activities and clubs; golf

PERSONAL DATA:

Married, one child, own home, excellent health

REFERENCES AND FURTHER DATA ON REQUEST

1822 Georgetown Street   Home (000) 000-0000
Point Pleasant, CA 95000   Office (916) 000-0000

R E S U M E

of

J. WILLIAM GRANT

OBJECTIVE

Opportunity to utilize skills in analysis, management
and languages, preferably in an international environment.

SUMMARY AND QUALIFICATIONS

***   Captain, U.S. Air Force, Office of Criminal Intelligence
dealing with criminal and fraud matters, worldwide. Entire
career of 12 years to present in USAF, and in OCI since
1970 as Special Agent in Charge except when attending
language schools. Achieved M.B.A. while in service. (B.A.,
History, 1968.)

***   Record of utilizing management principles and advanced
management techniques to increase efficiency of operations
during every tour of duty assignment.

***   Able to recognize deficiencies in methods and procedures
and find the means to correct them. Cited by supervisors
for numerous contributions to more efficient operations,
cost savings, curtailing frauds, smuggling, criminal
activities, and dedication to duty.

***   Multilingual in Vietnamese, Italian and French.

(FOR FURTHER DETAILS SEE FOLLOWING PAGES)

EXPERIENCE

__1968-Present__   U.S. AIR FORCE. Rank: CAPTAIN

__1979-Present__   SPECIAL AGENT IN CHARGE, San Diego, CA
                 Office of Criminal Intelligence (OCI)

OCI investigates criminal and fraud matters on a worldwide basis for the
USAF. Supervise eight Special Agents and three administrative assistants.
Line of command is Director (worldwide operations), Supervisor, Special
Agent in Charge.

Responsible for:
- investigation of frauds relating to millions of dollars of Defense Department funds for military contracts

Accomplishments:
- recognized need of specialized training of the Special Agents to bridge
  the gap between the business world and the military environment, including the proper briefing of senior officers; arranged for their training
  using an adaptation of civilian PERT and CPM techniques developed by
  the Western Regional Organized Crime Training Institute for the California Department of Justice.

__1974-1977__   SPECIAL AGENT IN CHARGE, Boot, Italy
              Office of Criminal Intelligence (OCI)

Supervised three language-trained Special Agents.

Responsible for:
- criminal and fraud investigations
- the territory South of Naples, including Sicily
- working jointly with the Italian National Police in matters such as
  international terrorism and smuggling

Accomplishments:
- discovered that the port of Boot and the isolated area along the
  Adriatic Sea was a source of smuggling contraband through Middle East
  shipping traffic, to Holland and central Europe
- arranged for extensive training by the U.S. Drug Enforcement Administration and other U.S. agencies in detection and identification techniques, for Italian National Police personnel; drug traffic decreased
  substantially.

__1973-1974__   LANGUAGE STUDENT, Italian
              ORD Language Institute, Monterey, CA

__1971-1973__   SPECIAL AGENT IN CHARGE, El Paso, TX
              Office of Criminal Intelligence (OCI)

Territory: all of northern Texas. Supervised 12 Special Agents, three administrative assistants.

                                        Over..... Please.......

1971-1973 continued

Responsible for:
- criminal and fraud investigations and inquiries regarding security
  clearances

Accomplishments:
- noted repeated trips to same areas resulting in unnecessary extra travel;
  set up territories by counties; concentrated assignments so that fewer
  trips had to be made with resulting lower operating costs and central
  billing instead of multilocation billing.

1970-1971   SPECIAL AGENT IN CHARGE, South Vietnam
            Office of Criminal Intelligence (OCI)

- as Vietnamese linguist represented District Supervisor in matters involving the OCI and the Vietnamese National Police.

1969-1970   LANGUAGE STUDENT, Vietnamese Language Department
            Ft. Ord Language Institute, Monterey, CA

1968-1969   SPECIAL AGENT IN CHARGE, Kansas City, MO
            Office of Criminal Intelligence (OCI)

Territory: Metropolitan Kansas City. Supervised 12 Special Agents, five
administrative assistants

Responsible for:
- criminal, fraud and security clearance investigations; credit investigations of persons entering the military

1967-1968   AIR FORCE INTELLIGENCE SCHOOL, Pueblo, CO

1966-1967   USAF OFFICER TRAINING SCHOOL, Boulder, CO

EDUCATION:

B.A., History, Council State College, Bluffs, IA, 1968
M.B.A. Management, Garden State University, Trenton, NJ. Special training as noted by the USAF

LANGUAGES:

(proficiency: (1) low, (2) average, (3) above average, (4) native:
Vietnamese: oral (3)   written (3)
Italian: oral (3)   written (3)
French: oral (3)   written (3)

HOBBIES:

Fishing, hiking, camping, travel

PERSONAL DATA:

Age 34, married, one child. Resided for extended periods in Vietnam and
Italy. Extensively traveled in the Far East and Europe

REFERENCES AND FURTHER DATA ON REQUEST

Naval Base Quarters   Home (123) 456-7890
Newport News, VA (zip)   Office (987) 654-3210

R E S U M E

of

JOHN P. JONES, IV

MANAGER/EXECUTIVE
in
GENERAL ADMINISTRATION or TECHNICAL CAPACITY

* * *   Entire career to retirement, 1 June at age 39, with U.S.
        Navy with present rank of Captain. Electronics and manage-
        ment specialties.

* * *   Accustomed to command positions involving as many as 600
        officers and enlisted personnel.

* * *   Reported on fitness by commanding officers consistently
        either outstanding or excellent.

* * *   Excerpts from fitness reports include the following:

        "a very dynamic officer" developing "a practical, effective
        and realistic organization" with "happy and well-motivated
        subordinates" . . . "cost conscious."

        "excellent command leadership ability, outstanding combat
        officer; ability to train staff in most effective use of
        new and experimental electronic equipment."

        "excellent manager, approaches all problems in rational
        manner; his Section has continued to respond in a timely
        manner to the numerous and varied demands placed upon it
        and successfully pursued existing programs for equipment
        modernization and improved systems performance."

        "demonstrated capability to handle positions of greater
        responsibility."

        and more.

(FOR FURTHER DATA, PLEASE SEE FOLLOWING PAGES)

EXPERIENCE

<u>1954-June 1975</u>   UNITED STATES NAVY

CAPTAIN, Combat Electronics Specialty. Total of 17 assignments in Medit-
terranean, Alaska, Bahamas, Charleston, SC, Thailand, Washington, DC and
Newport News, VA. Most important assignments as follows:

<u>Aug. 1972-June 1975</u>, CHIEF, ELECTRONICS SCHOOL BRANCH, U.S. Navy Training
Center, Training Division. Supervise 20 officers, 93 technicians, eight
radarmen, 18 clerks. Responsible for:

- training 600 students yearly.
- establishing the curriculum.
- preparation and administration of annual budget of $2 million.

Accomplishments:

- changed curriculum, which was not relevant to needs of U.S. Navy or students, from mathematical theory to practical utilization assuring capability to repair electronic equipment under battle conditions.
- changed basic theory of training from one based on negative advance
  evaluation of students to assumption of student intelligence and positive motivation by description of goals.
- grades curved upward and attrition declined from 28% to near zero.

<u>May 1971-July 1973</u>, CHIEF, FACILITIES SECTION, Electronic Engineering
Division, U.S. Navy Headquarters, Washington, DC. Responsible for:

- procurement, system design and installation of all electronic equipment on Neptune submarines.
- justification for and preparation and administration of $500 million
  budget.

Accomplishments:

- issued specific job assignments to engineers by class of ship and equipment.
- discovered that surface search radar installed previously exhibited design deficiencies such as inadequate antenna rotation, catastrophic
  power supply failures, poor video presentation, grossly inadequate mean
  time before failure (MTBF).
- increased MTBF from 16.7 hours to 260 hours within year.
- instituted program to monitor and certify all electronic installations.
- tested, developed and installed new type of transmitting antennas to
  better meet operational requirements.
- solved problem plaguing high-endurance submarines for many years.

<u>Sept. 1970-May 1971</u>, ELECTRONICS SYSTEM DESIGNER, Cruiser Design Staff,
Electronics Engineering Division, U.S. Navy Headquarters. Responsible
for:

- design of communications and navigation systems with bidding specifications.

Accomplishments:

- new U.S. Navy Cruiser (classified) has unmatched electronic fire system
  versatility and complete equal air control and navigation positions.

Sept. 1969-Sept. 1970, HIGH ENDURANCE DESTROYER SECTION, Communications Branch, Electronic Engineering Division, U.S. Navy Hdqtrs. Responsible for system design, procurement, installation of electronic equipment of 37 destroyers.

Accomplishments:

- developed system design for installation of new UHF, VHF/FM and VHF/AM communications equipment.
- improved upon previous designs of CCTV and MF communications systems.
- procured and installed new cameras capable of adjusting to varying light levels.

Sept. 1967-Sept. 1969, SPECIAL STUDIES.

June 1966-June 1967, COMMANDING OFFICER, U.S. Navy Command Station, Thailand. Supervised one officer, 28 enlisted men. Responsible for transmitting (classified) signal 99.97% each month throughout the year.

Accomplishments:
- transmitted usable (classified) signal of proper power and pulse shape 99.99% each month throughout the year.

HONORS:

Bronze Star, Silver Star, Purple Heart (3), D.S.M.

EDUCATION:

ABC Industries, New York, NY, 1967-1969. Advanced Electronics Technology. Graduated 20th in class of 80.
U.S. Navy Officer Candidate School, 1961 (5 months). Graduated first in class of 103.
U.S. Navy Electronics School. Graduated first in class of 67.

HOBBIES:

Wrestling, karate, hockey, water polo, boxing.

COMMUNITY ACTIVITIES:

Coach, Scout football team.

MEMBERSHIPS:

Retired Officers Association.

PERSONAL DATA:

Born 6/15/36, three children, excellent health.

371 Clinton Avenue
Irvington, NJ 07000

Home (201) 378-1657
Office (212) 377-4444

RESUME

of

TORAM XESTROS

HUMAN RESOURCES DEVELOPMENT SPECIALIST

OBJECTIVE: Human resource development and planning specialist providing technical assistance in the evaluation and development of corporate personnel and personnel programs.

QUALIFICATIONS: New York State certified Clinical School Psychologist, learning disability specialist, experienced coordinator of educational programs. Psychodiagnostician.

Wide experience in administering batteries of tests, evaluating, and producing recommendations.

Currently employed as corporate personnel consultant with additional assignment to develop stronger corporate image.

Graduate and postgraduate studies at New York University with specialty in Clinical Psychology.

EDUCATION: Advanced Certificate in Clinical School Psychology, Postgraduate work, Columbia University, New York, NY 1975
M.S., Clinical School Psychology, New York University, 1973
B.A., Psychology, Fordham University, New York, NY, 1970

ACCREDITATIONS: Permanent New York State certification as School Psychologist
Permanent New York State certification in science and special education teacher at junior high and high school levels.

PERSONAL DATA: Age 36, married, four children, own home; willing to relocate.

224

EXPERIENCE

1978-Present FOREMOST APPAREL INC., New York, NY

PERSONNEL CONSULTANT for major apparel manufacturer with plants in New York, New Jersey, Pennsylvania and overseas; several thousand employees.

Responsible for:
- analysis of employee records for application of psychological testing as indicated to be necessary
- assistance in adjusting a different cultural background to production requirements
- assistance in development of workshops on human relations
- bilingual evaluation system to increase employee effectiveness at the administrative level
- studies to improve trade name perception among buyers

1976-Present (concurrently) THE BRIDGETON (NJ) SCHOOL DISTRICT

LEARNING DISABILITY COORDINATOR for school district with 10,000 students, 600 teachers and 19 elementary, junior high and high schools. Supervise 4-8 professionals. Utilize tests familiarily known as Academic Achievement, W.A.I.S., W.R.A.T., Bender Gestalt, Projectives, Myers-Briggs Type Indicator, etc.

Responsible for:
- organizing, coordinating and implementing learning disability program (L.D.), developing budget, providing leadership and counsel to the faculty; hiring, training and supervising staff

Accomplishments:
- taking into consideration manpower, budget, student and faculty population, and existing programs; selected one of four alternatives for presentation to Board of Education; it was accepted and has remained in successful effect for 2-1/2 years (success measured by improvement in remediation)
- established all the policies and procedures to ensure uniform administration and delivery of the needed services
- held conferences with principals and teachers to create mutual understanding of procedures
- set objectives for testing, provided prescriptions and dates of completion
- maintained complete data file and progress reports

1975-1976 BONAVENTURE PSYCHIATRIC CLINIC

L.D. SPECIALIST. Supervised staff of six.
- developed individual remedial programs and education therapy for inner-city children

225

1975-1976 Continued

L.D. SPECIALIST.
- coordinated the reading center
- developed community workshops to enlarge and improve delivery of services

1975-1976 (concurrently)   THE NEW SCHOOL

SCHOOL PSYCHOLOGIST
- created programs for the exceptional children
- provided individual educational-career therapy
- acted as consultant to teachers to assist in providing most suitable programs to meet the specialized children's needs

1973-1976   PSYCHASSOCIATES, INC. (partially concurrent)

COORDINATOR of EDUCATIONAL THERAPY and ASSESSMENT
- developed programs and network of communications with staff and outside contacts

TEACHING EXPERIENCE

1977   Conducted monthly workshops with school staff to implement and follow program guidelines at the Bridgeton School District.

1974-1975   Seminar workshops for guidance counselors of the New Jersey schools.

1970-1974   SCIENCE TEACHER, Newark, NJ public junior high schools.

MILITARY SERVICE: Turkish Defense Forces, Naval, 1961-1964.

1829 Fairfield Avenue   Home (212) 123-4567
Forest Hills, NY (zip)   Office (212) 321-7654

R E S U M E

of

WILLIAM A. ARTHUR

Qualified as

COMMUNICATIONS EXECUTIVE

* * *   Experience in quasipublic tristate Authority in the
          management of complex EDP and other equipment for
          the input, reception, storage, security and retrieval
          of vital information.

* * *   Record as effective manager, trainer, administrator,
          implementer in a series of demanding positions re-
          quiring specialized expertise and leadership ability.
          Top government security clearance.

* * *   Strong communication skills - verbal, mechanical or
          electronic - with ability to maintain any communica-
          tions system at peak performance level.

* * *   Earlier, similar experience in the U.S. Navy as
          Commander.

(FOR FURTHER DATA, PLEASE SEE FOLLOWING PAGES)

* Demonstrating broad administrative, interpretative and budget skills, political aptitudes in exacting post with Tri-State Authority.

1974-Present   (NAME OF AUTHORITY ON REQUEST)

ASSISTANT CHIEF OF ADMINISTRATION for Fiscal Department responsible for all Authority funds. Supervise staff of 50 including accountants, administrators, guards, clerks, etc.

* Responsibilities and Accomplishments:

  - act as liaison officer between Chief of Administration and all Bureau and Division Chiefs in the selection of personnel.
  - administrate payroll, attendance records and efficiency ratings of personnel.
  - establish policy with Chief of Administration.
  - supervise purchasing, distribution; bindery and reproduction services; custody, preservation and retrieval of public records; physical inventories of machines, furniture, files.
  - control cash accounts for official and personnel disbursements.
  - issue directives and procedures affecting status of employees.
  - supervise processing of legal documents, court orders.
  - act as Chief of Administration in absence of Chief.
  - prepare annual estimates of the official Expense Budget.
  - authorize, by personal signature, important financial and administrative documents.

* Assigned responsibilities ordinarily accompanying rank of Captain, carried out assignments with distinction.

1972-1974   U.S. NAVY, U.K. COMMUNICATIONS REGION, Eastbourne, Scotland

* Responsible for:
  - monthly inspection of maintenance equipment, for personnel and their functions in ten Communications Sections.
  - coordination of training programs, installations, scheduling and administration of staff visits; implementation of security.

* Initiated, developed and supervised new Maintenance Officer Evaluation Program for purpose of improving competence and efficiency of Maintenance Personnel.

* Gained broad working knowledge of sophisticated wideband, microwave, multiplex and transospheric scatter communications systems.

1971-1972   U.S. NAVY, Bergen, Norway

COMPUTER AUTOMATIC SWITCHING CENTER MANAGER. Supervised 50 computer technicians in the proper transfer of computer activity from contractor to U.S.N.

* Responsible for maintenance, training and supply.
* Processed over one million messages without computer malfunction.
* Engineered program to discover computer trends. Received letter of appreciation from manufacturer.

1967-1971   U.S. NAVY, Newport News, Virginia

COMPUTER MAINTENANCE MANAGER. Responsible for:

* liaison and coordination among IBM, Dayco and Navy.
* maintenance of New York "Tanker Mining Defense System" (TDMS) 1441 computer.
* all training and supply programs.
* supervision of 70 computer technicians.

* Accomplished least amount of computer downtime within U.S. Navy over 3-year period.
* Had coordination and maintenance responsibility for unique Acronym network Digital Data Center (DDC) transfer program. Set up training program.
* Directed overall maintenance of 360/370 computer, transmitter/receiver site and cryptographic equipment, utilized to identify and control ship traffic throughout New York Harbor. Supervised all facets of installation, inspection, repair calibration, alignment and overhaul of complex digital computer systems, establishing best Force with 55% of authorized personnel.

AFFILIATIONS:

   National Automatic Data Association
   Association of Communications Engineers

EDUCATION:

   M.A., Education, 1969, Michigan State College, East Lansing, MI.
   B.S., Sociology, 1963, University of Toledo, Toledo, OH.
   1961, Graduate studies in Computer Art, New York University, New York, NY.

MILITARY SCHOOLING:

   Computer School, 1966-1967, U.S.N.A., Annapolis, MD, 50 weeks.
   Remington-Rand Computer School, 1970-1971, 20 weeks.
   Business Administration School, 1971, honor graduate.
   Management Art and Science, 1971, honor graduate.

PERSONAL DATA: Born 12/31/40, married, 4 children, excellent health.

REFERENCES AND FURTHER DATA ON REQUEST

1837 Caldwell   (123) 456-7890
Los Angeles, CA (zip)

RESUME

of

WILLIAM CLEVELAND

***   Record of achievement in advancing to Vice Presidency of
         major construction firm, after starting as supervisor of
         foremen.

***   Strong profit orientation with exposure in public rela-
         tions, marketing and sales; grasp of advertising strategy,
         direct mail campaigns, brochures; budget planning and
         forecasts; successful track record in competitive bidding
         situations.

***   Strength in planning new objectives, finding methods of
         implementation, creating millions of dollars of extra
         sales and profits.

***   Practical experience in project management, complete
         administration of work from start to finish; payment
         breakdown, monthly billing, percentage of completion,
         CPM or progress completion scheduling.

***   Proven skills in field supervision, evaluation of field
         personnel, labor relations, negotiations, material
         scheduling and expediting; purchasing - materials and
         vendor subcontracts.

***   Experience in quality assurance - quality control analysis
         and administration; job cost analysis, spec interpretation
         and negotiating.

(FOR FURTHER DATA, PLEASE SEE FOLLOWING PAGE)

<u>1965-Present</u>   (NAME OF COMPANY ON REQUEST)

With current annual sales of $50 million, this Mechanical Contractor employs 50 office personnel and from 200 to 400 people in the field engaged in a variety of construction projects, including a recently acquired complete plant with heavy R&D investment in a patented module unit.

Scope of activities includes: piping-heating, ventilating, air conditioning; industrial piping for manufacturing, chemical, petroleum, natural gas processing; gas for turbines, instrumentation, pollution control, power generation, cryogenic facilities, cold boxes, vaporizers, barge unloading systems, liquid natural gas storage plants, vehicle loading stations for LNG service, liquid propane handling and storage systems, and alterations to existing systems.

Employed as Supervisor (1966-1969); moved up to Senior Supervisor (1969-1970) and on to Assistant Manager (1970-1971). Since then have successfully met challenges in the following succession:

* Chief Project Manager
* Assistant to V.P., Marketing
* Assistant to Executive Vice President
* Vice President, Marketing Services

* <u>Specific Achievements</u>:

As Assistant Manager:
- developed new and better methods for estimating both HVAC and power piping
- increased sales by ten million dollars by end of year
- was given added responsibility as Project Manager

Analyzed market conditions, made recommendations and won approval for a plan to specialize efforts in power piping.

As Assistant to Vice President Marketing:

- given full responsibility to head all industrial projects including such areas as estimating, project manager, customer relations, subcontracts, engineering expediting, purchasing and cost control
- increased sales every year since 1970

* <u>Personal Data</u>:

35 years old, married, enjoy golf and sailing; active in community affairs; excellent health.

REFERENCES AND FURTHER DATA ON REQUEST

230 Albemarle West   Home (000) 123-4567
Constantine, NY   Office (000) 890-1234

R E S U M E

WILLIAM R. HAYES

OBJECTIVE

Position in corporate development department
of corporation or corporate finance division
of bank.

EXPERIENCE

1978-Present   BAXTER CYANAMID CORP., Camptown, NY

MANAGER, BUSINESS DEVELOPMENT, for $1 billion international manufacturer
of ethical pharmaceuticals, proprietary medicines, toiletries and household products. Report to Senior Vice President, International Consumer
Products.

Responsible for:
- defining targets and criteria for acquisition program at an expenditure level of $30-50 million annually, and for proposing and imple-
  menting strategy for acquiring approved companies or products
- accumulating, maintaining and analyzing a broad base of information
  suitable for making evaluations
- presenting reports and recommendations; conducting acquisition negotiations
- coordinating all activities in support of the responsibilities
  assigned

Accomplishments:
- investigated dozens of acquisition candidates, of which five were
  closed

1974-1978   INTERPOLE S.A., Aix la Chapelle, Belgium

DIRECTOR of MERGERS and ACQUISITIONS (starting in 1976) for investment
company engaged in consulting and arranging mergers and acquisitions among
manufacturing corporations for clients in the U.S. and overseas. Staff of
eight, including accountants.

Accomplishments:

- reorganized existing research and acquisition department which had been ineffective
- researched hundreds of major companies in Europe and the U.S. identifying size, financial strength, product line and areas of potential mutual interest among these companies
- expanded firm's contacts with banks and corporations, and outside of firm's European sphere; opened up American market
- introduced strict cost-controls within the merger/acquisition activity
- designed more effective method of recognizing acquisition candidates
- concluded nine successful acquisitions since 1975; acquisitions of U.S. and European corporations; participated in all negotiations.

Earlier, trained in arranging financing for major manufacturers in heavy industry for worldwide contracts

EDUCATION:

B.S., Business Administration, Oxford University, Cambridge, 1977. Attended evening classes, 1975-1978.

University Captain (top student leadership position). Captain of crew. Debating Society (honors student).

LANGUAGES:

French, German, Spanish, Hungarian

PERSONAL DATA:

Age 27 (born in Vienna, Austria); married.
Extensively traveled. Wide professional and personal contacts throughout Europe.

REFERENCES AND FURTHER DATA ON REQUEST

27 Ogilvy Drive
Monkton, NJ 07823

Home (201) 999-8888
Office (212) 888-9999

R E S U M E

of

ORIN THOMPSON

EDP EXECUTIVE

***   Extensive experience for more than 15 years in development of
      management information systems, EDP audits, EDP reorganizations,
      project management to accomplish improved reporting systems and
      lower costs for such major companies as Prudential Insurance
      Co., Citibank, Interpublic and Airco.

***   Competent in the utilization of medium, large-scale and mini-
      computer installations for comprehensive range of reporting,
      accounting, production, marketing.

***   Excerpts from letters of commendation include: Studebaker
      (Interpublic) client: "I would especially like to single out
      Orin Thompson for the important contributions he made to the
      overall success of the project" (LCS Industries).

      Interpublic: "We also want to recognize, in a very special
      way, the involvement of Orin Thompson. He provided Inter-
      public with the most professional guidance available any-
      where" (Army Recruiting Command).

***   Age 42, married, M.B.A and B.A. degrees

(FOR SUBSTANTIATING DATA PLEASE SEE FOLLOWING PAGES)

EXPERIENCE:

1975-Present   DATA CONSULTANTS, INC., New York, NY

SENIOR CONSULTANT, New York Office, for senior systems and project management consulting firm, for users of broad spectrum of large and minicomputers, with home office at Boston, MA and another branch in Richmond,
VA.

Current Assignment:
- development of seven multidivision users manuals for use with about-
  to-be-implemented wholesale Demand Deposit Accounting System (involving 20,000 customers and 90% of bank revenues) for Citibank,
  requiring the translation of a functional specification and a technical systems specification manual into user language for all levels
  of management and clerical operations: Reference Manual, Operation
  Manual, Data Dictionary, Bank Control File, Account Officer Manual,
  Cash Management Manual.

Earlier:
- Project Manager and Senior Analyst responsible for designing and implementing online computerized system covering 15,000 parolees for
  Albany County Parole Department
- responsible for development and implementation of comprehensive
  business support systems for new line of insurance by METROPOLITAN
  LIFE with annual premiums of $80 million and agent field force of
  8000

  Excerpt from letter from Metropolitan executive: "His (Thompson's)
  efforts in developing procedures, organization planning, personnel
  training, procedures documentation, and site planning were vital to
  the success of our project. The tasks set . . . were significant and
  the deadlines critical."

- for INTERPUBLIC RESPONSE DIVISION, evaluated responses to an RFP
  for a computer-based fulfillment system for the U.S. Army Recruiting
  Command; evaluated and selected new systems vendor and aggressively
  supervised the design and installation of the new system resulting
  in savings of $1 million per year and capability of answering in-
  quiries overnight, installed errorfree; influential in retention of
  $45 million in annual billing by Interpublic, and in substantial
  follow-up contracts for Interpublic client.

Recruited for position by former boss at Airco.

1971-1975   AMERICAN BIBLE SOCIETY, New York, NY

MANAGER, INFORMATION SERVICES, for international organization with revenues of $80 million, 500 employees.

Accomplishments:
- reorganized data processing, systems, and programming functions into
  a single Information Services Department with resulting increase in
  efficiency; accomplished timely distribution for first time in three
  years.

AMERICAN BIBLE SOCIETY (continued)
- Represented Society at international data processing conferences in
  Europe. Addressed conferences on data processing systems and utilization.
- planned and coordinated move of entire EDP staff and equipment to
  new installation; introduced major innovations: new documentation
  standards, tape library functions, data input/output control, a files
  program, and production scheduling; reduced operations from three
  shifts to two and increased production
- directed major systems implementation of forecasting program permitting accurate assessments of sale and distribution of modern bibles
  in scores of variations

1965-1971   AIRCO, INC., Parsippany, NJ

MANAGER OF STANDARDS, AUDITS AND CONTROLS (1967-1971) after progression as
follows: Senior Systems Analyst, Project Manager, Systems Training Administrator for billion-dollar international company.

Accomplishments:
- wrote and implemented corporation-wide procedures manual for stan-
  dardization of documentation of systems and programming; wrote and
  implemented handbook of tested and proven techniques to guide systems
  analysts and programmers; volumes were distributed to the Airco
  family of companies worldwide
- handled transfer of all systems and operations of newly acquired
  $10.2 million company from Michigan to New Jersey
- established corporation-wide training program for systems, programming and supervisory personnel
- performed systems audit of British subsidiary and reorganized entire
  EDP system to give improved performance
- designed personnel information system now used throughout Airco companies
- directed major systems conversion to IBM 1410 and later 360 under DOS

1956-1965   METROPOLITAN LIFE INSURANCE COMPANY, New York, NY

SYSTEMS ANALYST (1960-1965) after earlier clerical supervisor and administrative trainee

Accomplishments:
- participated in study of General Division resulting in reorganization
  and reduction of turnaround time in answering inquiries from 5-7 days
  to 2 days with fewer people
- participated in study of Group Insurance Department lasting over a
  period of two years; achieved substantial cost savings
- conducted study of New Business Office resulting in speedup of processing applications from five days to two
Received management training in all major departments earlier over a
period of two and a half years (1958-1960).

MILITARY SERVICE:

    U.S. Army, active duty VietNam, one year.

236

EDUCATION:

    M.B.A., Administrative Management, Rutgers University, 1965.
    Attended evening classes

    B.A., New York University, New York, NY, 1956

ADDITIONAL STUDIES:

    Project Management, IBM, 1975
    Data Processing Operations Management, IBM, 1975
    Systems Seminar, 1964

REFERENCES AND FURTHER DATA ON REQUEST

23 North Band Alley   (212) 213-7654
Benjamin, NY

R E S U M E

of

WILLIAM HARRISON

Qualified as

SYSTEMS/PROGRAMMER ANALYST

---

* * *   Twelve years of comprehensive experience in Data
          Processing including supervision, computer systems
          development, programming and operations.

* * *   Broad experience in systems design for IBM 379, 360,
          1400 computer series involving all types of computer
          application. Fully experienced with COBOL, BAL, System-3
          RPG II, autocode, IOCS and SPS programming applications.

* * *   Experience includes nearly six years as Systems Analyst
          planning and collaborating with departments to coordinate
          their activities with computer systems.

* * *   Designed and programmed departmental systems and proce-
          dures from conception to completion. Handled all phases
          of problem-solving related to these applications.

* * *   Age 32, excellent health.

FOR FURTHER DETAILS PLEASE SEE FOLLOWING PAGES

EXPERIENCE

__1974-Present__   MANUFACTURERS GREENWICH TRUST CO., New York, NY.

__1976-Present__   PROJECT ANALYST for major New York bank in charge of all
phases of all projects assigned. Responsible for:

- design and redesign of General Ledger System for entire bank; wrote
  programs in RPG II; implemented system.
- work in various phases of DDA system.
- work on branch clearing system, commercial loan system utilizing OS,
  JLC, DOS, JLC RPG, OCS including programming in RPG II, BAL, and COBOL.
- write specifications for modifications of systems and following through
  programming as supervisor up to implementation of systems.

Trained under Morgan-Hanover program by Burroughs in Information Management System (IMS)

__1974-1976__   TEAM MEMBER, Master Charge Credit Card Accounting Authorization
System.

Part of a team responsible for implementing a complete online Master
Charge credit card authorization system. Specific responsibilities were
to design and write program specifications and programs to convert the
merchant and cardholder data bases. In addition, designed test data to
test the entire system, modified and wrote additional programs and operation procedures. This included testing and solving problems which arose.
Frequently traveled out of state to work out implementation problems.
System successfully completed.

General Ledger System

Employed as Programmer/Analyst working as part of a system project team
to do feasibility studies, design, program specification, programming,
and implement a Manufacturers Greenwich online general ledger system. Responsibilities were data preparation and designing the online monitor
and 10 data processing modules. In addition, responsible for two trainee
programmers learning use of Assembly language. Project successfully completed.

__1962-1974__   GENERAL CORPORATION, New York, NY

__1970-1974__, employed as Programmer/Analyst responsible for design of programming specifications and programming of General's statistical geographical advertising system. System completed in eight months. April, 1968,
given responsibility to transfer the data processing operation from Los
Angeles to New York. Transfer successfully completed in three months.

Conducted feasibility study and impelmented NCR 735 and 736 magnetic
tapes encoder with communication logic to transmit data to and from six
geographical areas of the U.S. Frequently traveled to those areas to design and implement system to reduce clerical workload.

1961-1970, IBM Wiring Technician. In one year promoted to programmer; then to Supervisor of Programming Department, supervising three trainees. Designed and programmed systems for payroll application (operable within six months). Accounts Receivable, Accounts Payable, statistical statements, sales, invoicing and other financial reports.

Converted IBM programs to S/360 DOS operation while working with various Department Managers.

MILITARY SERVICE: U.S. ARMY, 1955-1959

Wiring Technical Specialist. Completed Army IBM Accounting Technical School. Selected as one of six technicians to attend advance wiring system and procedure school. Assigned to train U.S. and Korean technicians to process base inventory control data.

EDUCATION:

A.A.S., Ryder College, Trenton, NJ

Special courses as follows:
1968-1969: COBOL Programming
1967:   Introduction to IBM System 360
1965-1966: Advanced Programming: EDP System 1401
1964-1965: Programming 1401 System

Special IBM courses:
        BRAM MACROS and Facilities
        Introduction to System 360
        360 COBOL
        Advanced IOCS
        IBM School: Basic 1401 Programming

Additional courses U.S.A. Technical School: Systems and Procedures; Advanced Wiring, Systems and Procedures; Wiring, Machine Accounting.

PERSONAL DATA:

Age 39, excellent health.

REFERENCES AND FURTHER DATA ON REQUEST

1843 Niles Street   (516) 300-3000
Antrim, NY 23456

R E S U M E

of

<u>WILLIAM McKINLEY</u>

Qualified as

PROJECT ENGINEER - STRUCTURAL

Experienced, capable, innovative Structural Engineer with
record of effective participation and leadership in vitally
important and complex projects such as MOREX Building of
the (ABM) System, Kansas City Mall Power Plant Units.

Demonstrated management competence and broad engineering
comprehension by coordinating diverse engineering disciplines
to effect optimum results in adhering to completion schedules
and maintaining high quality, safe design and construction.

Excellent educational background with supporting graduate
courses in important engineering areas.

Record of remaining on job from inception to completion.
Recalled by former employers as new projects develop.

Registration: LICENSED PROFESSIONAL ENGINEER, State of
New York, No. 123456, December, 1960.

B.S. Degree, age 43, married.

(FOR FURTHER DATA PLEASE SEE FOLLOWING PAGES)

EDUCATION AND ACCREDITATIONS:

B.S., Civil Engineering, Structural Option, College of Engineering, University of Denver, Denver, Colorado, 1955.

Graduate courses in Structural and Industrial Engineering, New York University, New York, NY, 1960, 1961, 1962.

Read, write, speak German, Arabic, Polish.

EXPERIENCE:

1977-Present   ELY & SIMPSON, INC., Wichita, Kansas

SENIOR STRUCTURAL ENGINEER for consulting engineering firm. Responsible for major part of review and revision of design engineering of the Library and Museum Building in the "New Kansas City" Project. Checked design of posttensioning systems coordinating with contractor on manner and sequence of systems.

1973-1977   ELY & SIMPSON, INC., New York, NY

As SENIOR STRUCTURAL ENGINEER for Criteria and Design worked on:

Criteria:

- Complex Attack Umbrella Module System (AUMC) component in conjunction with mechanical, electrical, architectural and other engineering disciplines developing design criteria and specifications for structures designed to sustain nuclear blasts. Prepared cost estimates of project components. On project from inception to completion. (Studies available for inspection.)
- Specifications and design criteria for structures capable of withstanding nuclear blasts.

Design:

- Updating drawings to conform to latest Atlas Arms Convac interface requirements.
- Made field site visits, resolved deficiencies indicated in engineering memos.
- Supervised preparation of criteria for interdisciplinary groups.
- Maintained contact with all engineering groups, including mechanical and pipe support groups.
- Chosen to confer with A.U.M.C. Contractors and outside manufacturers' representatives.
- Remained on projects to completion.

242

Jan. 1973-July 1973   BALL & CHAIN ENGINEERING CORP., Kew Gardens, NY

As SENIOR STRUCTURAL DESIGNER:
- Supervised preparation of design drawings and reviewed industrial structures in steel mill plant (Italy) and gas processing furnace (Kuwait).

1969-1972   SENIOR STRUCTURAL DESIGNER employed through job shops for design, coordination of other engineering disciplines, and supervision of
drawings for the following firms:
- U.S. Electric Power, West Point, NY, floor systems and air intake en-
  closure ducts of Cape Horn thermal power plant.
- Maywood Corporation, Hopewell, NC, design of compressor building,
  foundations, superstructures, coordinating with other engineering disciplines to completion of project.
- Pasco Corporation, New York, NY, copper processing plants (Peru). Designed complete building in processing system from foundation to superstructure; remained on job to completion of project.

1968-1969   BALL & CHAIN ENGINEERING CORP., Smithtown, NY

As SENIOR STRUCTURAL DESIGNER in charge of:
- design and layout of reinforced concrete underground coal-handling structures and equipment for two 1000 MKW units, Wheelock Power, PA, project
  for Florida Electric and Power Company.
- design, layout, checking and supervising drawings of 500 KV substation
  switchyard, structural steel framing, on project for Charlestown Electric
  Power Company.
- complete superstructure and foundation - transmission towers for 500 KV
  switchyard on Denver Power Project.
Remained on all projects to successful completion.

1966-1968   MAKAIGH & FINCH, New York, NY

As STRUCTURAL DESIGNER participated in design of highrise commercial and
institutional buildings such as: Columbia Medical School, Church of the
Holy Virgin, Settlement, NY; Pownall College buildings; B'Nai Brith Con-
gregation, Pittsburgh, PA; Foley Square Arena, New York, NY; participated
in stress and stability investigation and preparation of a report on Kansas City Civic Center.

1964-1966   ELY & SIMPSON, INC., New York, NY

As STRUCTURAL ENGINEER, participated in design of Terminal Building, Ken-
nedy International Airport, New York, NY, and approach viaducts. Designed
floors and columns. Prepared complete pilot analysis and design of prototype concrete bent of viaduct fronting terminal; design used as guide for
design of other vents.

<u>1963-1964</u>   ARCO CONSTRUCTION COMPANY, Somaliland

ASSISTANT FIELD (CIVIL) ENGINEER for construction of underground reinforced concrete hangars for Somali Air Force. Supervised preparation of
concrete mixes, earth removal, road beds, paving.

<u>1962</u>   DIANA STEEL COMPANY, Jupiter, FL

STRUCTURAL DESIGNER working in structural steel detailing. Member of team
of seven structural engineers training in preparation for management of
consulting engineering business in Israel.

<u>1961</u>   SUSS, INC., New York, NY

STRUCTURAL DESIGNER. Designed various steel and reinforced concrete structures on a Chemical Processing Plant project for zinc plant.

<u>1960</u>   CHRYSLER ASSOCIATES, Chicago, IL

Worked as CIVIL ENGINEER in design, layout, drafting of municipal project
involving highway drainage, sewer and water services.

<u>PERSONAL DATA</u>:

Age 43, married, six children, own home and car. U.S. citizen.

Defense Department Security Clearance: SECRET.

Traveled extensively in Europe and Africa.

Member of American Steel and Aggregate Association.

<u>REFERENCES AND FURTHER DATA ON REQUEST</u>

244

3040 River View   (914) 123-4567
Hastings-on-Hudson, NY 10021

R E S U M E

of

ANNE MARIE TODD

qualified as

FASHION/FABRIC EDITOR

or for

FASHION-RELATED POSITION IN ADVERTISING, PUBLIC RELATIONS

* * *   Recognized authority and analyst in fashion and fabrics
         for men and women, with ability to write, lecture, train;
         imaginative in coordinating fashion elements; technical
         fabric knowledge; excellent trade relationships.

* * *   Experienced in large segment of fashion industry, in mer-
         chandising and promotion, store operations, fashion shows,
         public relations, organizing, editing. Familiar with home
         sewing and craft industries. Accept responsibility and
         execute. Trained in budget preparation and presentation.

* * *   Eighteen years as successful associate editor, fabric
         editor, promoter, trend forecaster, for three of the most
         important magazines in the field of fashion.

* * *   Made patterns and crafts segments of one magazine so
         attractive to readers that pattern pages were doubled and
         crafts pages increased fourfold.

* * *   Consistent record of career development in fashion in-
         dustry.

FOR FURTHER DATA PLEASE SEE FOLLOWING PAGES

245

BUSINESS EXPERIENCE:

1976-Present   SYNTHETIC YARN ASSOCIATION, New York, NY

DIRECTOR of promotional unit of synthetics industry representing about
90% of all U.S. producers, including all major mills. Report to Board
of Directors of Council. Responsible for:
  - publicity, merchandising, promotion, using all communications media
    in all markets for Men's, Women's and Children's Fashions.

Accomplishments:
  - Put together and staged fashion shows for TV across the country and
    arranged publicity, tying in with leading department stores; ac-
    claimed by manufacturers, designers, retailers and public for ex-
    cellence; strong press coverage, radio interviews.
  - conducted important fashion show annually, including Men's Wear;
    attended by more than 1,000.
  - prepared and presented budgets for board approval on monthly basis;
    made quarterly presentations to industry.

1973-1976   VOGUE-BAZAAR MAGAZINE, New York, NY

Employed in Fashion Department as FABRIC EDITOR, working for Executive
Editor of this internationally famous magazine directed to the 13-19
age market.

Responsible for:
  - coverage of fabric and fashion markets to be continuously current
    and ahead of trends in order to plan, coordinate and execute monthly
    fashion pages; study and reports on color evolutions.
  - conducting public relations programs, representing magazine as
    lecturing fashion authority; attend fashion shows and business con-
    ferences around U.S. and overseas; consulting with clients with re-
    spect to outlooks, fashion guidance.
  - autonomy to approve fashion pages in absence of editor.

Accomplishments:
  - pages devoted to fabrics doubled and tripled respectively due both
    to increased reader interest and better, more interesting pages.
  - first Fabric Editor at magazine to be sent to Europe to cover Frank-
    furt Fair to report on European influences.
  - made successful presentations to advertisers of such companies as
    Monsanto, J.P. Stevens, DuPont, Celanese.
  - new promotions, such as Dior Daytime Patterns, tied in with major
    department and specialty stores nationally.
  - responsible for new section and magazine cover tying in with Nieman-
    Marcus and Post-Teen Department.

1971-1973 CITY, TOWN & COUNTRY, New York, NY

ASSISTANT TO DIRECTOR OF MERCHANDISING AND PROMOTION with responsibility
for fabric and fashion promotion.
  - edited and supervised production of promotional brochures, including
    fabric reports.
  - made presentations to retail buyers on importance and effectiveness
    of editorial pages; worked cooperative advertising programs with
    multimillion-dollar corporations.

1956-1967 BUTTERY PATTERN COMPANY, New York, NY

Successively ASSISTANT SERVICE EDITOR, ASSOCIATE EDITOR.
  - as Fabric Editor, covered fabric market intensively, presented ideas
    and prognostications to staff, clients, buyers; acted in PR capacity.
  - predicted color and design trends; maintained library; epitomized
    market.

Work was widely recognized, resulting in unsolicited job offers from
three of the major fashion magazines.

EDUCATION:

    Jesuit College, Kansas City, MO, 1954-1958.
    B.S., Merchandising.

HOBBIES:

    SCUBA diving, gourmet cooking, travel.

PERSONAL DATA:

    Age 39, married.

                    REFERENCES AND FURTHER DATA ON REQUEST

RÉSUMÉ REPRODUCTION

In general we prefer a résumé that is reproduced as typed. It looks less studied than a page that resembles a book.

Some others, however, like the formal printed résumé with conformed right-hand margins.

The following résumé has been prepared in the formal manner to give you an opportunity to compare the styles and make your own choice.

Additional diversity and flexibility can be achieved by varying type sizes for headlining and emphasis and by using italic type and decorative typeset lettering.

87 Western Drive   (123) 456-7890
St. Louis, MO (zip)

CONFIDENTIAL RESUME

of

THOMAS MELLON

FINANCIAL EXECUTIVE

***   Consistent record, with various companies, of utilization of financial expertise to improve earnings, increase asset values, establish important lines of credit. Experienced in all facets of financial management; in handling financial public relations and corporate legal matters. Extensive experience in public accounting, taxes, E.D.P., corporate financing.

***   Using sophisticated financial techniques, sound accounting practice, advanced management methods, turned ailing company into highly profitable corporation, doubling its listed stock value in a period of three years.

***   Restructured multimillion-dollar corporation by changing established policies and eliminating losses after years of marginal operation. Accomplished outstanding turnaround for a third company.

***   Now employed, but seeking larger opportunity to exercise competence.

(FOR FURTHER DATA, PLEASE SEE FOLLOWING PAGES)

1973-Present   (NAME OF COMPANY ON REQUEST)

TREASURER, CHIEF FINANCIAL OFFICER, Member, Board of Directors for AMEX-listed industrial products manufacturer, with approximate annual sales of $35 million, four manufacturing plants, three warehouses. Supervise staff of 25, including Controller, Chief Accountant, Cost Accounting Manager, Manager, Inventory Control Manager.

* Responsible for all financial affairs and financial reporting of the Company, Legal Liaison, Financial Public Relations.

* Responsibilities:
  - set up corporate budgets, departmental operating budgets, factory overheads, R.&D., sales and G.&A. expenses; capital appropriations budget.
  - set up standard cost system and departmentalized overheads.
  - recommended profit goals as related to sales; as return on investment; measured progress by 15 relevant financial ratios.
  - calculated cash requirements, evaluated proposed capital expenditures.
  - invested cash in short-term commercial paper or otherwise as indicated currently.
  - handled Company insurance. Set up Company pension plan, secured Government approval; administered stock option and profit-sharing programs. Consulted with other officers on all compensation plans.
  - responsible for S.E.C. filings and all corporate taxes.

* Accomplishments:
  - recommended sale of and sold losing Division.
  - reduced factory costs by approximately $1 million lowering cost of goods sold from 67% of sales to 61%.
  - saved G.&A. expenses by over $1 million annually or a reduction of 37%.
  - reduced audit expenses by $80,000 annually.
  - speeded up billing and reduced receivables turnover time from 90 days to 48 days, with resulting increase of $1.5 million in cash flow.
  - earned $60,000 to $80,000 annually through short-term investments.
  - eliminated all short-term borrowing, reduced long-term debt, improved debt-equity ratio; created high credit rating.
  - increased utilization of EDP by 100% to include all corporate reporting at a cost increase of only 20%.
  - achieved Company turnaround from loss and poor credit position to annual profit after taxes of 9% and R.O.I. of over 22.7%, doubling value of stock in 3 years.

* Additional Accomplishments:
  - set up sales forecasting system for Sales Department using regression analysis techniques.
  - created successful PR effort for financial community.
  - reduced legal fees by $100,000 annually by handling matters within own competence.

1971-1973 SHERIDAN CANDY CORP., Hicksville, OH

GENERAL MANAGER, FINANCE and ACCOUNTING, Assistant to President of $10 million company with staff of five including Vice President-Finance, Treasurer and Controller.

* Administered all financial affairs of Company; by analysis of operations and effective application of financial techniques, succeeded in overcoming losses and achieving breakeven point in first year.
    – established breakeven point for products; closed out production of poor sellers.
    – established departmental budgeting that signaled loss areas, permitting correction and reducing expenses by $25,000.
    – successfully led Company defense against attempt to unionize.

1968-1971 LEED CORP., Hudson, CT

CONTROLLER for this manufacturer of electrical components.

* Operations much as described previously.

1954-1968

Provided financial management for N. HOPPER CO., INC. (paper manufacturer), OVERHEAD DOORS CORP. (garage doors); worked for Certified Public Accounting firms.

* *Education:*
  B.S., Accounting, 1955, University of Michigan.
  M.B.A., Finance, 1979, University of Chicago (attending evenings).
* *Accreditations:*
  C.P.A.
  * *Memberships:*
  The National Association of Financial Executives
* *Personal Data:*
  Age 49, married, one child, excellent health.

REFERENCES AND FURTHER DATA ON REQUEST

Seranade Drive   (107) 000-7711
Las Vegas, NV 00000

R E S U M E

of

HENRY SCARNE

HOTEL EXECUTIVE
for
HOTEL CHAIN or FIRST CLASS HOTEL

***   Comprehensive early training and education in all phases
        of hotel management and for the last ten years significant
        successes in profitable operations and in turning losses
        to profits in large enterprises; in directing construction
        and accomplishing successful opening of major resort hotel
        complex.

***   Accustomed to complete management responsibilities for
        accounting and controls, front office, food and beverage,
        golf course, club house, entertainment and all other
        facilities; and to financial reporting, profit and cash
        flow projections; planning and development.

***   Accomplished also in developing convention business,
        arranging entertainment, providing gourmet food service
        and high level of other services. Experienced in close
        analysis of operating figures and correction of trouble
        areas; in the use of E.D.P. to assist the managerial
        function.

***   Capable in selecting, training and developing management
        talent; possess leadership and empathy.

(FOR FURTHER DATA, PLEASE SEE FOLLOWING PAGES)

252

BUSINESS EXPERIENCE

<u>June 1974-Present</u>   CAESARS HOTEL, LAS VEGAS

GENERAL MANAGER of 800-room hotel, with additional 400 rooms scheduled for opening in January 1976; six specialty restaurants, 600-seat main dining room, three golf courses, club house, beach operation, two pools, convention hall and meeting rooms, night club, discotheque and restaurant, water distillation and recycling plants, housing for staff of 1,000 with staff cafeteria and transportation service.

Responsible for:
- supervision of construction and opening of new $74-million hotel complex.
- staffing and training, marketing, pricing, menu planning.
- September 1975 opening with reception and five-course banquet for 1,100 with floor show.
- reaching occupancy rate in October 1975 of 87% with gross October sales of $1.3 million and average room rate of $80.00 MAP.
- attaining immediate results of 37% food cost, 24% beverage cost; with monthly payroll of $400,000.
- complete plans which will permit additional 400 rooms to be available for occupancy with full services immediately upon completion.
- booking $8.0 million conventions back to back September through June 1976 and similarly for 1977.

Other responsibilities included union negotiations, advance planning, budgeting, guest relations, advertising and all other management activities for entire operation.

<u>1963-1974</u>   KNOTT INTERNATIONAL HOTEL CORP., (Bermuda)

VICE PRESIDENT and GENERAL MANAGER. Hotel opened in 1969 with poor start. Persuaded by President of Knott International to operate this new hotel. Accomplishments included:
- made complete necessary reorganization to save money including Sales Department.
- by 1971 an increase in gross sales of $1.2 million.
- improvement in operating profit by $800,000.
- sell-off of unprofitable operations reducing corporation to half its original size.

<u>1965-1973</u>   BERMUDA BEACH HOTEL, Bermuda

VICE PRESIDENT and GENERAL MANAGER. Unit suffered loss of $453,000 in 1962. Following four-month loss of $301,000 in four months 1961.
- instituted immediate cost reduction programs.
- reoriented marketing and advertising to highlight travel agency sales.
- established personalized services.
- created management development program.
- took other necessary steps.

The following figures show results accomplished (000 omitted):

1967 $277
1968 $325
1969 $375
1970 $427
1971 $482
1972 $523
1973 $670
1974 $940

The audited results for this 200-room hotel in 1969 showed $4.2 million gross revenue with a gross operating profit of $1.7 million. Corporation recovered all losses during this period.

1964-1965   CORAL BEACH CLUB, Bermuda

RESIDENT MANAGER.

1963-1964   KNOTT INTERNATIONAL HOTEL CORP., New York, NY

NEW YORK SALES MANAGER for Coral Beach Club

1962-1963   WATERLOO HOUSE, Bermuda

U.S. SALES MANAGER. Directed sales activities of hotel until sale of property was announced.

1961-1962   HENRY ADDISON, 800 Fifth Avenue, New York, NY

NEW YORK DISTRICT SALES MANAGER for Hotel Representative firm. Handled sales in the New York District.
- responsible for 59% of convention sales ($2.3 million).

MILITARY SERVICE:

1959-1960   U.S. ARMY, Lieutenant

EDUCATION:

B.S., Hotel Administration, Cornell University
Seminars in Advanced Management, Decision Processes
Grid School. T. Groupings
Worked in hotels during summer vacations.

PROFESSIONAL MEMBERSHIPS:

Board of Directors, A.H.M.A.; Executive Committee, A.H.M.A.; Member, Board of Directors, Florida Knott International Corp.; SKAL; ASTA.

PERSONAL DATA: Born 5/14/40; married, two children, excellent health.

REFERENCES AND FURTHER DATA ON REQUEST

1831 Log Cabin Drive   Home (201) 327-5251
Cuyahoga, OH 23320   Office (212) 001-1111

R E S U M E

of

WILLIAM ABRAM GARFIELD

OBJECTIVE

Vice President or Director of Marketing, domestic and/or international, or General Manager in the U.S. of division of multinational company.

SUMMARY and QUALIFICATIONS

*** Nearly 18 years of success in the chemical and textile industries
for major companies, plus extensive educational background in
both areas.

*** Experience includes full marketing direction with staff of 70
after stages in R.&D., manufacturing, production planning, sales
management, product management, technical promotion, advertising,
key account liaison, pricing strategy, profit margin improvement.

*** Experience also encompasses these activities both in the U.S. and
overseas. Possess intimate understanding of European business
attitudes and needs with the ability to merge differing philosophies
into successful common objectives. Multilingual

*** Record of success in introducing new products and increasing market
share with continuously increasing responsibilities to present position. Participated in spectacular turnaround for present employer.

*** Able to train, lead, motivate; to recognize and exploit business
opportunities.

*** Chemical Engineering degree and continuing educational involvement.

(FOR FURTHER DATA PLEASE SEE FOLLOWING PAGE)

255

EXPERIENCE

<u>1971-Present</u>   STEVENS & BURLINGTON CORP., Cleveland, OH
                (Dyes & Chemicals Div.)

VICE PRESIDENT, Marketing and member of Management Committee for $100 million division of $720 million manufacturer of dyes and chemicals for the textile and paper markets, fragrances, and other chemical products.

Earlier (1976-1980), Director of Marketing with staff of 40-50 and direct reporting group of eight.

1973-1975, successively Sales Manager, Middle States; Product Manager, Senior Product Manager.

Achievements:
- accomplished spectacular turnaround for Division, which since 1976 has become a leader in the industry noted for its marketing and earnings.
- earlier as Product Manager produced significant sales gains.

<u>1960-1970</u>   AAKEN A.G., Geneva, Switzerland and Dayton, OH

   <u>1970</u> Permanently relocated to the U.S. to aid company in divestiture of Division, caused by merger. Aided in formation of Estoril Corp. for acquisition by Stevens & Burlington.

   <u>1969-1972</u> Temporarily relocated to U.S. to introduce chemical agents to textile industry. In 1971, additional responsibilities were assigned for the promotional coordination of dyes and chemicals in the U.S.
   - accomplished high share of market for synthetic fabrics.
   - increased company market share in all dyes and chemicals.

<u>1962-1968</u>   APPLICATION and DEVELOPMENT GROUP LEADER, Geneva

- aided in development of FWA application technology; awarded patents
- created technical literature including comprehensive volume on new technology.
- wrote for many publications; held many speaking engagements; made promotional visits to the U.S. and many other markets; became leading expert in the field.
- Aaken became leader in chemical agents worldwide.

<u>EDUCATION:</u>   C.E., Chemical Engineer, Stevens Institute, Hoboken, NJ, 196
                 Subsequent training included spinning, weaving, dyeing, finishing, printing, accounting, supervisory experience in all departments of two of the largest companies in New Jersey.

<u>LANGUAGES:</u>   German, French, Spanish, Portuguese, Italian

<u>HOBBIES:</u>   Tennis, skiing, soccer, opera

<u>PERSONAL DATA:</u> Age 40, married, three children, excellent health. Father was a chemical executive who traveled extensively in Europe with his family, giving me an opportunity to exercise my ability to learn languages with relative ease.

<u>REFERENCES AND FURTHER DATA ON REQUEST</u>

28 Bainbridge Place
New York, NY (zip)

Home (212) 123-4567
Office (212) 765-4321

R E S U M E

of

RICHARD STERN

Qualified as

SALES/MARKETING EXECUTIVE

*** Learned the techniques of sales management in the field
as a salesman. Developed new accounts, opened up new
territories. Handled key accounts.

*** Devised programs, displays, assortments to meet the
needs of new classes of trade. Expanded distribution.
Created new selling units producing better profits.
Recruited, trained, managed salesmen.

*** Excellent contacts nationally among mass merchandisers,
chains, department stores, stamp and mail order companies, drug chains and hardware wholesalers, supermarkets.

*** Experienced in budgeting, forecasting, advertising,
sales presentations, sales meetings, remuneration, new
product development.

(FOR FURTHER DATA, PLEASE SEE FOLLOWING PAGES)

EXPERIENCE

<u>Sept. 1973-Present</u>   (NAME OF COMPANY ON REQUEST)

NATIONAL SALES MANAGER for manufacturer of household products, casters, waxes, stains, cleaners, venetian blinds, plastic covers; 200 employees and a sales force of 40 covering the entire United States. Report to President. Responsible for:

- recruiting, training and directing salesmen.
- planning participation in appropriate trade shows.
- key account development, sales and supervision.
- sales forecasts, budgets, pricing and profitability.
- new product development, displays and packaging.
- preparation of essential sales tools such as sales training material, catalog pages, advertising planning.

Successful in:
- replacing unprofitable line with highly profitable new lines, increasing volume.
- effective repackaging of entire line.
- increasing sales by means of unique and exclusive exchange plan.
- opening new accounts which added 20% to Company volume.
- developing strong accounts throughout the U.S. in areas where Company had been traditionally weak.
- meeting and outselling competitors in such accounts as Mass Merchandisers, Catalog and Mail Order Companies, Variety Chains, Drug Chains, Supermarkets.
- making Company number one in field among all above classes of trade.

Travel extensively throughout the U.S.; maintain excellent contacts with major buyers nationally.

<u>1971-1973</u>   HAMILTON CREATIONS, INC., New York, NY

<u>1972-1973</u>, FIELD SALES MANAGER (Assistant to National Sales Manager) supervising sales force of 40 manufacturers representatives with department store line and separate brand for mass merchandisers.

Responsible for:
- discovering ways to increase sales.

Accomplishments:
- worked with salesmen on short trips; achieved immediate results in opening new accounts for new department store line; appointed Field Sales Manager.
- found Company department store oriented; developed concepts for mass merchandisers to fit individual customer needs such as prearranged assortments using existing displays, for drug and hardware chains.
- sold hundreds of small new accounts and rack assortments without which new line would have been dropped.

1971-1972, SALESMAN, New York Metropolitan Area, for parent company and
subsidiary selling consumer equipment: hampers, space savers, baskets,
brushholders, tank cabinets, ice buckets, picnic kits, etc.

Responsible for:
- selling to major department stores and independent retailers.

Accomplishments:
- created effective promotions with major accounts.
- sold to new accounts including major home furnishings chain.
- increased volume over 20% in one year.

MILITARY SERVICE:

U.S. Navy, 1964-1966, Boatswain's Mate First Class.

EDUCATION:

B.S., Rutgers University, New Brunswick, NJ, 1970.

HOBBIES:

Tennis, bridge, chess.

PERSONAL DATA:

Age 31, married, two children, own home, excellent health. Willing to
relocate.

REFERENCES AND FURTHER DATA ON REQUEST

100 Pound Ridge Road
Clayton, MO (zip)

Home (123) 456-7890
Office (246) 321-4567

R E S U M E

of

JOHN T. MORRIS

Qualified in

FINANCIAL MARKETING

*** Strong personal motivation with successful background in management, sales, corporate and individual financial planning, systems and organization and excellent record of volume and profit contributions in every position held from beginning of career. Able to conceive and implement broad, complex programs to reach new goals.

*** History of numerous top awards and commendations for setting and achieving high sales objectives as well as for developing marketing plans, motivating staff and raising branch offices to national leadership.

*** Experienced recruiter and trainer of top producers in the industry, consistently sought by competitive firms because of known qualities of outstanding leadership and empathy and ability to communicate.

*** Accustomed to negotiations at highest levels, assigned responsibilities for large accounts with resulting growth and development to major status under most competitive conditions.

*** Experienced in profit sharing, pension and insurance planning for major corporations, and in maximum E.D.P. utilization.

(FOR FURTHER DATA, PLEASE SEE FOLLOWING PAGES)

EXPERIENCE

<u>1977-Present</u>   NEW HORIZONS RESEARCH CORP., St. Louis, MO

DIRECTOR of CLIENT RELATIONS for investment research company providing investment management for portfolios of individuals, pension and profit-sharing funds, corporate accounts, trusts and institutions. Investment recommendation featured in Forbe's (1/15/78). Responsible for:
- marketing management, marketing research, gaining new clients, liaison with existing clients.

Accomplishments:
- created complete marketing program where no program existed.
- trained network of Registered Representatives working for N.Y.S.E. member brokerage firms to sell our services.
- gained listing on Hemphill, Merrill, Hayden, Bache & Smith, Inc. approved list of investment advisors.
- initiated tax advisory program for professional individuals through a prominent Missouri law firm to assist with:
  * incorporating individuals
  * pension and profit-sharing plans
  * deferred compensation
  * Keogh plans.
- achieving letter of intent to manage $50 million in-house investment management program for large brokerage firm to begin in January upon expiration of contract with another firm.

<u>1972-1977</u>   CORVATH, HAYES CO., St. Louis, MO

MANAGER, St. Louis Office (earlier Assistant Manager), for national brokerage with 80 offices from coast to coast and total assets approaching $1 billion. The company handles retail, commercial and corporate accounts and deals in preferred and common stock, corporate and municipal bonds, mutual funds and insurance for corporations. Supervise 29 salesmen through three Assistant Managers and back-office staff of nine. Responsible for:
- setting up new salesmen, training program, establishing guidelines for sales approaches, encouraging customer contacts.
- handling new stock and bond offering calendar.
- personal selling, providing investment ideas, generating sales.
- liaison with leading corporations whose stock is recommended.
- corporate profit-sharing, pension and insurance planning for major companies.

(continued)

Accomplishments:
- brought office to second most profitable nationally from a position seldom among top 20.
- recruited and trained the two top producers in the office who now rank among the top ten nationwide.
- personally generated substantial sales while concurrently effective in administrative duties.

1966-1972 CONROY ELLIMAN SECURITIES, Mission Hills, KS

SALESMAN FOR BROKERAGE FIRM.
- increased personal sales production over 200% in six years.
- awarded gold prize for generating $10,000 in commissions in one month.
- awarded diamond prize for generating $20,000 in commissions in one month.
- chosen to speak to 200 salesmen on Salesmanship at headquarters meeting.
- won five-day trip to Hawaii in Mutual Funds Sales Contest.

1964-1966 MERRILL, SMITH & MORGAN, New York, NY

SECURITY ANALYST, RESEARCH TRAINEE for large brokerage firm. Received excellent training for future personal development in financial selling, service and analysis.

EDUCATION:

B.S., Economics, University of Kansas, Kansas City, KS 1964.

OUTSIDE ACTIVITIES:

Instructor, Adult Education Classes, N.Y. Stock Exchange program. Coach, Youth Athletic Association baseball team.

MEMBERSHIPS:

Bond Club of Missouri; Member, Chamber of Commerce

PERSONAL DATA:

Age 37, married, three children, own home, excellent health.

REFERENCES AND FURTHER DATA ON REQUEST

1856 Staunton Path
New York, NY (zip)

Home (212) 123-4567
Office (212) 957-6543

RESUME

of

WILLIAM WILSON

Qualified

MARKETING EXECUTIVE in PETROLEUM/CHEMICAL INDUSTRIES

*** Widely experienced in marketing, economic and forward
planning in petroleum and chemical industries with strong
background in chemistry; for large independent international oil company, and formerly for Getto Chemical Co.

*** Record of major contributions in increased revenues, cost
savings; in leadership and revitalization of underproductive
departments; in research, analysis and recommendations
with respect to feedstocks, tankage, storage, production
and marketing maximization, cost control, economics, forecasting, budgeting.

*** Accustomed to P.& L. responsibility requiring comprehensive knowledge of all operations; frequently called as
expert witness at Federal hearings affecting the petroleum
industry.

*** Consistent growth with present and previous employer to
positions of increased responsibility and excellent record
of achievement in each position. Equipped for leadership
in search for new energy sources and better use of energy.

*** Rhodes Scholar, First Class Honors in Chemistry. Fluent
in French.

(FOR FURTHER DATA, PLEASE SEE FOLLOWING PAGES)

263

BUSINESS EXPERIENCE:

1969-Present   ENERGY OIL CO., New York, NY, $500 million independent oil
                refiner and manufacturer of chemicals.

1977-Present, DISTRIBUTION PLANNING MANAGER. Report to V.P. Planning.
Responsible for planning and economics associated with marketing, distribution, feedstock purchase, storage and shipping of Company products.
- developed data on costs, profit margins, availabilities permitting
  superior decision-making with risk and sensitivity evaluations.
- drew up share-of-market, distribution terminals, feedstock, optimum market, dockage comparison, tankage plans under normal and
  "energy crisis" conditions.
- acted as expert witness at Government hearings on costs and
  prices in the oil industry.
- developed cost bases for increased profitability.
- thorough analysis of fuel and feedstock contracts provided basic
  plan for renegotiations, saving millions of dollars.
Result of work: raised Company margin on its petroleum and L.P.G.
volume from $6 to $8 million.

1976-1977, OPERATIONS PLANNING MANAGER, Virgin Islands. Supervised
15 graduate chemical engineers, clerical personnel. Responsible for
all aspects of planning and economics for large petroleum and petro-
chemical plant including plant utilization, costs, feedstock alloca-
tions, scheduling, storage planning, forecasting, budgets, new plant
economics.
- exercised leadership to revitalize organization and encouraged
  completion of studies on costs, tankage development and use, optimum blending, optimum component use, plant shutdown economics.
- from these studies made recommendations which were implemented
  and are now drawing benefits.
Asked to assume similar but increased responsibilities at New York
office.

1959-1970   ARABIAN CHEMICAL ET CIE, Paris, France, for the French
             affiliate of Arabian Chemical, U.S.A., largest chemical
             company in France with revenues of $550 million, 2,700 em-
             ployees. Company produced Ethylene, Propylene, Butadiene,
             synthetic rubber, solvents, fuel and lubrication additives
             and specialties.

1967-1970, PLANNING GROUP MANAGER. Reported to Manufacturing Manager.
Supervised graduate engineers. Responsible for:
- feedstock evaluation
- scheduling
- yield monitoring
- cost control and development
- financial and production forecasts
- economic planning

Achievements included:
- development of department as the authoritative source of economic data and planning for the Company in France and internationally.
- saved more than $2 million annually through a mass balance/yield reporting system permitting refinement of feedstock evaluation and monitoring of plant yield deterioration at early stage.
- 4.5% reduction in utility consumption.

1965-67, ASSISTANT MARKETING MANAGER, Paris, France. Responsible for marketing Ethylene, Propylene, Butadiene, Benzene and other industrial chemicals through contract negotiations, spot sales, development of existing customers; responsible for profitability.

- negotiated two major contracts involving several million dollars.
- maintained and developed a series of highly profitable spot sales.
- successfully developed markets for new products.

1959-1965   HUMBLE OIL CO., Foxworth, London

1962-1965, MARKET RESEARCH. Made detailed reports on Polyolefins, oxo alcohols. Ethylene oxide and Nitriles, alcohols, plastics and worldwide economic conditions. Visited Spain, England, Kuwait, Iran.

1962, LABORATORY ASSISTANT. Worked on oxidation of hydrocarbons, aromatic and aliphatic.

MILITARY SERVICE:

1957-1959   United Kingdom. Demobilized as 1st Lt./Royal Artillery.

EDUCATION:

1960-1965, Cambridge College of Technology, Cambridge, England, B.S.
1960, Associate King's Institute of Chemistry (equivalent to M.S.).

LANGUAGES:

Fluent French.

PERSONAL DATA:

Age 38, married, two children, own home, excellent health.

REFERENCES AND FURTHER DATA ON REQUEST

37 East Corsica Street
Blooming Grave, NY (zip)

Home (212) 765-4321
Office (212) 123-4567

R E S U M E

of

FLORENCE DeW. HARDING

PERSONNEL EXECUTIVE

*** After receiving Master's Degree in Sociology at the University
of Chicago, employed as Stewardess by United Airlines; promoted
after six months to PR and training assignments.

*** Since that time and for 12 years to present, engaged in Personnel
Administration and continuing study with increasingly important
responsibilities for 3 employers. Currently Personnel Director
of $50 million manufacturing company.

*** Experienced in labor relations, new employee indoctrination programs, benefits, remuneration, job descriptions, employee review
programs, security, recruiting to $50,000 annual salary level,
Federal and State employment laws. Saved present employer hundreds
of thousands of dollars in potential liability by instituting
wage and salary increases under salary equalization program between men and women more than 3 years ago.

*** Invited to conduct seminar in labor relations by leading international management association. Complimented on organization
and content.

*** Age 35, married, B.B.A. and M.S. degrees, excellent health.

(FOR FURTHER DATA PLEASE SEE FOLLOWING PAGES)

EXPERIENCE

<u>1975-Present</u>   (NAME OF COMPANY ON REQUEST), New York Area

DIRECTOR OF PERSONNEL (started as Assistant Director) for well-known manufacturer of communication equipment for industry, municipal, State and Federal law enforcement agencies, transit authorities and the Military. Supervise staff of 10. Report to President. Responsible for:

- recruiting, wage and salary administration, records and procedures, employee benefits, employee relations and social activities and plant security.
- labor relations, settlement of union grievances, participation in union contract negotiations; appearances before the National Labor Relations Board.
- preparation of job descriptions for all clerical, administrative and executive personnel.
- manpower development planning.
- budget administration.
- employee food services.
- development and improvement of work flow forms; continuing study to improve existing programs.

Accomplishments:

- recognized potential impact of Fair Employment Practices Act; studied job responsibilities and titles; upgraded female employees; avoided litigation for unfair practices; estimated saving to company in potential liability of $780,000.
- credited with superior judgment in hiring middle and upper management executives to $50,000 annual remuneration.
- studied national labor scales by job classifications; recommended upgrading salary and piecework rates; avoided strike in 1978 which had previously occurred during every three-year negotiation period since 1969.
- improved employee cafeteria with better food quality, attractive lounges, recreation area.
- conducted regular program of employee indoctrination; reduced turnover rate by 43%.

<u>1970-1975</u>   CONTINENTAL AIRWAYS, INC., Kansas City, MO

MANAGER, Employee Motivation Services. Responsible for:

- in-flight and ground crew uniforms, training, motivation, grooming (3,000 women, 2,000 men) involving Flight Attendants, Pursers, Ticket Desk, Passenger Assistance, Mechanics, Porters, Marketing Personnel.
- grievance hearings and settlements as possible.
- budget of $3 million.

Accomplishments:

- selected uniforms for 14 different employee categories, gained management approval, organized simultaneous changes for all employees and met established deadline. Changes previously had been accomplished in classification segments and were invariably late.

267

1970-1975 (continued)
- set up training programs for Flight Attendants in smaller groups with superior results as shown by tests.
- improved employee service to public by initiating employee relations programs: meetings with top executives, better interemployee communications, prizes recognizing exceptional service, better employee ground facilities.

TRAINING SUPERVISOR, Flight Attendants.

- set up new training program.
- conducted PR seminars throughout Greater Chicago area.

Earlier STEWARDESS (Flight Attendant) for six months.

EDUCATION:

  M.S., Sociology, University of Chicago, 1966.

  B.A., University of Chicago, Chicago, IL, 1965. Dean's List Junior and Senior years. Elected to honorary society; Homecoming Queen.

  Special courses over a period of five years (evenings) at New York University in Personnel, Labor Relations for Non-Lawyers, Manpower Development Planning, Laws Relating to Employment.

HOBBIES:

  Golf, tennis, swimming, travel.

PERSONAL DATA:

  Married, one child, excellent health.

REFERENCES AND FURTHER DATA ON REQUEST

213 Seesaw Avenue   (201) 000-1234
Belmar, NJ 07000

R E S U M E

of

OTTO HELMSTETTER

PLANT/PRODUCTION MANAGER
METALWORKING AND PLASTIC

***   Qualified manager, experienced in metalworking production, equipment maintenance and supervision. Learned as apprentice in Germany; added to skills in assignments in the U.S. over a period of 19 years.

***   Competent in tool and die making, fixturing, welding, production planning and scheduling, purchasing equipment and materials, adapting equipment to accomplish better production, fabricating machines or parts from blueprints or sketches, engineering development work; and repair and rebuilding of industrial equipment.

***   Experience includes forging, heat treating, machining, EDM machines, design of fixtures and custom-made tools, plastic extrusion, compounding machinery, packaging machinery, industrial and marine pumps.

***   Record of improving production efficiency, reducing costs, minimizing downtime, contributing to profitability.

***   Accustomed to supervision, setting standards, leading. A shirt-sleeve manager who can accomplish any mechanical job personally and show others how it should be accomplished.

(FOR FURTHER DETAILS SEE FOLLOWING PAGES)

EXPERIENCE

1977-Present   S.M.C. COMPANY, Carlstadt, NJ

PRODUCTION MANAGER of the largest shop for freight car and industrial repair on the East Coast. Report to the Vice President.

Responsible for:
  - entire plant production

Accomplishments:
  - improved planning and flow of work through shop by establishing new
    procedures and methods
  - increased production and profits by proper delegation of responsibility
  - competed successfully against other O.E.M.'s by providing quality
    workmanship with shorter delivery times

1975-1977   WESTINGHOUSE ELECTRIC CO., Service Shop, Saddle River, NJ

MECHANICAL SPECIALIST in the mechanical department of one of the largest
Westinghouse service shops in the U.S.A.

Responsible for:
  - quoting, selling, planning and follow-through of all mechanical work
  - repair and rebuilding of industrial equipment

Accomplishments:
  - promoted from mechanical supervisor to mechanical specialist within
    four months
  - designed custom-made tools to perform equipment repairs in the shop,
    as well as for on-site work
  - made suggestions and submitted cost improvements resulting in savings
    in excess of $125,000.

1969-1975   WILLIAMS STEEL CO., INC., Purchase, NY

PLANT SUPERINTENDENT of $1.5 million manufacturer of tools and dies, en-
graving tools, molds, hobs and coining dies. Supervised 20 to 30 machinists,
tool and diemakers, engravers; with complete general machine shop.

Responsible for:
  - all manufacturing operations

Accomplishments:
  - reorganized inefficient shop
  - changed production flow; purchased new equipment; built new fixtures;
    separated inefficient personnel; reduced work crew from 36 to 16 top
    craftsmen and increased production

270

1968-1969   WESTOVER EXTRUDER CORP., Irvington, NJ

Manufacturer of plastic extruders, compounding machines and blow molding
equipment. GENERAL FOREMAN of fabricating, welding, grinding, assembly,
machine shop, auxilliary department and plant in Ohio. Supervised labor
force of 100 to 125.

Responsible for:
  - administrative supervision
  - production from engineering to finished products

Accomplishments:
  - made needed corrections in disorganized and unsafe shop
  - set up new procedures, reduced downtime

Company moved to South Carolina.

1966-1968   STUMPF & KOERNER CORP., Chadwick, NJ

This U.S. branch of Germany-headquartered company manufactures plastic
extruders and compounding machines. TECHNICAL SERVICE ENGINEER.

Responsible for:
  - installation of equipment, startups and troubleshooting
  - customer service

1960-1966   PROCTER & GAMBLE, Elizabeth, NJ

TOP ENGINEERING/DEVELOPMENT MACHINIST in packaging machinery plant of this
giant international company. ACTING SUPERVISOR in absence of Supervisor.

Responsible for:
  - parts fabrication and assembly of prototype packaging machinery

Accomplishments:
  - fabricated automatic and semiautomatic machines from engineering in-
    structions and drawings
  - started as machinist first class; promoted after six months

1956-1959   M. M. HOECHST GmbH, Waldenheim, Germany

WORKING FOREMAN, MAINTENANCE for manufacturer of paper-making machinery,
power turbines, hydraulic transmissions and clutches.

1951-1956   FIELD SERVICE TECHNICIAN for above. Traveled throughout Europe.

1950-1951   IN TRAINING with above company.

1945-1949   Served MECHANIC APPRENTICESHIP with Zuyderzeeschleiferel Oelze,
Waldenheim.

EDUCATION:

    Junior College, Germany, 1944-1945; Trade School, Germany, 1945-1948
    B.S., Rutgers University, 1964-1965.

LANGUAGES: Fluent German

PERSONAL DATA:

    Born March 31, 1930, married, two children, excellent health
    U.S.A. citizen

REFERENCES AND FURTHER DATA ON REQUEST

30 Hermitage   Home (212) 070-3131
Chappaqua, NY 00000   Office (212) 111-2222

R E S U M E

of

JOSEPH R. MAZDA

MANUFACTURING/OPERATIONS/GENERAL MANAGER

SUMMARY

***   From beginning of career, 1964, to present with leading
         manufacturer of metal components, starting as Engineer
         in Training through seven promotions to present position
         as Director of Manufacturing.

***   Record of creating cost savings, increasing R.O.I., con-
         sistently gaining greater productivity, innovating in
         technology. Hold three patents. Author of papers on
         worker motivations and precision instrument ball bearings.

***   Accomplished turnaround for deficient division, including
         new products, new image, new customers and tripling of
         sales.

***   As head of new products committee worked with major con-
         sultants, found new product now ready for marketing,
         participated in two acquisition negotiations.

***   Experienced in all forms of metalworking from forging
         and stamping to plating and assembly. Able to lead, com-
         municate, motivate, decide.

(FOR FURTHER DETAILS, SEE FOLLOWING PAGES)

EXPERIENCE

<u>1964-Present</u>   PNEUMATIC BUSHING CO., Div. DATRON INC.
            Belgrade, NY

<u>1977-Present</u>, DIRECTOR OF MANUFACTURING for $160 million manufacturer of
precision parts. Operations include forging, stamping, heat treating, machining, precision grinding, polishing, plating, coating, assembly. Supervise five U.S. plants with 5,000 employees.

Responsible for:
- complete operations of all plants which include 12 profit centers;
  participation in labor negotiations.

Accomplishments:
- monitor and document continuous cost performance analysis; reorganized
  staff to achieve 13% productivity improvement in 1979; reached 6% productivity improvement in 1978 with saving of $5 million
- sponsored foreman efficiency reward programs involving series of personal meetings with 140 foremen providing leadership and communications,
  and establishing goals and incentives
- improved on-time performance with customers; reduced overdue commitments
- set, and with few exceptions met, R.O.I. objectives by profit centers
- participated in factory computer control project expected to contribute
  further improvement in productivity
- appointed to represent Company at elite Industrial Machinery Institute,
  member of Manufacturing Council; delivered paper before Institute "Improved Operations Through Tier Training"
- company received two awards for plant safety record - from Datron - and
  more are forthcoming in 1980
- appointed to labor negotiating committee
- improved scrap by 12%

<u>1974-1977</u>, GENERAL MANUFACTURING MANAGER

Responsibilities much as described before, for four plants in New Jersey

<u>1973-1974</u>, DIRECTOR OF PRODUCT DIVERSIFICATION

Headed new products committee; employed and worked with management consulting firms such as Booz, Allen, Hamilton; personally recommended new
product (transmission units) now ready for marketing. Also involved in
two acquisition negotiations.

<u>1970-1973</u> PROJECT MANAGER

Assigned to correct operating deficiencies in division:
- conducted marketing research; called on prospective customers; created
  new product line and identity; added major new high precision product
  line for computers, missiles, space vehicles; <u>tripled sales</u>

<u>1964-1970</u> Successively, Engineer in Training, Application Engineer, Senior Engineer in Charge, Engineering Manager

EDUCATION:

Degree, <u>Management Engineering</u>, M.I.T., Cambridge, MA. Minor: Mechanical Engineering with Electrical Engineering, 1964

Harvard University School of Business Administration, intensive Executive Development Program sponsored by Datron

EXTRACURRICULAR ACTIVITIES:

Secretary and Honor Board (elected) Interfraternity Council.

Summer jobs each year 1958-1961; Engineering Assistant; Crib Attendant (Pratt & Whitney); Maintenance, Connecticut General.

PROFESSIONAL MEMBERSHIPS:

Science Foundation, Air Force Association, Component Manufacturers Association (Tech subcommittee), MPI (Machinery Products Institute)

COMMUNITY ACTIVITIES:

Vice Chairman, Zoning Board of Appeals, Chappaqua
Chairman, Corporate Gifts (raised $250,000, 1977-1978)
Vice Chairman, Board of Special Assessors
President, High Gee Association
Justice of the Peace

COMPANY ACTIVITIES:

Chairman, U.S. Savings Bond Drive
Company won three awards for percent of participation, increases in new enrollments, increases in amounts deducted, 1977
New York Committee on Business Planning

HOBBIES:

Tennis, platform tennis, sailing, cross country skiing, hunting, fishing, travel, electronic assemblies

PERSONAL DATA:

Age 38, married, three children, own home, excellent health

<u>REFERENCES AND FURTHER DATA ON REQUEST</u>

196 Garth Road
Scarsdale, New York 10583

Home (914) 725-5687
Office (212) 687-2323

R E S U M E

of

ALLEN ROOSEVELT

OBJECTIVE

Involvement in real estate analysis and acquisition for company with large funds available for investment in real estate at optimum yields.

SUMMARY AND QUALIFICATIONS

* * * Competent in real estate portfolio evaluation, and real estate appraisal and analysis, including all elements involved in the decision-making process for investment, divestment or use.

* * * Special expertise in analysis and valuation of regional shopping centers; in the restructuring of all components of an income statement to estimate market value of income-producing properties of all kinds; for "Blue Ribbon" clients.

* * * Experienced in interfacing with and advising clients - developers, bankers, corporations, major law firms.

* * * Record of reliable analysis and creativity in the identification of real estate investment opportunities.

* * * J.D. and B.A. degrees. Age 32.

(FOR FURTHER DATA, PLEASE SEE FOLLOWING PAGES)

EXPERIENCE

1976-Present ANALYTICAL ASSOCIATES, INC., Houston, TX

ASSOCIATE (investment analyst/appraiser) for widely respected real estate consulting firm with "Fortune 500" clients.

Responsibilities and Accomplishments:
- land use, valuation, investment analysis, market and feasibility studies from inception to consummation; including net operating income and expense projections, tax and operating expense escalations, lease expirations, overage and/or percentage rent projections, discounted cash flow analyses; after considering physical condition, demographics (trends), location, debt structure and costs; to arrive at market value for the purposes of investment, portfolio review, disposition, mortgage financing, internal financial planning
- work of this nature nationally involving such diverse projects as regional shopping centers, office buildings, land development, apartments, industrial complexes, ranging in value from a few million dollars to $350 million or more
- specifically, such assignments include valuation of fees underlying major office buildings on Michigan Avenue (Chicago); land use and market studies for proposed large scale multifamily residential developments; appraisal of regional shopping centers in Ohio, Indiana and New Mexico; portfolio reviews of major REITS; valuation of properties net leased to A&P, Burger King, Singer Co and other major retailers; appraisal of 25 industrial warehouses in eight different cities; investment analysis of real estate arm of major investment banking institution; valuation of office buildings and air rights over buildings in Houston involving such clients as B.I.G. Property Investors, Standard and Poors, Metropolitan, Houston Public Library, Illinois Consolidated Gas, Citibank, Baltusrol Development Corp., Western Pacific.
- the preparation of opinions used as the basis for multimillion-dollar investment or divestment decisions
- most of the above activities require the computation of pretax and aftertax yields
- interfacing with clients as to advisability of purchasing fees, air rights, major tenant equity interests in proposed office buildings, and lease negotiations (for major office space)

1974-1976 EQUITABLE LIFE ASSURANCE COMPANY, Dallas, TX

REAL ESTATE INVESTMENT ANALYST for insurance company with assets of $1.4 billion.

Responsible for:
- analysis of purchase and development of raw land into apartments, condominiums and office buildings

- recommendations with respect to problem loans
- legal review of purchases, sales, underwritings; selection of and coordination with local counsel for bankruptcies and foreclosures
- appraisals for insurance and valuations for sales
- work on major bankruptcy involving company loans of $8 million

Accomplishments:
- recommended better utilization of accelerated depreciation, prepaid
  interest and other tax advantages to shelter income
- recommended studies of residual value of property, maximization of
  useful life, projection of income and expenses, capital gains, and the
  recapture of excess depreciation on individual properties to increase
  return on invested assets
- instrumental in arranging $6 million in tax-free income by putting to-
  gether a package of five wholly owned apartment complexes and avoiding a capital gain from their sale by retaining ownership and mort-
  gaging through a California S.&L. company

1973 CLAYTON ADVERTISING INC., Dallas, TX

ASSISTANT ACCOUNT MANAGER. Decided to return to real estate field.

1972-1973 SMITH & CO., Salt Lake City, UT

REAL ESTATE BROKER for largest full-service real estate company in the
Rocky Mountain region, managing more than $250 million in property and
with sales exceeding $100 million.

1971-1972 DOBERMAN & PINCHER, Salt Lake City, UT

LAW CLERK, INSTRUCTOR in real estate school owned and operated by this law
firm. Students achieved the highest examination-passing percentage in the
state.

EDUCATION:

J.D., Moravian University, Logan UT; Legal Aid and Defender Program; National
  Moot Court Competition, interschool
B.A., History, Miami University of Ohio, 1968. Active in intramural sports.
  Editor of compos mentos paper.
Rice University Real Estate Institute, 1974-Present (six courses)
Courses 1A and 1B sponsored by the American Institute of Real Estate Ap-
  praisers.

ACCREDITATIONS:

Licensed Real Estate Salesman in third year at law school
Licensed Real Estate Broker immediately upon graduation
Member, Real Estate Board of Texas, Inc.

HOBBIES:

Handball, platform tennis, tennis, bridge, riding

PERSONAL DATA:

Single, engaged to be married, excellent health

REFERENCES AND FURTHER DATA ON REQUEST

1905 Plymouth Street   Home   (212) 362-9232
New York, NY 10023   Office (212) 736-8900
                                                                           X39

R E S U M E

of

GRACE COOLIDGE

OBJECTIVE

Sportswear buyer; buying office market
representative

QUALIFICATIONS and SUMMARY

Experienced sportswear buyer (5 years) for chain of
23 quality department stores with record of planning
and producing volume multiplication, and introducing
new departmental subdivisions, new concepts and new
lines.

EXPERIENCE

1974-Present   FEDERATED RETAILERS, INC., New York, NY

1978-Present BUYER, SPORTSWEAR, for chain of 23 department stores in
12 states throughout the Midwest. Total volume approximately $41 million;
sportswear $12 million. Quality moderate to better; emphasis on brand
names using such resources as Trissi, Devon, Fire Islander, Ship 'n Shore,
Koret, Levi, Dunloggin and some lower-priced lines. Report to Divisional
Merchandise Manager.

Responsible for:
- buying for all stores, with an open-to-buy of $5.0 million
- all missy sportswear - coordinates, separates, blouses, skirts, sweaters;
  also large sizes
- all swimwear, with $500.000 O-T-B
- junior and missy designer jeans
- exercise wear
- planning; accompanying individual store executives on market trips

280

Accomplishments:
- instituted Danskin program using warehouse as a distribution center; developed volume as follows: 1978, 4,000 units; 1979, 10,000 units (est.)
- introduced Calvin Klein jeans in 2 stores, now featured in all stores; volume rose from zero to 7,000 units (denim and corduroy), 1979
- developed "large size" sportswear department started in 4 stores, now expanded to 13, all successful
- started rapidly growing basic denim and stretch gabardine programs throughout chain

1974-1978   FEDERATED RETAILERS CORP., Dayton, OH

DEPARTMENT MANAGER, Sportswear Department, for $1.5 million junior department store. Reported to Store Manager.

Responsible for:
- all aspects of day-to-day departmental management including stock, inventory, scheduling, markdowns
- regular New York buying trips

Accomplishments:
- increased departmental volume from $230,000 in 1974 to $480,000 in 1978; doubled space of department
- found and built important new resources
- contributed highest percent increase in sportswear of any store in chain in 1977-1978
- promoted and assigned to buying for all stores at New York City headquarters

EDUCATION:

B.A. degree, Bowdoin College, Brunswick, ME, 1974.
Major: Fashion Merchandising and Retailing; Dean's List.
As extracurricular activity, coordinated four fashion shows, two each for Butterick and Vogue. Designed the sets, arranged lighting, selected models, prepared and did the commentary.

SUMMER JOBS (high school and college):
1972-1974   THOM McAN SHOES, Hanover, NH. SALES PERSON, CASHIER
1970-1972   BELLIN'S DEPARTMENT STORE, Portland, ME. STOCKROOM CLERK; CASHIER

HOBBIES:

Reading, skiing, tennis, cooking

PERSONAL DATA:

Age 24, (born 8/8/55), single, good health

REFERENCES AND FURTHER DATA ON REQUEST

37 Robe Boulevard
Pasadena, CA (zip)

Home (123) 456-7890
Office (123) 654-3210

R E S U M E

of

TAYLOR GIMBEL

RETAIL EXECUTIVE/DIVISIONAL MERCHANDISE MANAGER/STORE MANAGER

***   Progressive and successful career in retailing
from Trainee to Merchandise Manager with major
Los Angeles department store.

***   Record of efficient departmental reorganizations,
consistent volume increases; innovative promotional ideas, new display and packaging concepts.

***   Develop buyer confidence and find strategies to
maximize profits and volume.

(FOR FURTHER DATA, PLEASE SEE FOLLOWING PAGES)

BUSINESS EXPERIENCE

<u>1971-Present</u> WILSHIRE DEPARTMENT STORES, Los Angeles, CA, internationally
known $1 billion plus department store retailer with branches
in major metropolitan areas.

<u>1978-Present</u>, MERCHANDISE MANAGER, Pasadena, CA, with additional assign-
ment as Supervisor of $24 million branch store. Responsible for:
- merchandising Major Appliances, Television, Radios and Stereo Sound
  Studio, Air Conditioners, Housewares, Budget Store, Auto Shop; with
  departmental sales of $10 million.

Examples of Accomplishments:
- overcame poor sales of T.V.'s, stereo systems and service contracts.
- changed location, improved display with new display concept, improved
  product emphasis and sales presentation; increased sales 27% in first
  year (20% over plan and best increase among all branches).
- surmounted loss of housewares space reduced 40%, by better identification
  of potential bestsellers, placing orders accordingly, conceiving new display presentation; increased sales 12% above plan, and only 15% below
  previous year in larger space.

<u>Jun. 1977-May 1978</u>, MERCHANDISE MANAGER, San Diego, CA, for Leisure Living,
Housewares, Budget Store, Toys, Auto Shop.

Examples of Accomplishments:
- developed new floor plan for poorly organized Housewares Department; created new displays, impulse shopping atmosphere, improved traffic flow.
  Major elements of plan were adopted as prototypes for all Wilshire
  stores; increased Fall sales 13% in first year (10% above plan), the
  highest percentage increase among all departments and stores in Division.
  Increased spring sales 9%, second largest Housewares increase among all
  stores.
- for entire departmental responsibilities achieved first, second or third
  best percentage increases among all stores.

<u>Jan. 1976-Jan. 1977</u>, MERCHANDISE MANAGER, Long Beach, CA, for Men's Store,
Silver, Luggage, Cameras, Fine Jewelry.
- increased volume 7%.

<u>July 1974-Feb. 1976</u>, BUYER, Men's Underwear, Hosiery, Handkerchiefs and
Scarves, Los Angeles, CA.
- started new trend in men's accessories; imported new and different
  products from Europe; created $100,000 new volume in six months.
- conceived handkerchiefs promotion based on new approach; used with
  great success by manufacturer nationally after Wilshire introduction.
- designed new men's underwear display fixture now used in all stores.

<u>1971-1974</u> BUYER, Men's Underwear and Hosiery, Main Store

- originated theme "Look as Well Inside as Outside"; sold $27,000 in three days.
- rated most profitable Buyer for Company 1968.
- gave vendors responsibility for departmental mark-on percentages.
- appointed Chairman, Corporate Buying Committee.

<u>1963-1971</u> MEYER AND DANIELS, Portland, OR

<u>July 1971-Dec. 1971</u> BUYER, Men's Shirts, Hosiery, Pajamas, Robes

<u>1969-1971</u> BUYER, Men's Dress Shirts, Hosiery

- created unique promotion still used by Company; at first promotion sold entire stock in one day.
- achieved departmental net profit of 20.5%.
- increased volume from $4 million to $6 million in one year.

<u>June 1968-Feb. 1969</u> BUYER, Appliances

<u>1963-1968</u> Successively Trainee, Head of Stock, Assistant Buyer, Associate Buyer.

<u>MILITARY SERVICE</u>: U.S. NAVY, Shore Patrol, 1961-1963

<u>EDUCATION</u>:   B.A., History and Business Administration, University of California at Los Angeles.

                 Ph.B., Political Science and Philosophy, 1960.
                 Certificate, Stanford University of Retailing, 1965.

<u>PUBLICATIONS</u>:   "What's Wrong with Housewares," Housewares Magazine
                 "Merchandise Review," Men's Furnishings.
                 "Merchandise Review," Men's Underwear.

<u>HOBBIES</u>:   All sports, hiking, travel.

<u>PERSONAL DATA</u>: Born 2/15/39, married, two children, excellent health. Willing to relocate.

<u>REFERENCES AND FURTHER DATA ON REQUEST</u>

845 Fifth Avenue
New York, NY 10003

Home (212) 000-0000
Office (212) 000-0000

R E S U M E

SUSAN ANTHONY

OBJECTIVE:	Position in sales

QUALIFICATIONS: Experience in dealing with people and problems in present position and in earlier part-time jobs during high school and college years. Extensive theater experience and education. Some earlier teaching experience in drama and dance.

PERSONAL DATA: Age 22, single, excellent health.

EDUCATION: B.S., Theater/Literature, Vassar College, Poughkeepsie, NY, 1978. Dean's List. Departmental Honors. Served Theater Internship at Kansas City Theater Center, December 1977-February 1978, and at Connecticut Theater Festival, June-August 1977. Managed Vassar Theater box office; brought Broadway actors to Vassar.

EXPERIENCE: 1978-Present   TICKETRON, INC., New York, NY

TICKET AGENT. Responsible for:

- booking groups from around the world into a variety of cultural events in the U.S., including Broadway productions
- suggesting suitable visits for various kinds of groups: club, religious, singing, etc.

On own initiative, provided itineraries, hotel and restaurant reservations, activity schedules, tours, and meetings with performers. (This is not a regular service of the company.)

SUMMER JOBS: 1976 LORD & TAYLOR, New York, NY

ASSISTANT TO GENERAL MANAGER, Better Dresses

- analyzed sales reports from 11 stores
- analyzed inventories
- aided in selection of Fall merchandise

1974-1975 (two years) DANA WOMEN'S FASHIONS, New York, NY.

ASSISTANT SALES MANAGER.

1973, Taught drama at the New School; drama and dance in Afghanistan

1972, Taught drama at children's camp

THEATER: Participated in leading or chorus parts in 9 shows,
                    Vassar

EXTRACURRICULAR: Student of ballet and modern dance

HOBBIES: Skiing, tennis, dance, gourmet cooking

REFERENCES: On request

1874 Blacksmith Drive
West Branch, NJ (zip)

Home (201) 123-4567
Office (212) 654-3210

R E S U M E

of

WILLIAM HOOVER

DISTRIBUTION/TRANSPORTATION EXECUTIVE

*** Record of profit contributions in millions of dollars to two employers in 15 years through transportation cost savings and efficiencies arising from wide experience and continuing studies of transportation administration.

*** Qualified for executive management of corporate operations involving personnel, facilities, equipment, procedures, inventory control and policies. Strong experience in using computer technology to establish programs and arrive at answers to complex problems including inventory control and better turnover to generate improved cash flow.

*** Experienced in organization structure, manpower development, space analysis and layout including sophisticated warehouse planning. Demonstrated leadership qualities.

*** Experienced conference, association, seminar speaker, negotiator with government commissions and all major rate bureaus.

(FOR FURTHER DATA, PLEASE SEE FOLLOWING PAGES)

RECORD OF EMPLOYMENT

January 1970-Present   ESBEE QUALITY PRODUCTS CO., INC., Boonton, NJ

MANAGER, TRANSPORTATION of $250 million Company with 1,000 direct-to-dealer salesmen calling nationally on retail stores. Staff of 15 including Analysts, Routing, Passenger, Travel, Private Transportation Supervisors, Automobile Fleet Coordinator, Transportation Clerks.

Responsible for:
- direction and coordination of all transportation functions including recommendations of policies and procedures.
- coordination of established programs and procedures.
- providing direction to Branches and Manufacturing Units in establishing and maintaining adequate and efficient transportation services.
- all transportation costs and expenditures.
- administration of leasing of 1,250 automobiles for salesmen and executive staff and 250 delivery trucks.
- personnel travel and hotel accommodations.

In execution of responsibilities:
- issued Transportation Department Manual, Delivery Service Manual, Guidelines for Transportation Profit.
- assisted all units by counseling during periodic visits.
- participated in selection of Transportation personnel.
- maintained and communicated data in connection with newest development in transportation.

Accomplishments include:
- development of expanded own carriage program with a 1979 saving of $318,000.
- trucking cost savings: 1979, $100,000; 1978, $200,000; 1979, $400,000.
- utilization of Air Freight Forwarding for a $300,000 saving in first year.
- substitution of an automobile lease program for automobile allowance program reducing salesmen's out-of-pocket expenses and saving Corporation $100,000 annually.
- establishment of LCL and Truckload Commodity Rates to eliminate premium rates on mixed shipments resulting in annual corporate savings of $400,000 (prior to expansion of own carriage program).
- setting up additional consolidation terminal in Omaha supplementing New Jersey terminal. Created transportation savings of $250,000 annually.
- by computer program eliminated scales, UPS and postage meters and operators in 12 branches. Saved $175,000 annually.
- developed Unitized Shipping Plan in-bound from Vendors. Expanded plan to include out-bound shipments to branches. Annual saving of $600,000.

1963-1970   ALLIED STORES, INC., New York, NY

GENERAL TRAFFIC MANAGER for $1 billion plus chain of 100 leading department stores, supervising department of 85 people.

288

_1963-1970_ (continued)

Accomplishments included:

- reduction of staff from 85 to 70 with annual saving of $150,000.
- development of Company Vendor Routing Guide.
- reduction in number of Shipper Association Memberships.
- improvement of shipping time to West Coast.
- increase in claims recoveries of $250,000.
- establishment of New York warehouse to handle imports.
- computer program to control imports. Reduced pier handling time by
  seven days per shipment.

_1958-1963_ PROPANE GAS COMPANY, Indianapolis, IN

Tank Car Supervisor, Rate Clerk, Transportation Clerk.

EDUCATION:

B.A., University of Indiana, Indianapolis, IN. Major, Business; Minor,
Transportation. Attended evening classes.

SPECIAL SEMINARS:

Attended advanced seminars in Transportation 1965-1975, evening classes.
The Management Grid, Scientific Methods, Inc., Washington, DC.

COMMUNITY PARTICIPATION:

Chairman, Community Chest, three years. Citizen-of-the-Year Award.

MEMBERSHIPS:

President, The National Shippers Association
Board of Directors, Carrier Conference of BNT.
American Traffic Club

HOBBIES:

Chess, bridge, golf.

PERSONAL DATA:

Born 8/30/41, married, 2 children, excellent health. Willing to relocate.

REFERENCES AND FURTHER DATA ON REQUEST

289

APPENDIX B

USEFUL WORDS AND PHRASES

There are certain words that may help you to express yourself better and phrases and sentences typical of the succinct and vivid language of a résumé. The examples given below are intended only to guide you and to suggest style. Appraise them carefully before choosing a word or phrase that fits you best. Your résumé should be as distinctive as are your fingerprints.

ABOUT YOUR EXPERIENCE

consistent record (of progress, growth, achievements, promotion)
demonstrably (successful, capable, effective)
effective
experienced
extensive
intensive
in-depth, comprehensive, of

wide scope, wide, broad, diversified, varied
intimate (familiarity with rules, regulations, procedures)
progressive
solid
complete
thoroughgoing
successful

ABOUT YOU

---

accustomed, used to

an administrator

analytical

broad gauge

(possess) communication skills

competent, capable, able

contest or award winner

contributor

contributory

controlled

a coordinator

dedicated

developer

distinguished

dynamic

educated, schooled, trained

efficient, effective

exceptional (avoid
   "unexceptionable")

an executive

a generalist

harmonious

imaginative, conceptual

indoctrinated (with)

ingenious, inventive

talented

innovative, creative

a leader

a manager

motivated

a motivator

multilingual, bilingual

a negotiator

an organizer

outstanding

planner

a producer

reliable

responsible

skilled

a specialist

strategist

stress resistant

student of

a supervisor

a trainee

a trainer

traveled

ABOUT YOUR SKILLS AND ABILITIES

---

analyze	lead
assist	organize, systematize, install
communicate	plan
conceive (an idea)	qualify for
contribute	recruit
create	solve problems
create profit, profitability	supervise, manage, administer
delegate	train, indoctrinate, teach
develop	understand
economize, save money	work well with others, work in
implement	harmony
innovate	write, compose, create copy
learn	

ABOUT YOUR ACCOMPLISHMENTS

---

accomplished	progressed
achieved	reduced, expanded
achieved company or	reorganized
division turnaround	restored profit
contributed	saved
increased, multiplied profit	sold
increased, multiplied sales	succeeded
introduced new concepts	

In the examples that follow these words and phrases are put to work.

Comprehensively trained in every aspect of procedures.

Product student, market researcher, competition evaluator, sales planner, salesman.

Competent in developing existing customers; in finding new customers; in implementing sales plans; in maintaining customer loyalty.

Single, young, motivated, willing to travel, willing to relocate.

Accomplished in organizing efficient production, in production control planning and in the effective utilization of the complete range of metal fabricating equipment.

Able to bring effective solutions to complex (mechanical, engineering, financial, marketing, pricing) problems.

Willing to undertake training. Capable of learning. Possess imagination to conceive goals and find ways to accomplish them, quality of leadership, and ability to communicate.

Author of program to expedite critical data to management leading to expansion (other).

Proven skill in defining requirements, procedures, methods, display, and report formats to keep management informed of progress.

Experienced in managing salesmen, training, recruiting, sales planning, utilizing all techniques (audiovisual, flip charts, advertising, contests, tie-ins, advance merchandising) to stimulate sales.

Labor intensive, capital intensive (industry).

Experienced recruiter and trainer of top producers in the industry, consistently sought by competitive firms because of known qualities of leadership and ability to communicate and identify with others.

Ability to analyze and reorganize corporate administrative procedures and use advanced techniques (word processing, communciations center, electronic data processing) to achieve greater efficiency at lower cost.

Talent for recognizing better ways to accomplish business objectives through coordination, consolidation, systematization, retraining.

Able to see interdisciplinary relationships and express them effectively.

Credited with novel concepts and creative approaches to the production of scores of recognized 30 and 60 second primetime TV spot commercials for leading national advertisers.

After 15 years in public service interested in making a career change to the private sector and qualified in personnel, college administration, recruiting, manpower development, general administration.

Six years of secretarial and other office experience as receptionist, bookkeeper, filing clerk, and PBX operator with a variety of service companies: law firm, management consultant, insurance company, advertising agency. Type accurately 60 to 65 words per minute, with skills increasing continuously.

Awareness of legal needs of business and ability to provide clear answers and effective remedies for corporate legal problems.

Broad administrative background as senior executive with giant public authority; special expertise in the planning and operation of major seaports and transportation centers. Competent in negotiation, persuasion, leadership, and motivation. Record of consistent promotion to greater responsibilities throughout career.

Intimately familiar with U.S. markets, business methods, requirements, strategies. Record of creating sales and profits of significant proportions, measured in millions of dollars in diverse industries involving marketing to supermarkets, chains, department stores, government agencies, institutions, whole-salers, using brokers, agents, direct salesmen.

Comprehensively trained and experienced in brokerage and investment banking, in both "front office" and "back office" procedures: portfolio management, daily transactions and administration, cash flow management, Exchange and S.E.C. compliance. Record of profit contributions to employers.

Experienced in establishing effective management information systems; in the expanded use of E.D.P. to provide critical data expeditiously; in cost accounting, inventory control, production control; in reducing lead time; in measuring productivity; in creating controls at all levels of production to identify profit leaks; in applying innovative methods of accomplishing corporate objectives and increased profitability.

Talent for analysis and organization of complex administrative problems. Innovative. Enthusiastic. Ability to train others. Record of important contributions in management, timesaving systems and profit to major multimillion and billion dollar corporations. Record of conscientious application, reliability and loyalty in every position held and ready acceptance or responsibility to get improved results in every assignment.

Experienced in most aspects of insurance, with emphasis in the investigative and adjusting field, which includes extensive legal negotiations, with autonomous discretion from major insurance companies to settle cases at the highest levels. Also general brokerage experience, including solicitation and development of accounts, counseling relative to insurance needs, complex underwriting evaluations, and placement of coverages by various carriers.

Accustomed to complete management responsibilities for accounting and controls, front office, food and beverage, golf course, club house, entertainment, and other facilities; and to financial reporting, profit and cash flow projections; planning and development. Accomplished also in developing convention business, arranging entertainment, providing gourmet food service and high level of other services. Experienced in close analysis of operating figures and correction of trouble areas; in the use of E.D.P. to assist the managerial function.

Successful record as president of own business; formerly director of industrial engineering for multimillion dollar corporation. Experienced in the selection and evaluation of capital equipment needs, production control, rate setting, productivity standards and measurement, systems and procedures, plant layout, incentive plans; in power plant operation.

Record of major contributions in increased revenues, cost savings; in leadership and revitalization of underproductive departments; in research, analysis, and recommendations with respect to feedstocks, tankage, storage, production and marketing optimization, cost control, economics, forecasting, budgeting.

Successful career as financial analyst, securities salesman, knowledgeable in all areas of brokerage including municipal bonds, commodities, underwritings, placements, individual and corporate portfolio management. Competent trainer, leader, developer of manpower. Excellent public speaker, widely experienced in conducting seminars and adult education courses in securities and investment.

Expert in marketing wide range of ethical and proprietary pharmaceuticals and complex electronic health instrumentation products, with in-depth knowledge of markets, sales techniques, training methods. Skilled in communications. Numerous company awards for sales and other achievements. Accustomed to leading, training, and motivating large staffs and hundreds of employees.

Leader and developer of sales personnel for effective administration of greater responsibilities.

Expert in accommodating promotion programs to regional, trade, and consumer characteristics; in developing innovative packaging to enhance consumer response.

Ability to see what needs to be done, to do it or get it done in a general management capacity.

Exceptionally consistent record of turning loss-operated companies into profitmakers; recently increased sales and production fourfold in less than three years.

Ability to conceptualize and implement broad, complex programs to reach new goals.

Effective market researcher, sales leader, and trainer with expertise in all kinds of packaging and creative sales ideas.

Complete knowledge of the application of graphics to good design with ability to curtail cost.

Demonstrated management ability in national marketing with strong following among chains, discounters, distributors; excellent personal salesman.

School psychologist and counselor, self-starting and innovative.

Record of continuous promotion to positions of greater responsibility; currently holding P.&L. responsibility for multimillion dollar division where sales have tripled and a profit objective has been met. Fully equipped in all aspects of management; in developing management information systems; in full utilization of data processing; in long-range planning and implementation.

Comprehensive experience in the financial and administrative management of huge engineering and construction projects overseas and in the United States involving diverse heavy industrial and military installations; assured their profitable completion.

Extensive educational background and practical experience in human relations, the latter as program developer for nonprofit

organization working in South Africa to improve the effectiveness of the organization's structures, human relations, and economic and health conditions of the nationals of Tanzania and
Kenya; and of the organization's personnel. Conceived program and assigned to implement it.

JOB RESPONSIBILITIES IN MAJOR JOB CLASSIFICATIONS

Y ou may find it helpful to review the activities in certain job classifications. The list below does not include *all* job responsibilities.

Not all companies specify the same responsibilities. R.&D. as well as warehousing and shipping may sometimes be assigned to marketing and sometimes elsewhere. As a vice-president of marketing you would be expected to be familiar with all the elements listed under that heading depending on a company's organizational structure. As a sales manager you would be responsible only for the areas shown under that heading. You will get ideas about other responsibilities, such as product manager, from one or more of the résumés reproduced.

The classifications include most of the duties within the major functions of a company: marketing, finance, and production. Select your area of activity within these categories.

The list also includes personnel, purchasing, retail, data processing, and others selected somewhat arbitrarily; it could have

been expanded ad infinitum. We wished to show that, whatever the job classification, your résumé should discuss the responsibilities and accomplishments normally associated with
that job. A sales manager, for example, must know the markets
of the industry in question.

Use this section as a reminder of your responsibilities, so that
you do not omit relevant and important activities with which
you should be familiar.

ACCOUNTING

Act as cashier
Adjust entries
Age accounts receivable and accounts payable
Analyze intercompany expenses
Approve petty cash and checks
Bank reconciliations
Budgets, forecasts, and financial planning
Closing entries
Collect from debtors; pay creditors
Consolidate reports for parent company with recommenda-
tions as to standing and results of operations of local branches
Correspondence
Dispose promotional items
Examine salesmen's collections and promotional remittances
Examine weekly reports of branch managers and regional offices
Footings
Maintain books of original entry, general ledger, and subsidiary
ledgers
Maintain records and control costs of inventory
Posting to the general ledger

Prepare regular payroll
Prepare reversing entries
Prepare taxes
Prepare various supporting schedules
Take off and post closing trial balance
Trial balance

AUDITING

Age receivables and payables
Analysis and evaluation of cash flow, fiscal and interim statements, and projected statements
Analytical audit of books of original entry and records
Analyze turnovers of receivables and payables
Cash counts
Close books
Comparative analysis of sales and financial statements between two or more fiscal periods
Compute breakeven inventory, estimated inventory, and estimated profit or loss
Conduct physical inventory
Confer with company's officers and accountants
Continuous reconciliations
Detailed analysis of balance sheet and P.&L.
Evaluate D.&B. ratings
Examine and check other audit reports
Examine bonds, stocks, important documents, contracts
Examine canceled checks and checks being held
Examine notes
Examine shipping documents
Examine pension fund, welfare fund, vacation fund, unemployment fund, education fund, accrual fund

Examine taxes
Financial and accounting analysis of diversified multidivisional corporations
Observe factory inventory flow and operations
Post to general ledger
Prepare entries: journal, adjusting, correcting, reversing
Prepare financial statements with opinions
Prepare, present, discuss, explain reports
Prepare taxes
Prepare various schedules
Send out trade checks and verification
Systems suggestions
Take off trial balance and post closing trial balance
Work on books of original entry

DATA PROCESSING

Applications to inventory, production, accounts receivable, accounts payable, payroll, sales, shipping order processing

Budgets
Data centers
Diagnostic systems
Econometric models
Economic models
Educational systems
Forecasting
Hardware, selection of
Leased time
Management information systems

Minicomputer use
Models—financial, marketing, production
Procedural manuals
Programming
Real time
Scientific systems
Softwear, selection of
Training
Utilization, maximum

FINANCE

Acceleration of financial reporting
Accounting
Acquisitions and mergers
Audits and controls
Balance sheets
Bank reconciliations
Bank relationships
Budgets
Capital resource planning
Cash flow
Cash handling
C.P.A. accreditation
Chart of accounts
Compensation
Consolidations
Cost analysis
Credits and collections—bad debt ratios, accounts receivable, aging
Economic correlations
E.D.P. systems
Financing
Financial models
Financial public relations
Financial reporting
Forecasting
Foreign currency fluctuation
Insurance
Inventory control, turnover
Investment
Invoicing systems

Long range planning
Management information systems
Negotiations
New York Stock Exchange, AMEX reports
New York Stock Exchange, AMEX listings
Pensions, fringe benefits, profit sharing plans
Pricing formulas
Profit and loss reporting
Profitability
S.E.C. reports, registrations, prospectuses
Staff training
Taxes
Terms of sale
Training
Underwritings

MARKETING

Sales management
  Budget
  Compensation
  District sales
  Expenses
  Field sales
  Incentives
  Markets
  National sales
  Organization
  Quotas
  Regional sales
  Sales meetings
  Sales planning
  Sales training
    Territory routing
Sales promotion
  Brochures
  Budget
  Circulars
  Direct mail
  Display
  Merchandising
  Packaging
  Presentations
  Promotions

Public relations
  Budget
  Employee public relations
  Media liaison
  Planning
  Press releases
  Speechwriting
Legal liaison
  Advertising agreements
  Co-op advertising,
  discounts, pricing
  Sherman antitrust
Computer utilization
Planning
Product management
(marketing in microcosm)
Research and development
  Budget
  Market evaluations
  New products
  Obsolescence
  Old products

Product evaluation
  Quality comparisons
Advertising
  Agency relations
  Budgets
  Contests
  Copy, copy testing
  Legal liaison
  Media: print, TV, radio
  Production
  Themes
Market research
  Cost projections
  Demography
  Market testing
  New market planning
  Pricing
Forecasting
Pricing (pricing for profit)
Warehousing and shipping
(distribution)

PERSONNEL, INDUSTRIAL RELATIONS, AND MANPOWER DEVELOPMENT

Administration, wage and
salary
Arbitrations
Bonding

Budget
Community relations
Computer utilization
Credit unions

Disability
Discipline
Employee orientation
Employee public relations
Employee productivity re-
views
Fair Employment Practices Act
Food service
Grievances
Group insurance
Hiring
Interviewing
Job description
Labor negotiations
Legal liaison
Loans
Major medical insurance
Manpower development

Manpower planning
Medical department
Morale
National Labor Relations
Board
OSHA (Occupational Safety
and Health Administration)
compliance
Policy and procedure
Records
Security
Social functions
Training programs
Unemployment compensation
Unemployment insurance
Welfare and pension plans
Workmen's compensation

PRODUCTION

Automatic equipment
Automation
Budgets
Chemical engineering
Civil engineering
Computer utilization
Construction
Conveyorization
Cost control
Electrical engineering

Electronics engineering
Environment
Industrial engineering
Inventory control
Manpower planning
Mechanical engineering
Metallurgy
New construction, startup
Patents
Personnel

Plant layout
Power
Production control, scheduling, planning, flow
Purchasing, materials management
Quality control
Quality engineering
Recruiting
Research and development

Space planning
Stampings, forgings, castings, extrusions
Safety engineering
Systems
Tools and dies
Training
Warehousing and shipping
Waste disposal, recycling

PURCHASING AND MATERIALS MANAGEMENT

Alternate option purchasing
Blanket and annual contracts
Budget
Computer utilization
Economic Order Quantity (EOQ) purchasing
Economics
Environment
Inventory control

Legal liaison
Make or buy
Market studies
Packaging
Price trend analysis
Shortages
Strikes
Turnover
Value analysis

RETAIL

Acquisition
Administration
Advertising
Branch store administration, expansion

Budgeting
Buying
Cash flow
Computer utilization
Credit

Department layout
Display
Expansion
Financial planning
Financial reporting
Housekeeping
Inventory control
Leadership
Management information
systems
Market analysis
Market changes
Markup, mark-on
Merchandise selection

Merchandising
Open-to-buy
Operations
Promotion
Quality control
Retailing mathematics
Receiving
Security
Shipping
Staffing
Store layout
Systems
Training

APPENDIX D

PROFESSIONAL RÉSUMÉ SERVICES

Like doctors, lawyers, and advertising agencies, professional résumé services do excellent, mediocre, or poor work. It is therefore important to select your professional résumé service carefully.

In addition to résumé writing, a résumé service may perform the following tasks:

Reproduction
Mailing
Supplying mailing lists—custom and standard
Broadcast letter writing
Interview technique assistance
Aptitude testing
Psychological testing
Third party services
Organization of complete job campaigns
Corporate "out placement"
Executive search
Career counseling
Compensation guidance

Though some consider professionally prepared résumés to lack the stamp of personality evident in a "homemade" résumé, many successful leaders in business, the professions, and the arts have used them. Writing is a difficult task, requiring practice and a knowledge of the rules. Writing about yourself can be even more difficult. You might wish to employ a professional writer for the following reasons:

You have been unable to organize your employment history.
You find the task of writing about yourself tedious and exasperating.
You cannot express "you" in a way that you like.
You speak better than you write.
You have neither the time nor the patience to write your own résumé.
You cannot decide what to omit and what to include.
Your experience is narrow.
You don't know whether your experience is narrow or comprehensive with respect to the job you want.

Ask the professional résumé service to show you samples of their work. Arrange to meet the individual who will be writing your résumé.

The cost of a résumé varies with the time and expertise required to write it. In a large city such as New York the prices will range from $75 for a single page résumé to $400 for a complex one. Like any business, your résumé service has such overhead expenses as rent, heat, light, taxes, and secretarial help. Preparing a résumé involves its planning, writing and rewriting, proofreading, interviewing, and researching reference material. Fees of $50 an hour are about the minimum needed to run a professional résumé service in a large urban center. The following typical fees for a professionally written résumé are based on information supplied by six résumé writing firms:

By mail
  $50 to $150
  $50 to $75 per page (maximum: $150)
  $50 to $75 per page (no maximum)
By personal interview
  $50 per page
  $85 for first page, $35 for second page, and $25 for third page
  $40 to $75 per hour
  New entrant to job market: $50 to $75
  Clerical: $50 to $75
  Lower middle management executive: $100
  Upper middle management executive: $150 to $200
  Vice-president for small company: $200
  Vice-president for large company: $300
  Chief executive officer or president: $300 to $400
Some writers change on the basis of the subject's annual income:

$ 10,000	1.0%	$100
20,000	0.75	150
30,000	0.75	225
40,000	0.75	300
50,000	0.75	375
75,000	0.6	450
100,000	0.5	500

The professional résumé writer has three big advantages compared with the average individual writing his or her own résumé: experience, objectivity, and organized information about the subject. The professional résumé writer also has two great disadvantages. First, he or she must please the client. If this need is paramount, it can kill the spontaneity and effectiveness of a résumé. The other disadvantage is cost. Most people do not want to spend much money on a résumé; yet a workman-

like job is time consuming and requires skill. Once written, it
may have to be rewritten; or one résumé may not suit all
needs. A superior résumé is invaluable; a poor one may not
only be a waste of money, but may harm your employment
future. If you want a superior résumé, be willing to pay for it.
If you need only a stereotype, say so, and it will be inexpen-
sive—that is, under $100. The charge is usually lower for a re-
cent graduate.

How can you tell whether a professional résumé writer is
competent? The same way in which you find out whether a
doctor, lawyer, or advertising agency is competent.

A good résumé writer is a combination analyst, writer, psychologist, and experienced business executive, willing to take
the time necessary to know you; he or she must be reimbursed
accordingly. Sometimes, like a doctor who makes the wrong
diagnosis, he may lose a patient; trying to treat yourself for an
illness, however, is usually worse than calling the doctor.

INDEX